# The Michael-Mystery

Sergei O. Prokofieff

# The Michael-Mystery

*A Spiritual-Scientific view of
the Michael-Imagination and
its representation in Eurythmy*

Sergei O. Prokofieff

Wynstones
Press

"Thus we speak of a proper comprehension of the
Christ-impulse when we speak of a proper comprehension
of the Michael-impulse in our time."
*Rudolf Steiner, 29 May 1913*[1]

"Michael wishes in future times to take his seat in the hearts, in the
souls of earthly human beings, and this is to begin in the present
age. It is about a guidance of Christendom into more profound
truths, inasmuch as Christ is meant to find more understanding
among human beings; to live His way into humanity as a Sun-being
through that Sun-spirit – Michael – who has always ruled over the
intelligence, and who now can no longer administer it in the
cosmos, but in the future wishes to administer it through
the hearts of human beings!"
*Rudolf Steiner, 21 August 1924*[2]

"Michael will be the actual spiritual protagonist of freedom."
*Rudolf Steiner, 13 January 1924*[3]

"Once a human being begins to meditate, he/she carries
out what amounts to the only actually completely free deed
in human life… We are entirely free in so doing.
Such meditating is an utterly free action."
*Rudolf Steiner, 20 August 1922*[4]

Published by
Wynstones Press
Stourbridge
England.

www.wynstonespress.com

First English edition 2015

Originally published in German under the title
*Das Michael-Mysterium*
*Eine geisteswissenschaftliche Betrachtung der Michael-Imagination*
*und ihrer Darstellung in Eurythmie.*
Verlag des Ita Wegman Instituts, Switzerland, in 2014
(edited by Ute E. Fischer).

Translated from the German by
Maria St. Goar.

Grateful thanks for the kind permission to include the Michael-meditation
translated by George and Mary Adams, from *Verses and Meditations*,
published by Rudolf Steiner Press, England 1993.

Jacket illustration: Christine Cologna: *Michael with the Dragon*
Frontispiece: Thaddäus von Rychter: *Michael with the Dragon*

Cover layout based on original design by
© Walter Schneider www.schneiderdesign.net

Printed in EU

ISBN 9780 946206 780

# Contents

# Preface

From 6 to 8 May 2011, a conference took place at the Goetheanum in Dornach, Switzerland with the title "Alchemy of the Soul Forces, Three Meditations by Rudolf Steiner". They were dedicated to the 150th anniversary of his birthday. Likewise, this conference was to demonstrate the central significance that Rudolf Steiner from the beginning of his activity as a spiritual teacher attributed to meditating as the most important means for promoting the inner development of the human being. This actually occurred based on personal experiences. For already beginning around age 35, he could state in regard to himself: "In *soul experience* I recognized the nature of meditation and its significance for insights into the spiritual world... Now something appeared in my inner being that demanded meditation as if it were a necessity of existence in my soul life. This striven-for soul life required meditation just as the organism on a certain stage of its development requires breathing of the lungs... what now happened was that meditation became a mental necessity of life" (GA 28, Chapter XXII; italics by Rudolf Steiner).

It is therefore understandable that in the individual guidance of his students, but likewise on other occasions, Rudolf Steiner always gave meditations as a daily practice so that the spirit forces slumbering in every human being could thereby awaken and be supported.

Thus, in the centre-point of the conference, there were three meditations by Rudolf Steiner, concerning which three individuals offered explanatory and deepened contributions. The Rosicrucian "Butterfly- meditation" was highlighted by Florian Roder of Munich. The "Heart-meditation" was Peter Selg's theme and appeared soon afterwards as a book in the publishing house of the Ita Wegman Institute. Selg was also the one who had discovered this meditation in Rudolf Steiner's handwriting at the Ita Wegman Institute and had published it for the first time.

The third contribution was my various explanations of the "Michael-Imagination" through which Rudolf Steiner had concluded his *Last Address* of 28 September 1924, and for the performance on stage of which he had been able to create a eurythmy form shortly before his death.

In the composition of the entire conference, the explanations for the first meditation were to depict the path of transformation for thinking, the second for that of feeling, and the third for that of willing, something that corresponds to the threefold alchemy of the soul forces on the path of initiation, as had been announced in the title of the conference.

The basis for what has been presented in this book is my lecture about the Michael-Imagination by Rudolf Steiner. In his written elaboration, the original content of the lecture was given an essential expansion, whereby the deeper nature of this unique meditation[1] – aside from the Foundation Stone Verse – brings to expression the actual mission of Rudolf Steiner on earth like no other meditation, or at the very least brings that mission better to revelation.

Among the most important tasks for Rudolf Steiner was the union of esoteric or Rosicrucian Christendom with the cosmic or Michaelic Christendom.[2] The first stream found its point of departure and its main source on earth in the Mystery of Golgotha, the death and resurrection of Christ Jesus. The origin of the second stream is located on the Sun from which, at the Turning Point of Time, the Christ descended in order to link up at the Baptism in the Jordan with the human being, Jesus of Nazareth. Michael remained on the Sun as ruling power of the great cosmic kingdom of the Christ, and guardian of the Christ-mysteries in the cosmos. Even today, the spiritual key is still to be found on the Sun for comprehension of the Mystery of Golgotha, not only as an earthly but likewise as a cosmic event, the forces of which are needed by all hierarchies in the spiritual world for the continuation of humanity's further development. In this sense, the conference was meant also to contribute to this significant meditation; towards a better understanding of Rudolf Steiner's earthly task in this regard. For, it is the power of Christ as the spiritual Sun of the universe that can link esoteric and cosmic Christendom in the heart of every human being, as Rudolf Steiner exemplified for us during his life on earth. He also opened up completely new perspectives for us and a deeper dimension of Christendom.

Following the first two introductory chapters of this book and beginning with the third chapter, the reader may well be a little surprised by the complexity of the Michael-mysteries, concerning which one might perhaps know only a few aspects. In the totality of Rudolf Steiner's work, however, one can decidedly discover further viewpoints regarding these mysteries that are dealt with here in a more detailed form. The overall picture that gradually arises out of the last three chapters will transmit a striking impression of the many levels of the Michael-mysteries in the cosmos and evolution of humanity. In studying Rudolf Steiner's work, by no means can all aspects be focused upon that could in fact be gleaned from his work. Thus, further research is necessary. And what is more, for a complete grasp of the indispensable value and significance of the Michael-mysteries in the life and work of Rudolf Steiner – this must be left to future researchers.

This book can therefore only represent a first attempt at taking the initial steps in the indicated direction. And its content may therefore be an encouragement for those Anthroposophists who, based on Rudolf Steiner's spiritual research, seek for more profound access to the Michael-mysteries. For after all, as Anthroposophists, we bear all the basic facts of these mysteries within our own selves.

In conclusion, I would like to thank Peter Selg for the suggestion of publishing these contents as a book by the publishing house of the Ita Wegman Institute.

Whitsun 2012
Sergei O. Prokofieff

# I
# Three Meditations

The three meditations that stood at the centre of the conference mentioned in the preface, reveal the main stream or central impulses that are inseparably linked with the nature and being of Anthroposophy on earth. For they relate to the three actual entities in the spiritual world and on the earth that play a decisive role for the origin and development of Anthroposophy.

The first, the "Butterfly-meditation", is connected with profound secrets of the Rosicrucian stream.[1] In itself, it harbours the secret of death and resurrection in the Rosicrucian-alchemistic sense; a secret that has always stood at the centre of all true Rosicrucian esoteric instruction since the establishment of this stream (in the middle of the thirteenth century). The second meditation that speaks of the spiritual nature of the heart in connection with the Sun, points simultaneously to the cosmic secret of the Christ in connection with His working in the human heart, in the way this became possible following the Mystery of Golgotha. This meditation addresses and describes the modern path to Christ.[2] The third meditation – that stood in the centre of the presentations on the last day[3] and could be watched on stage after the lecture as a Michael-Imagination in the eurythmy performance – shows the existential and unique connection of Anthroposophy with the presently reigning Time-spirit, Michael.

If one follows the inner paths that open up these three meditations to us, one soon discovers that quite accurately they correspond to the first three parts of the Foundation Stone Meditation. For, the first part stands in a connection with Rosicrucianism; the second part is linked with the Sun-secret of the Christ that was later guarded in the Grail-mysteries; and the third part stands in a close relationship with the Michael-mysteries in the spiritual world.[4] All of them together are embraced and supported by the fourth part of the Foundation Stone Meditation that unites them esoterically with the Christ-Sun that lit up at the Turning Point of Time. Since then the destinies of earth and humanity have become inseparably united through the Mystery of Golgotha.

Since the 150th anniversary of the birth of Rudolf Steiner was commemorated[5] in the year 2011, the following depiction will begin with the question: In what kind of relationship does Rudolf Steiner himself stand with the contemporary Time-spirit and the cosmic mysteries of Michael? For we must be very much aware of the fact that even today, more than eighty years after the death of Rudolf Steiner, Anthroposophy remains the only fount within humankind where a true cognition of the cosmic-telluric Michael-Mystery can be found in the present age. In our time there is no other place, no other possibility to approach these mysteries concerning Michael – first in a cognitive sense, then with one's whole heart, and ultimately even with human will.

And what does it actually mean to approach these mysteries concerning Michael? It means nothing else than to occupy oneself with the great tasks of the Time-spirit in contemporary humanity. This, however, also means that it is only when one occupies oneself with these mysteries in depth that in the true sense of the word one is a human being of the present time. For, one is not part of the present age simply by means of hobnobbing or mingling with today's civilization with all its tendencies of decline. In that way one erroneously considers all kinds of possibilities for what is timely or modern; matters that frequently indwell the present day as anti-Michaelic impulses. In reality none of this is by any means modern. What today uniquely and alone is correct and measures up to the great tasks of contemporary humanity stands in connection with Michael. Or expressed differently, all that finds no access to the Michaelic impulse of the present age must be designated as hopelessly old-fashioned and, according to its nature, belonging to an earlier epoch, even if it appears in a different light to begin with and imagines itself to be modern. The truly modern element is always linked with the ruling Time-spirit in every epoch of human evolution, and only emerges out of such a spirit's inspirations.

# II
# Rudolf Steiner and
# his relationship to Michael

From his earliest youth, Rudolf Steiner had a unique relationship with the coming impulses of today's Time-spirit, Michael. Already as a boy, his further path as a purely Michaelic task was preordained. It was a task of decisive significance not only for the time then, not only for today, but a task of profound importance for mankind still for many centuries to come. As an eight-year-old, Rudolf Steiner thus formulated the central task of his entire life, not exactly in the following words but more on the level of feeling: How can one carry the spiritual experiences, spiritual awareness, and spiritual impressions – he said this to himself following his first acquaintance with geometry – so accurately in one's soul as is the case with the theorems of this precise science? Such questioning or inquiry is of a fundamentally Michaelic character and completely modern.

Spiritual perceptions were natural for him already by his seventh year.[1] Later as an eight-year-old, he did not want to remain at these experiences, but rather determined completely on his own that he should take the first steps in the direction of his later task in life. "As a child, I of course did not clearly tell this to myself but I felt that, just like in geometry, one must carry the knowledge of the spiritual world in oneself." (GA 28, Chap. 1). At the end of his life, in his autobiography, *The Course of My Life*, he recalled this decisive moment and added to this: "In my relationship to geometry I must consider the first budding of a view of life that gradually developed in me. It lived in me more or less unconsciously during childhood and around age twenty assumed a certain fully conscious form" (ibid.).

Now, in order to arrive at this "fully conscious form" of his life's task that later culminated in the founding of spiritual science, a few other issues had to be resolved in Rudolf Steiner's life. The question may therefore be posed: What did the young man do around the year 1879 during the beginning of the contemporary Michael-epoch? Precisely around this time, he asked himself the decisive Michaelic questions which he then pursued consistently and without any break through all the high and low points of his inner development until the end of his life.

Around this same year Rudolf Steiner becomes eighteen-years-old, he begins to occupy himself intensely with the riddle of the human "I", and this alone brings him into the vicinity of Michael. For as Time-spirit, Michael is that hierarchical entity whose outer sheath consists of "I"-substance. This means that Michael turns to human beings out of a substance that is intrinsically related with their own ego. We humans on the earth live in a physical body. Angels have as their outer sheath the ether body, and the Archangels the astral body. The Archai (the Time-spirits) on the other hand, wear the "I"-substance as their outer garment which corresponds to the most important aspect in the human being. And through this, Michael finds his access to humankind.

Thus, in this same year, Rudolf Steiner poses for himself, as well as for his own further inner path, the crucial question concerning the human "I" in order then to answer it based on his own spiritual experience. In the book, *The Course of My Life*, we can read the following on this subject: "There existed a world of spiritual beings for me. That the 'I' which itself is spirit dwells in a world of spirits was for me a direct observation" (GA 28, Chap. III). In these words, Rudolf Steiner's supersensible ego-experience is described which he had experienced already by age eighteen.

In the same year, a further likewise purely Michaelic striving enters his life which he describes in his later review [his autobiography] as follows: "I now worked more and more consciously on pouring the direct *observation* I had of the spiritual world into the form of *thoughts*" (ibid.; italics by Rudolf Steiner). This means that around this same time he already worked consciously and aimfully with the problem: How can thinking be transformed in such a way that it no longer destroys or even kills spiritual perceptions, but illuminates them in such a way that human beings can participate quite freely – and with a strong "I"-consciousness in full composure – with the events and processes of the spiritual world?

In other words, how can the human being become a conscious brother-in-arms and co-worker among spiritual entities, and above all with the new Time-spirit?

These are precisely the questions – although not exactly in the above formulation – that Rudolf Steiner was intensely occupied with around the year 1879. It was also the time of his first Moon-node. In the ten lectures adding to Rudolf Steiner's biography that I gave in the year 2011 for the anniversary of his 150th birthday at the Goetheanum, this theme stood entirely in the centre. In doing so, the inner path that guided Rudolf Steiner directly to Michael was described in much greater detail.[2]

A short time later when he was eighteen and a half-years-old, there likewise belongs to Rudolf Steiner's biography the encounter with the Rosicrucian Master who has remained un-named. This initiate transmitted to him a sort of esoteric "tool", by means of which Rudolf Steiner could attain his goals that he indeed had already set for himself. Thus, he entered the path to Michael as a true modern Rosicrucian, however not in connection with any ancient institutions or traditions but purely under the guardianship of the present Time-spirit.

And what happened then? In order to be able to answer this question, we must briefly go into a particular quality of Rudolf Steiner's. His spiritual research fills more than 350 volumes, and despite this infinite wealth of communications he rarely spoke of his own personal supersensible experiences. This not only speaks to his special humility, but stresses above all the great discipline with which he himself approached his own experiences in the spiritual world. Concerning communications to other human beings, he waited until he could bring to the public in books or lectures (as objective results of his spiritual scientific research) what he had experienced in the supersensible realm.[3]

In this sense, Rudolf Steiner stood, and stands to this day, in stark contrast to many contemporaries who – in the case of most incipient spiritual experiences – feel the irresistible urge immediately to talk about their own spiritual experiences everywhere. By contrast, the very rare and seldom discovered "personal remarks" by Rudolf Steiner regarding his own experiences in the spiritual world means that such communications, when they are imparted, are of very special significance. One can appreciate them as precious pearls strewn around in his work that one may receive with special devotion and thankfulness.

Thus, towards the end of his life in Torquay, England, he reports of his conscious encounter with Michael during the time in Weimar, where he witnessed the battle of the Time-spirit with the Ahrimanic dragon in the spiritual world adjoining the earth. In this connection he likewise heard the mighty cosmic questions that indwelled Michael's spirit-realm concerning the future of humanity. (See the words by Rudolf Steiner concerning his encounter with Michael further on in this chapter.)

Now, how did this encounter with Michael come about? How did it come to that? This encounter with Michael could only occur on a modern path of initiation, no longer on the path of the ancient Rosicrucians. This begs the question, how could this event become possible solely and only after the beginning of the Michael-epoch in the year 1879 within the modern Michaelic-Rosicrucian path of initiation? This was for the reason that Michael had now descended from the Sun into the surroundings of the earth, whereby the entire relationship of Michael to humankind had radically changed.

The path for such an encounter had been pre-planned by the ancient Rosicrucians. At the end of the Middle Ages and the beginning new age, they had conscientiously studied the Copernican system. They spiritualized this knowledge with the methods of the Rosicrucian spirit-schooling in their souls and carried it up to the gods. This is how Rudolf Steiner described this in the lecture of 13 January 1924. And on this path, the Rosicrucians of that time actually encountered Michael, and in a special form at that. In the entire context of the lecture one can think particularly of Christian Rosenkreutz himself. Rudolf Steiner points out that, prior to the year 1879, even the most advanced Rosicrucians could meet up with Michael on this path only in a dream-like condition and not yet fully consciously. In this regard Rudolf Steiner's actual words were: "Rosicrucianism is defined by the fact that its most *illustrious minds* had a powerful longing for encountering Michael. They could do this only as if in a dream" (GA 233a).

This casts a strong light on the biography of young Rudolf Steiner: For what did he do as a student at the Viennese Technical College after his meeting with the Rosicrucian Master? He diligently studied all the sciences offered there. The list he mentions in his autobiographical lecture includes nine disciplines: "chemistry, physics, zoology, botany, biology, geology, mathematics, geometry and pure mechanics."[4] Added to this is the intensive study of modern philosophy, all the way to Kant, Fichte, Hegel, Schelling and other less known philosophers of the second part of the nineteenth century. Without exaggeration, one can therefore say that in these few years Rudolf Steiner had made the entire wealth of humanity's thoughts his own, and in particular its main directions – the scientific and the philosophical one.

In Vienna and later in Weimar, he is moreover very interested in art. At that time art was becoming more and more naturalistic under the influence of the prevalent materialism. In the same way, he also harbours similar impressions in his mind concerning religion, which in the nineteenth century turned increasingly materialistic and dogmatic.[5] And what does he do with religion? Initially, he illuminates everything with the light of Goethe's all-embracing world-view. Already beginning at age eighteen, Rudolf Steiner occupied himself intensely with Goethe's art, and then starting at the age of twenty-two, he occupied himself with Goethe's unique access to the sciences in order – in this way – particularly to deepen and transform the first learned and thus acquired natural sciences.

A thorough study of Darwin's and Haeckel's writings was pursued in Weimar. Rudolf Steiner later added their teachings to the second volume of his treatise, *Views of World and Life in the Nineteenth Century*[6] (GA18) in accordance with Goethe's conception for an understanding of nature. Rudolf Steiner himself states the following about this: "I was just at the point of working on the second volume so that in a *spiritual form* Darwinism and Haeckelism, as seen in the light of Goethe's world-view, would be the starting points of a spiritual deepening into cosmic secrets" (GA 28, Chap. XXX; italics by Rudolf Steiner). Thus an inner transformation of Haeckelism occurred in accordance with Goethe already during Rudolf Steiner's time in Weimar.

This first stage of transformation concerning the modern natural scientific thinking was superseded by a further one, namely its spiritualization according to the guidelines that Rudolf Steiner had received from his Rosicrucian Master. All this he brought up towards the gods so that in his own words natural scientific thinking could be given back the content of evolution as depicted in his book, *Occult Science, an Outline*. He himself reports on this: "Study it today inasmuch as you have been touched by the Rosicrucian initiation-principle referred to here; study Heckelism with all its materialism; study it and let yourselves be penetrated by what are methods of cognition according to *Knowledge of the Higher Worlds and Its Attainment*"[7] ... Learn all ... that can be learned through external natural science, and bring it towards the gods and you will receive what is narrated in my book *Occult Science* concerning evolution" (GA 233a, 13 January 1924).

When in this way during the time following the beginning of the Michael-epoch art, religion and science – that had all turned increasingly naturalistic (meaning materialistic) – were brought upward towards the gods in the spiritual world, then one could actually encounter Michael as the contemporary Time-spirit. "And what one does there – namely that one carries upwards into a spiritual world the natural insights or likewise creations of naturalistic art or feelings of religion that work naturalistically in the inner nature of the soul – for even religion has basically become naturalistic – inasmuch as one carries this upwards to the gods one in fact encounters Michael if one develops the faculty for doing so" (ibid.). Now this took place no longer in a dream-like state – as was still the case among the ancient Rosicrucians – but in a new quite conscious manner. For human beings can encounter Michael in a conscious way in the spirit "since the end of the last third of the nineteenth century," (ibid.).

It was in a conscious way that Rudolf Steiner had his first Michael-encounter during the Weimar-period (1890-1896). Rudolf Steiner met Michael in the spiritual world directly adjacent to the earth in full consciousness based on his own free "I" that was carried through the purest forces of his spiritualized "thinking" which he had developed in particular from occupying himself with philosophy, the sciences, and

Goethe's natural scientific writings. Thus in our Michael Age, Rudolf Steiner is *the first Rosicrucian* that in a fully conscious manner (and as a modern "I"-endowed human being) has encountered Michael. He himself describes this in the following words: "Through living outside the physical world with the intellectual- or sentient-soul,[8] one could live in the region (in the sphere) into which Michael was just entering earthly life" (GA 240, 12 August 1924).[9]

This joining together with the ruling Time-spirit stood in the background of Rudolf Steiner's work on his book, The *Philosophy of Freedom*, which was published in 1894, the year when its author had reached his thirty-third year of life. His later description makes it clear how this book is connected with Michael: "Michael can work into all that I have called, for example, in my book *Occult Science*, pure free thinking – something that in freedom must become the impulse for individual willing on the part of human beings in the modern age. And regarding actions that spring from the impulse of love – for them Michael has a special affinity (GA 219, 17 December, 1922).

What Rudolf Steiner described in *Occult Science, an Outline* as the extension of "pure thinking" into the supersensible world beyond the threshold was founded by him on a more philosophical basis, meaning for regions still on this side of the threshold as early as in his *Philosophy of Freedom*.[10] With that, above all in this book's first part, is given the substance into which Michael can work his way in order gradually to unite himself with the purified thinking of human beings. And in the second part of the same book, we deal with the establishment of free deeds that can only truly be free when they appear out of "love for the object" (GA 4, Chap. IX). For it is only with such deeds that "Michael has his special affinity". Thus already at that time, Rudolf Steiner had written the first Michaelic book that has the task – both in the present and for a long time to come in the future – of preparing human beings for conscious cooperation with Michael. For in both its parts, nothing less is described than what it signifies to think and to act Michaelically.

After that, Rudolf Steiner was told – from out of the spiritual sphere in which he now consciously found himself – what as the cosmic

Michael-Mystery he could bring to presentation and what he could only put into effect at the end of his life after the Christmas Conference (see more on this below). These Michael questions were above all the mighty questions dealing with the development of humanity and world-evolution that could be dealt with in the spiritual sphere. "But there, behind the scenes, behind this thin veil in the region of Michael – there the great questions of life were raised" (GA 240, 12 August 1924).

A hard spiritual battle was also linked with the revelation of these cosmic questions; a battle against the Ahrimanic dragon that Michael had to wage for the future of the earth and for humankind dwelling on it. Here, it was above all those souls standing by his side that previously, under his guidance, had concluded the supersensible Michael-school in order then, as anthroposophical souls living during the twentieth century, to work on the earth for the tasks of the Time-spirit. "Behind the veil, mighty phenomena occurred that were all grouped around the spirit-being whom we call Michael. There were great adherents of Michael; human souls that at that point in time were not in a physical body but between death and a new birth. There were in addition, however, powerful demonic powers that under Ahrimanic influences revolted against what was supposed to come into the world through Michael" (ibid.).

During his time in Weimar, Rudolf Steiner beheld all of this behind the veil of the physical-sensory world in the spirit-sphere directly adjacent to the earth. It was at the same time that the nature of the Michael-mysteries gradually dawned on him, which he likewise beheld in this sphere. With that, already in his youth – he was even then already initiated into these Mysteries in a rudimentary form – he still needed decades until he was allowed to communicate these matters to humanity. Only through the Christmas Conference, did it become possible for Rudolf Steiner to speak quite openly about this. For in so doing it was only through his esoteric action that certain Ahrimanic demons could be defeated; demons that earlier had not allowed expression of these secrets. "Indeed, since the Christmas Conference, through all of what has become possible to give to the Anthroposophical Society – through the ways and means I myself am allowed to work since that time in an esoteric sense –

these are not new matters, but in esotericism one cannot immediately communicate insights today that one has just discovered yesterday. These are old matters, things that were experienced in the way I have depicted it to you, but what has now been added is that the demons who earlier did not permit matters to be spoken about openly must now remain silent" (GA 240, 12 August 1924).

Particularly in the lectures concerning the karma of the Anthroposophical Society and in the so-called *Michael Letters*, Rudolf Steiner recounted the Michael-Mystery in great detail; and in the same way also pointed there to the Michaelic path towards the Christ, which can only be trod by human beings in our time (since the beginning of the present Michael-epoch), a path that Rudolf Steiner himself trod as the first human being to do so.

Let us select just one description out of the *Michael Letters*: Michael – who not on his own, because he respects our freedom fully, but through his image, which is at the same time our model, our example – guides human beings up into the sphere of the Christ and out of the realm of Ahriman where today materialistic science, and with it the entirety of western civilization, is stuck. It is a unique and modern Michael-path to Christ, on which what Rudolf Steiner sums up in one sentence, turns into complete inner reality, namely: "Such people see[11] how the human being in freedom is to be guided in the Ahrimanic sphere through the image of Michael away from Ahriman to the Christ" (GA 26, article of 19 October 1924).

From what has been stated, one can now understand even better why Rudolf Steiner studied all sciences so intensively already at the Technical College in Vienna at the time when materialism in the nineteenth century had attained its highest point in the development of western humanity. For, only in this way was it possible for him to find the way into Ahriman's realm so that later on, through his union with Michael, he could attain from there the ascent into the Christ-sphere.

This unique path to Christ can be characterized in yet a somewhat different way. To begin with, the human being is led into the kingdom of the Ahrimanic beings where – inasmuch as he or she has the picture or imagination of Michael as an example in his or her mind – one learns to vanquish the Ahrimanic dragon out of his or her own strength. Thus, the human being has entered into Michael-service here on earth and becomes a fellow-fighter with the Archangel as regards the further guidance of humankind in accordance with Christ.

Rudolf Steiner describes this aspect of the Michaelic path in the following words: "This is an important imagination: Michael, subjugating the dragon. To receive spiritually flowing life into the sense world: Michael-service it is henceforth. We serve Michael in being victorious over the dragon, the dragon that wants to achieve more growth in ideas, which have brought about materialism during the past epoch; ideas that today and in the future want to become even more abundant. To overcome this means to be in the service of Michael. That is Michael's victory over the dragon" (GA 152, 20 May 1913).[12]

In this way, Rudolf Steiner "stood in the service of Michael" since his early years. For like no other human being during the Michael-age that had begun in 1879, he was ready and willing to slip into the skin of the dragon that confronted him in the materialistic thinking-manner of his age in order to vanquish and transform this dragon in a Michaelic sense from within so that among human beings the path from natural science to spiritual science could be established.

In a conversation during 1907 with Edouard Schuré at Barr in Alsace, France, Rudolf Steiner used the picture of slipping into the skin of the Ahrimanic dragon to represent today's materialistic science in regard to Rudolf Steiner's own development. Edouard Schuré related these words later on as follows: "How was he to gain victory over, or at least tame and convert, this mighty opponent that – comparable to a huge armour-covered dragon spreading itself out over a great treasure – represents modern materialistic science? How would it be possible to secure this dragon of modern science in front of the carriage of spiritual truth? The only answer to this Michaelic question that could have been given to the young Rudolf Steiner by his Rosicrucian Master was: "When you wish to battle the adversary, you must understand him. You can only vanquish the dragon when you put on its skin"[13].

How this slipping into the skin of the dragon actually appeared is described by Rudolf Steiner only at the end of his life in his autobiography: His intensive occupation with materialistic natural science had already led him in his youth "into the vicinity of beings in the spirit-world ... who try to make such a [materialistic] direction of thinking the only prevailing one" (GA 28, Chap. XXVI). Then Rudolf Steiner continued: "Later on, I spoke of Ahrimanic beings when I wished to point in that direction. For them, it is an absolute truth that the world should be a machine". Now, here is the decisive sentence: "Likewise, my own inner struggle was that much more consciously directed against the demonic powers who did not wish to turn natural scientific cognition into spirit-beholding but into a mechanistic-materialistic way of thinking. One who seeks for spiritual cognition must *experience* these worlds" (ibid.; italics by Rudolf Steiner). These sentences are found in his book, *The Course of My Life*, in the chapter at the end of which he refers to his own spiritual experience of the Mystery of Golgotha.

It was this path with all its abysses and depths that Rudolf Steiner pursued in particular after his moving from Weimar to Berlin (1879). "I had to save my spirit-viewing in inner tempests. These storms stood behind my external experiencing" (ibid.). Based on the pure Michael-power in his heart – as a result of his earlier encounter with the Time-spirit in the spiritual world – Rudolf Steiner now sought for the possibility of discovering in the Ahrimanic sphere the new Michaelic path to the Christ. "After the time of trials that had exposed me to hard soul-struggles, I myself had to delve into Christianity, namely into the world where the spiritual speaks about it" (ibid.). But this is only possible when the human being discovers in this Ahriman-sphere and in the depths of his or her soul the power of Christ, which can be found there since the Mystery of Golgotha in freedom. For that too, Michael can be seen as an example and 'pointer of the way' for the human being. "Michael accomplishes what he has to accomplish in such a way that he does not influence human beings thereby, but so that they can follow *him* in freedom in order, with the power of Christ, to once again find the way out of the Ahriman-sphere into which they had to enter by necessity" (GA 26, article of 10 October 1924; italics by Rudolf Steiner).

The meaning of this is indicated by Rudolf Steiner at the end of his commentary, *The Freedom of Man and the Age of Michael* (GA 26). In order to attain freedom in thinking, human beings must consistently extinguish the thought-content that they bring in spiritually alive forms out of pre-natal existence for the build-up of the physical body on earth. In doing so, the Ahrimanic forces unavoidably move into our inner life. For they make it possible for us to eliminate our pre-earthly thoughts and transform them into mere shadow-images which then increasingly fill our consciousness.

These shadow-images, that in regard to their nature are 'nothings' and therefore cannot force human beings to do anything, nonetheless do permit us subsequently to experience freedom in our own soul. In all this, the Ahrimanic spirits participating in this process in no way wish to allow human beings to benefit. For through transforming human thinking into a "nothing" – something that is certainly the case in materialistic science – they ultimately try to break our connection to the spiritual hierarchies that guide us. In this way they hope eventually to separate all of humanity from the spiritual cosmos so as to hold us spellbound in their own illusory kingdom.[14]

So that this does not happen, human thoughts – without human beings losing the freedom that they have struggled to attain through these thoughts – must in a quite new way re-attain their connection with the spiritual existence of the cosmos in a manner that Anthroposophy makes possible today. For, "it is a path of knowledge that would like to lead the spiritual in the human being to the spiritual in the universe" (GA 26, Leading Thought 1).

In order to construct a bridge between the non-being of human thoughts and the spiritual being of the cosmos, a leap across the cosmic abyss is necessary, and Rudolf Steiner reports that with the help of Michael *and* Christ this is possible today. In accordance with what has been stated before, it is Michael himself who guides the human being in our time to this cosmic abyss of non-being through his spiritual example. Standing there, the human being must now dare to carry out the leap based on his or her own "I"-force. Then, at the other shore of the cosmic abyss, he or she is awaited by Christ himself in order to receive into his/her true "I" the spiritual communion with the World-"I", the Sun-Logos.

Rudolf Steiner sums up what has been said above in the following words: "In humankind's evolution, the abyss of non-being is indicated here, over which human beings must leap inasmuch as they become free individuals. Michael's activity and the Christ-impulse make the leap possible" (GA 26). Rudolf Steiner could utter these words without doubt based on his own inner experience,[15] which at the Turning Point of Time in Berlin he had passed through as a modern Christian initiate. For this is the true path to Christ in the Michaelic sense, or in Rudolf Steiner's formulation, "the Michael-path that finds its continuation in the Christ-path" (GA 194, 23 November 1919).[16]

One can therefore say: The first individually formed and individually fulfilled Michael-ceremony was therefore realized in Rudolf Steiner's soul. And in his soul the highest meaning of this Michael-festival was to stand in front of the Mystery of Golgotha in a *celebration of knowledge* from which Anthroposophy was founded on earth in the twentieth century. "The above-described probation of souls came about before the turn of the century. In my soul's development, having spiritually stood before the Mystery of Golgotha in innermost earnest celebration of knowledge is what mattered" (GA 28, Chap. XXVI).

With these words, reference is made at the same time to the purely *Michaelic* path of cognition and co-experiences with the Mystery of Golgotha; the path on which Rudolf Steiner himself journeyed, and on which around the turn of the last century he reached his loftiest goal. Still later, he also characterized this path as follows: "It is therefore so important for human beings of the present age to attain to the possibility of experiencing the Mystery of Golgotha *as something purely spiritual*. Then they will experience other spiritual matters and find access to spiritual worlds, the paths to spiritual worlds through the Mystery of Golgotha."[17]

As the conclusion of this chapter is reached it should particularly be emphasized that, despite all hindrances and abysses, Rudolf Steiner's inner path – from his earliest youth to the establishment of Anthroposophy in the twentieth century – ran its course consequentially without any breaks. For that reason any reader of the book, *The Course of My Life*, can have full confidence in the following words[18]: "I did not move forward in contradictions, as many believe. If that were the case, I would gladly admit it. But it would not be reality in my spiritual progress. I moved forwards in such a way that I added new realms to what lived in my soul" (GA 28, Chap. XXX).

For it was nothing else than the Rosicrucian impulse that initially led Rudolf Steiner to his Rosicrucian Master, then into the depths of the Ahrimanic sphere of the present, and subsequently – in one unique leap across the world-abyss – to the connection with the Christ-"I" on the other shore of world-existence through which the spiritual co-experience of the Mystery of Golgotha became possible for him.

And it is the same Michael-impulse that guided Rudolf Steiner to the founding of Anthroposophy that he served up to the end of his life, the impulse that united itself in him further and further with the Christ-being, so that at the end of his life he could even coin the new word-creation *Michael-Christ*.

*"But he appears with the direction-giving sword, through which he indicates the higher nature of the human being."*
*Rudolf Steiner (GA 229, 15 October 1923).*
*"Michael with the Sword." Russian Icon from the Archangel Michael Cathedral in the Kremlin in Moscow, beginning of 15th Century.*

# III
# The Nature of the Michael-Mystery

The Michael-Mystery, existing as it does in the cosmos and on earth, forms the esoteric basis for Anthroposophy in its totality. When we trace Rudolf Steiner's work and the developmental course of Anthroposophy systematically, the following is discovered: To begin with the Rosicrucian impulse (or that of esoteric Christendom) stands in the foreground – an impulse that Rudolf Steiner had unfolded within the Theosophical Society from the beginning. Why within the Theosophical Society? The reason was that this society, established in 1875 in New York, had likewise proceeded from a Rosicrucian inspiration, and only later was it diverted into a non-Christian or even anti-Christian impulse of eastern occultism.[1] Thus, Rudolf Steiner joined this society so as to lead it back to its original sources that are situated in esoteric Christendom.

Now, what about the second fount of inspiration – the message by the Time-spirit, Michael? When one pursues this question, one becomes aware that the revelation of the Michael Mysteries in Anthroposophy moves forward with a step-by-step separation from the Theosophical Society. The more the distance grows, the more powerfully Rudolf Steiner then places the Michaelic impulse into the foreground. In his early lectures of 1905/1906, the secret of the Michael-epoch is merely touched upon in a few sentences, and at that point only to a quite limited circle of listeners (see GA 93a, 3 November 1905).

Then during 1907 in the background of the Congress in Munich, something takes place that in no way is less important than the birth of anthroposophical art that stood in the foreground, namely the separation of Rudolf Steiner's Esoteric School from the Esoteric School led by Annie Besant. The western Christian-Rosicrucian School – guided on earth by Rudolf Steiner and inspired out of the spiritual world by the two great

masters of esoteric Christendom, Christian Rosenkreutz and Master Jesus
– ultimately separates from the eastern school that is henceforth led by
Annie Besant in an increasingly one-sided non-Christian direction and
inspired by two eastern mahatmas.[2]

What happened next after this separation during Whitsun of 1907
in the then liberated purely Christian-oriented esoteric school which was
now under the sole leadership of Rudolf Steiner? As early as during the fall
of the same year and within the framework of this school, Rudolf Steiner
gave several esoteric lessons dedicated to the Michael-Mystery[3].
Unfortunately, only around two and a half pages of notes based on
memory have survived from these lessons. Yet, we can imagine that during
such opportunities Rudolf Steiner typically offered an entire lecture often
lasting for one to one-and-a-half hours. Surely, with such a high volume
of communications, even the first (still introductory) description of the
Michael-Mystery of the present time was given.

The separation, however, continued further. As is known, Rudolf
Steiner and his friends were excluded from the Theosophical Society in
1912. For him personally, this was a great relief and liberation. And thus,
at Christmas of 1912 in Cologne, an independent Anthroposophical
Society could be established. At the beginning of May 1913, Rudolf Steiner
then travelled to London – where the majority of the old Theosophists
who followed H. P. Blavatsky existed at that time – now no longer as an
official within the Theosophical Society but as the free representative of
Anthroposophy – then still termed "Rosicrucian Theosophy".

We do not know exactly to what audience Rudolf Steiner spoke
at that time, nor how many people were present on the 1st and 2nd of
May 1913. However, Rudolf Steiner spoke in the second of the two lectures
– which belongs among his greatest and most powerful lectures – about
the contemporary Michael-Mystery[4] in connection with the supersensible
Mystery of Golgotha that had occurred in the world adjacent to earth in
the second half of the nineteenth century, and the consequence of which
is the appearance of the etheric Christ beginning in the twentieth century.

The first announcement concerning the second (spiritual)
Mystery of Golgotha was inseparably united with, indeed fully embedded

in, the Michael-theme: Michael who as the "Countenance of Christ" and as his "mediator" and "herald" now brings humanity the insight of the supersensible Mystery of Golgotha.[5] Thus, Rudolf Steiner reports at the conclusion of the above-mentioned lecture concerning Michael's new contemporary revelation to humankind: "Although many people will not acknowledge this new Michael-revelation, it will nevertheless unfold over all mankind" (GA 152, 2 May 1913). Then, concerning anthroposophists, he also adds: "Although we are only a small society in all of humanity – a society that tries to make the effort of grasping this new truth about the second Mystery of Golgotha, this new revelation by Michael – we nevertheless build up a new strength that depends least of all on our faith in this revelation, but solely and alone on this revelation itself; on truth itself" (ibid.). The meaning is that this revelation can and must be received in accordance with true Rosicrucianism.[6]

This unique connection of Michael with the supersensible Mystery of Golgotha has as a result for himself the direct cooperating with the appearance of the Christ in the etheric realm starting in the twentieth century. In this regard, Rudolf Steiner reports in a lecture from the year 1914 that Michael can today become visible essentially as a kind of 'fighter' for the purity of the spiritual horizon[7], so that the etheric Christ does not appear in a false image distorted by Ahrimanic demons, but instead as a pure – one would like to say Michaelic – imagination that can become visible to more and more human beings. Quoting him directly, Rudolf Steiner said: "This event of the appearance of the Christ in the way Theodora referred in the First Mystery Drama, can only be brought about when the rule of Michael becomes ever more wide-spread.[8] At present this is still a process in the spiritual world.[9] It is as if on the plane adjacent to our world, Michael does battle for the approach of the etheric Christ ... So that we can as it were actually behold a kind of incursion by Michael for the approach of the Christ" (GA 158, 9 November 1914). And the reason for this battle was characterized by Rudolf Steiner in the following way: "So that He, the Christ, does not appear in a wrong form, that is to say in a subjective imagination on the part of humanity; so that He appears in the right image, Michael must fight the battle that I have indicated" (ibid.).

In the quoted words, one sentence is of special significance, namely that the etheric second coming can only take its course properly if the Michael impulse spreads out over humankind widely enough. Why is this passage so particularly important? For, as some Anthroposophists have by now correctly noted, in the second half of his anthroposophical activity Rudolf Steiner refers more frequently to Michael than to Christ. (One could almost bemoan the fact that the great Christological deliberations between the years 1908 and 1913, which are summed up in several lecture cycles, appear in later years as if they are pushed into the background). Yet it becomes clear from the last quoted sentence that every word which Rudolf Steiner has uttered is in reality connected with the second coming of Christ, for in today's civilization the Michael impulse must gain ground *first* so that the etheric Christ can then appear among humankind. This is why Rudolf Steiner committed himself untiringly with so much energy until the end of his life to the Michael-impulse and the new Michael-culture on the earth.[10] For in the background of this dedication, the hard struggle was being fought out until the very end in order to make it possible that Christ could appear to humanity in the etheric world, and in the proper Michaelic manner at that.

One can therefore say that every word which Rudolf Steiner spoke about the Michael-Mystery until the end of his life points at the same time to the Christ-Mystery in its present etheric form. And for Rudolf Steiner himself, throughout all of his supersensible research and cognition, it was always a matter of the "Michael-Christ-Mystery".

To all that has been mentioned, the following should also be added. Already during his second London lecture, Rudolf Steiner speaks not only of the "new" revelation of Michael since 1879, but likewise about Michael's "second" revelation which takes place during the present age. "In order to take a firm stand here, we need only recall today that we remember that this contemporary age is the age of the *second* Michael-revelation" (GA 152, 2 May 1913).

During 1913, Rudolf Steiner only mentioned these two Michael-revelations in passing. Almost seven years later on the other hand, he defines them much more accurately and provides detail in the lecture of

22 November 1919 in one concise sentence: "The Word becoming flesh is the first Michael-revelation; the flesh becoming spirit must be the second one" (GA 194). And he formulates this somewhat differently elsewhere in the same lecture: "For true as it is that it says in the Gospels: In the beginning was the Word, and the Word has become flesh and has dwelled among us [Jn. 1,1; 14] – it is equally true that to the [second] revelation we must add: And the human flesh must again become spirit-pervaded so that it becomes capable of dwelling in the kingdom of the Word in order to behold the divine secrets" (ibid.).

With this second Michael-revelation there is moreover linked the fact that beginning in our time – for every human being, proceeding from his or her free "I" – the path to the higher spirit-members of his/her entity, Spirit-Self, Life-Spirit and ultimately to Spirit-Human – becomes accessible. For the transformation of the physical body (the "flesh", to use biblical terminology) into the spiritual Word is only possible with and out of the power of Spirit-Human. This is why Rudolf Steiner speaks in the Michael-Imagination about the "cosmic time of Spirit-Human" that begins in the present age. (See more on this in the fourth chapter of this book.)

Likewise, in another verse that he wrote for Marie Steiner, Rudolf Steiner mentions this activity of the forces of Spirit-Human that takes place already in our time:

> "Stars spoke once to human beings,
>   Their becoming silent is worlds' destiny;
>   Awareness of the silence
>   Can be sorrow for earthly people.
>   In the silent stillness, however, ripens
>   What human beings speak to stars;
>   Becoming aware of the perception
>   Can become strength of Spirit-Human."
>   (GA 40, 25 December 1922)

As will be shown later on in this chapter, the speaking of human beings to the stars, meaning to the spirits of the higher hierarchies, is directly linked with the Mystery of Michael in the present age. For, the transformation of human intelligence – so that it can be brought back to the heavenly kingdom of Michael – is indeed the modern path on which a human being today can learn consciously to speak to the hierarchies, something out of which the power of Spirit-Human gradually grows forth.

To all that has been said, the following indication by Rudolf Steiner still needs to be added, namely that the earth itself can only make possible the development of the "I" for human beings. Christ on the other hand, particularly through His present appearance in etheric form, can guide us to the higher members of being – Spirit-Self, Life-Spirit and Spirit-Human.[11]

In earlier times, it was only possible for the highest initiates or "Masters" consciously to work on the transformation and spiritualization of the physical body out of the forces of Spirit-Human. In the lecture of 28 October 1906, Rudolf Steiner describes how nowadays the entire earthly civilization works on the transformation of the astral body's changing into the Spirit-Self, but this is the case especially in humanity's most outstanding representatives. These are the Spirit-disciples (or Chelas) who also begin already now with the transformation of their etheric body into Life-Spirit through spiritual exercises. Finally, it is only the Masters that attain this stage of spiritual development on which they are able to already work on the spiritualization of their physical body out of the forces of Spirit-Human. "And when the 'I' receives the Spirit-Human stage into itself, it thereby receives the powerful strength to penetrate the physical body with it ... Precisely what has become Spirit-Human in the physical body is what has been spiritualized" (GA 9, Chap. IV, "Body, Soul and Spirit").

Rudolf Steiner sums up the last two stages like this: "Conscious working into the ether body is the stage of the 'Chela' (in German literally 'Chelaschaft'). Conscious working into the physical body is the stage of 'Master' (in German literally 'Meisterschaft')" (GA 94).[12]

Along with the appearance of Christ in the etheric, however, it is not only the work on the astral and etheric bodies that becomes possible for human beings but likewise work on the physical body now becomes possible for all human beings who unite themselves consciously with the Christ-force. "But for that, all of us need the permeation by the Christ-Spirit, and with that we also need the faith in the Christ-Spirit in its true essence; faith that the Christ entity is something which we can (and must) unite with the element in us that makes us human and which guides us to what is beyond earth; makes us into completed personalities inasmuch as faith in the Christ-Spirit helps us to develop Spirit-Self, Life-Spirit and Spirit-Human" (GA 197, 23 November 1929).

Here too, Michael once again steps forward preparing the way for Christ as his servant and helper because, during the time when he leads humanity as the Time-spirit, his forces likewise work out of the spiritual world *all the way down into the physical body of man.* "But Michael's impulses are strong and powerful, and they work from out of spiritual realms through the entire human being; they work into the spiritual, then from there into the soul-element, and from there into the bodily element of the human being" (GA 237, 3 August 1924). The reason that Michael possesses such spiritual strength is due to the fact that as the hierarchical being that today stands on the level of an Archai, he has his "I"-consciousness in the Spirit-Human stage and from this level can guide his spiritual impulses all the way into the physical world, imprinting them in this world.

We can now trace the Michaelic impulse further in Rudolf Steiner's work. In the autumn of 1917 he speaks about a new mighty deed undertaken by Michael. Now, the time has come that the spiritual world ultimately must be cleansed of the opposing forces that seek to prevent the approach of the etheric Christ. And "in front of Him" strides Michael, no longer with the scale – the way he was frequently pictured in former times – but now with the sword. He no longer points to the dragon with the sword, but instead points upwards to the higher ego nature of the human being[13] out of which alone a conscious relationship to Christ is possible. Michael appears before humanity today as the "Spirit of Courage" that never compromises with anything Ahrimanic. He is a serious stern spirit who – while he encompasses the entire earth and despite his openness to the world – never makes concessions to the

Ahrimanic spirit. He is active as the highest representative of "Cosmic-will", the will of Christ Himself.[14]

In the autumn of 1917, these opponents of the etheric Christ are also called "spirits of darkness" by Rudolf Steiner, spirits that have been cast down to the earth by Michael.[15] And one recognizes immediately where during the same year they gain a nesting among human beings, for during that year the Bolsheviks gain power in Russia with their reign of terror that lasts more than seventy years. Furthermore, Rudolf Steiner defines these spirits of darkness as those Ahrimanic powers that like a pestilence will spread racism and nationalism amongst humankind in our age. And where do we find this epidemic in the dark history of the twentieth century? In National Socialism! Just as the Bolsheviks, so too the National Socialists are likewise possessed by these anti-Michaelic demons. And since then, these Ahrimanic spirits continue to have their field of activity on the earth. Human beings must now deal with them, meaning that they must overcome these Ahrimanic spirits through their own strength. In the spiritual world on the other hand, they have already been overcome by Michael. Thereby, the path for the etheric Christ has been cleansed, and has thus become free. On this Michaelic path Christ strides into humanity.

As early as the following year, 1918, Rudolf Steiner points to a further characteristic of the Christ and Michael working together. Simultaneously with his ascent from the level of Archangel to that of a Time-spirit, Michael descended into the direct spiritual circumference of the earth between the years 1841 and 1879 in order, since then, to dwell in the hearts of human beings. Replicating this cosmic path on which Christ descended to earth, Michael then followed Him into the realm of human beings during the nineteenth century so as to connect himself still more deeply with them. "The Archangel Michael had to prepare himself for his descent to earth itself in a sense to emulate and follow the great downward journey of Christ Jesus Himself to earth; to live through this grand process: here on earth to take his point of departure and to continue with his work from out of the viewpoint of the earth" (GA 174a, 17 February 1918).

What this 'earthly' activity by Michael consists of is then characterized still furthermore. Here, it is above all important to ascertain that
Michael had chosen the same path in his journey from the Sun to the
earth that Christ – together with the soul of the later Jesus of Nazareth –
had previously traversed in the so-called cosmic 'pre-stages' of the Mystery
of Golgotha.[16] In so doing, he wished to connect himself anew with these
cosmic deeds of the Christ entity so that he would be able to fulfil his task
in regard to the coming appearance of Christ in the etheric realm. For,
the Christ's contemporary second coming, as viewed cosmically with
regard to the Mystery of Golgotha that stands in the centre of world-
evolution, is none other than the mirror-image of the third pre-stage of
the Mystery of Golgotha in which Michael participated in a particularly
active manner.[17]

The present-day collaboration between Michael and Christ
is additionally described by Rudolf Steiner in the following words:
"In our age, Michael is destined increasingly to become the ministering
entity for the Christ so that the statement that 'the Michael-reign enters
into humanity's destinies in an ordering fashion' means at the same
time that 'The Christ-reign will extend into the world' holds true.
In the front Michael bears the light of spiritual cognition, as it were.
Behind him Christ carries the challenge of overall human love"
(GA 218, 19 November 1922).

In this quote, the words "humanity's destinies" indicate that
in our age Michael also works together with Christ as Lord of Karma.
This is something that the later karma lectures affirm, given as they were
based on direct Michael inspiration. And the reference that Christ
bears the impulse of "overall human love" in mankind stands today in
a direct relationship to His etheric second coming. For the etheric
body in which Christ appears is at the same time a "body of love"
(GA 130, 2 December 1911); a body to which Michael guides the human
being in spreading the light of spirit-cognition.

When we trace the Michael-effects further in Rudolf Steiner's
work, we come to the special year following the burning of the First
Goetheanum when everything in the Anthroposophical Society

threatened to fall apart. And to the listeners who had to walk past the ruins of the First Goetheanum to the Carpentry Hall, Rudolf Steiner said in his introductory lecture at the Christmas Conference that these ruins were likewise a sign for the world conditions (GA 260, 24 December 1923).

Yet, these ruins were more than a symbol for the conditions in the Anthroposophical Society of that time. And about what does Rudolf Steiner speak to the members in this year of decision? He speaks about the annual festivals; he speaks about what can unify human beings in an especially strong spiritual sense, and for the first time he poses to them the unique task in humanity's history that out of their own initiative – not through the guidance of the gods above – to inaugurate a new festival. A new Michael festival is to originate on earth based on full human freedom on the foundation of Anthroposophy.

As early as May of 1913, Rudolf Steiner had told the members of the Theosophical Society in London that the totality of spiritual society was nothing less than "Michael's gift" to humanity (GA 152, 2 May 1913). And this is precisely the basis for the new Michael festival. Its inauguration, however, can take place only based on human freedom, and this festival thereby becomes a modern path to Michael because "Michael ... [is] the spirit that in the most eminent sense works with the freedom of human beings" (GA 174, 17 February 1918).

In this an inseparable connection towards Anthroposophy also exists that has its roots already in the content of *The Philosophy of Freedom* (GA 4) in the unique path that is only depicted in this book; a path of inner transformation for the entire human being that proceeds from spiritualization of his or her entire thinking.[18]

As already mentioned above, it is ultimately through the esoteric impulses which had come into the society during the Christmas Conference, that the Ahrimanic demons were brought to silence, whereby Rudolf Steiner could begin with the full revelation of the Michael-Mystery. Some elements of this he had already discussed earlier. Now, however, he was able to explore this in much further scope and in greater depth than had ever been imagined by the members before.

At this point, it appears necessary to quote a quite bewildering section from the *Michael Letters*. For these words affirm like no others the true dimension of the cosmic activity on the part of Michael in regard to nascent humanity. At the same time it becomes clear from them how intimate Michael's relationship to humankind, and its entire process of development, was in the cosmos from the very beginning, although the formulation used in the *Michael Letters* sounds a bit strange: "The spiritual entity that from the beginning had directed its glance on humanity was Michael. In a manner of speaking he organized the actions of the gods in such a way that in a cosmic location humanity can endure."[19] The barely imaginable dimension of this hierarchical spirit in its primal connection with mankind becomes observable at this point.

Already in 1919, Rudolf Steiner posed the question concerning who it might have been in particular that cast the Luciferic spirits out of the higher worlds and into that sphere which the Bible has spoken of as the Paradise in which those serpent-like spirits dwelled who then mislead the human being? And from Rudolf Steiner's reply it becomes unmistakeably clear that it was Michael himself. At the behest of the higher hierarchies, he had transferred the Luciferic spirits out of their 'Cosmic-will' into Paradise so that, with the aid of Luciferic beings, humanity could pursue its path to the earth. Not freedom itself, but the *conditions* for becoming free – something that is often mixed up – are created by Lucifer. Freedom in its highest aspect originates from a completely different sphere. (See more on that in this chapter.) Through the so-called Fall into Sin only the necessary conditions for their later realization are generated.

It follows from what has been stated that the spirit who cast the Luciferic spirits into the human sphere[20] was without any doubt the one who saved a being for the future of humanity's evolution at the same time and protected it from this fall. This being was the Nathan soul who remained in spiritual worlds in order to appear at the Turning Point of Time as Jesus of Nazareth for the first and only time on earth, and who became for three years the Christ-bearer.[21] It is probably obvious that in both cases it was Michael who was responsible for the fall of Lucifer as well as for the protection of the Nathan soul.

Why is this so? This is because, after the fall of the primal human being from Paradise, Michael became the guardian of the two Trees of Paradise. Since the Fall into Sin, these two trees – the Tree of Knowledge and the Tree of Life, like a primal image for the entire future – are no longer separated from each other but in their crowns are woven into one another; indeed are grown into each other all the way through. And the Guardian of these grown-together trees is Michael (see GA 96, 17 December 1906).

An essential aspect of these two trees relates to the separate paths pursued after the Fall into Sin by the primal human being Adam – who had partaken of the Tree of Knowledge and had therefore to begin his journey on the earth – and the Nathan soul whom Rudolf Steiner moreover designated as the heavenly "sister-soul of Adam" (GA 142, 1 January 1913) and who had remained in Paradise (in the spiritual world), connected with the Tree of Life (see GA 114, 18 September 1909).

In this way, the primal image originated in the spiritual world for what was supposed to happen on earth so that Christ could incarnate in a human body at the Turning Point of Time. As the first event, the Nathan soul came to earth as bearer of the forces of the Tree of Life. In its twelfth year, this soul received the individuality of Zarathustra into itself, who as an initiate had worked the most on himself (through many initiations) in order to transform the fallen forces of the Tree of Knowledge so that the fallen forces could then serve the further develop-ment of humankind. These two beings – the Nathan soul and the Zarathustra entity incarnated in it – now worked together. And this working together made it possible for Christ to incarnate on earth through the Baptism in the Jordan. The primal image for this entire event, however, lay in the two woven-together trees which Michael guarded in the spiritual world from the primal beginning.

From spiritual research by Rudolf Steiner we know that the Nathan soul had already in pre-Christian times been unceasingly occupied; that previously on three occasions during its cosmic existence this soul had surrendered itself to the Christ so that He could save mankind. We therefore come across three so-called "pre-stages" of the

Mystery of Golgotha. And in all this Michael was also involved, for he is always present when it is a matter of the struggle against the counter-forces. Above all, Michael has a profound connection with the last of the three pre-stages, of which Rudolf Steiner reports that all images that have pictured Michael or the Holy Spirit in the course of time as doing battle with the dragon are earthly replicas of the third pre-stage of the Mystery of Golgotha.[22] At that third pre-stage, Michael with his cosmic power is particularly and intensely involved. If his cooperation in the first two pre-stages still took place as if in concealment, now where events draw closer to the Mystery of Golgotha, his participation in it becomes quite evident. And the remarkable thing in all this is that when we consider the Mystery of Golgotha as the axis of world-evolution, these pre-stages are mirrored in the stages afterwards.

Thus, the third pre-stage – in which the imagination appears of Michael battling the dragon – is reflected in the first stage *after* the Mystery of Golgotha. And what comes about in this first stage afterwards? It is the beginning of the Christ appearing in the etheric realm. For, as early as in the third pre-stage, Michael had already preconceived this event that some day after the Mystery of Golgotha would take place, something would also happen, the foundation of which he had created at the same time earlier to enable his later participation in it for our time. These matters mutually mirror each other when one places the Mystery of Golgotha into the centre of world-happenings.[23]

Then a great decisive event follows for Michael. As guardian of the kingdom of the Sun, he has to experience how the Christ – that spiritually represents the centre of the Sun bestowing on this Sun-kingdom its world-significance – departs from this realm so as to link up with the destinies of humankind on earth.

It goes without saying that Christ stands immeasurably higher than the entire Sun-region. In primordial times, He descended out of hardly-imaginable heights of the spiritual cosmos down to the Sun, in order from there gradually to take over the guidance of earthly humankind. (Rudolf Steiner states in this regard, "The Christ descended down from still farther heights to the Sun".[24]) And already from this "time" onwards Michael became the servant and herald of the Christ on the Sun.[25] Now, however, Christ departs from the Sun-kingdom; a remarkable experience for Michael as the reigning spirit of this sphere.

Rudolf Steiner describes this in moving words. Down on earth all the true insightful initiates felt: At last, Christ is coming to the earth! It was an Advent-mood. Conversely for all the beings on the Sun, and above all for Michael himself, a completely different mood held sway: "He is leaving! That was the overwhelming experience" (GA 240, 19 July 1924).

And what happened then? From out of the Sun, Michael had to experience how even what he had administered for aeons from the very primal beginning – the cosmic intelligence and all creative deeds and rules of conduct for all divine-spiritual beings amongst themselves – was gradually descending to the human beings on earth.[26] In all this, one fact is of great significance, namely, that this "slow descent" of the cosmic intelligence from Michael's Sun-kingdom is in the same way a consequence of the Mystery of Golgotha. For according to Rudolf Steiner, "*under the influence of the Mystery of Golgotha* this Michaelic intelligence underwent this move ... from heaven to earth" (GA 260, 21 August 1924).

When one moreover takes into consideration that in another lecture Rudolf Steiner described this descent of "intelligence" as a "cosmic gift" out of the spiritual world to earthly humanity (see further in this chapter), the thought then comes to mind that even the loosening and leaving of the cosmic intelligence that Michael had until then administered, was a kind of sacrifice for this being that he offered up from out of the Sun in beholding the Mystery of Golgotha.[27]

For, along with the Mystery of Golgotha, Michael has ventured onto the path of becoming the "countenance of Christ", meaning the cosmic countenance of that being who in all mysteries was venerated and recognized as the "Great Sacrifice" (GA 102, 27 January 1908). Hence, Michael was prepared to move onto a sort of "sacrificial path" in the spiritual world that was moreover to become a path of renunciation and silence for him. (See more on this further in this chapter.)

There is one more magnificent image that stands in the sign of the Michael-Mysteries: The cosmic intelligence departs the Sun-kingdom on the same path that the Christ had taken earlier – from the Sun to the earth. Like a "sacred rain" (GA 240, 20 July 1924) this intelligence now drops down and beginning in the 8th and 9th century AD can be increasingly received by human beings. Now on the earth, the first "individuals arise who think for themselves" [in German "Eigendenker"]. A completely new development gradually begins that, with the start of the consciousness-soul-epoch (AD 1413), becomes the destiny, or fate, of all mankind.

On this formerly Michaelic but now turned human intelligence, people of more recent times establish their most precious possession – their freedom – which is rooted in thinking and has become independent. For at the moment when human beings could be certain that they no longer received their thoughts from the spiritual world but produced them on their own – that they were the creators of their world of thoughts – from then on they could fully and consciously grasp hold of their freedom.

From what has been said, it becomes clear how human freedom and intellectuality are inseparable, simultaneously determining each other. For when cosmic intelligence became purely human intellectuality or rationality on earth, it transformed itself out of the living condition it had possessed in the cosmos into the dead merely shadowlike thoughts of ordinary human consciousness. Yet, because the lifeless shadows are mere replicas of outer reality and do not compel us in any way, they turned into the foundation for the inner experience of our freedom. This is why Rudolf Steiner says: "Both had to come eventually: Free personal use of intelligence [and] freedom of the human will" (GA 237, 28 July 1924).

There exists a wondrous lecture from the year 1923 in which Rudolf Steiner describes this process as if in code, without bringing it directly into a connection with Michael[28] as was the case after the Christmas Conference. Yet, we can conclude with certainty from the later karma lectures that we are concerned here principally with Michael. So Rudolf Steiner asks in the above-mentioned lecture: Where in fact does the intellectuality come from that establishes our individuality and freedom nowadays? This intellectuality comes out of spiritual worlds, so he states, which also happens to mean that same world where human beings ascend to following their death. And to his further question how this became possible, he himself replies:

through a *celestial* gift. "Our freedom and our faculty for abstraction ['intellectuality'] is a *celestial* gift that moved into earthly worlds out of the supersensible worlds" (GA 257, 30 January 1923).[29]

And then he links this twofold gift of heaven with the descent of Christ from the Sun, for both derive from the same cosmic realm and have descended on the same path down to the earth and therefore stand in a profound connection with each other.[30] "What occurs in the world is that the Christ, the Spirit-Sun, has moved down into earthly worlds from spiritual heights, so that what has humanly moved out of the supersensible into the sensible [freedom and intellectuality] joins with what has cosmically moved out from the supersensible into the sensible [the Christ-entity] so that human beings can find themselves together with the Spirit of the Cosmos in the right way. For only then can we as human beings stand properly in the world, *when the spirit in us finds the spirit outside ourselves*" (ibid.).[31]

The italicized words express the entire essence [nature] of Anthroposophy in the same way that Rudolf Steiner formulates it a year later in the First Leading Thought: "Anthroposophy is a path of knowledge that would like to guide the spiritual in the human being to the spiritual in the universe" (GA 26).

Now, how can this transition from the spirit in the human being to the spirit of the cosmos consciously be carried out? In our age, this can only be done if the human being finds a new inner relationship to Christ and then pervades the two celestial gifts – freedom and intellectuality – with the Christ's power in order, thereby, to attain a completely new relationship to the divine-spiritual. "And inasmuch as these celestial elements – intellectuality and freedom – moved into earthly life, a completely different outlook towards the Divine has become necessitated for humanity than was the case up to now" (GA 257, 30 January 1923).

These days, Anthroposophy would like to bring this new way of "looking up towards the Divinity" to human beings; it would like to teach us "in a pure way to think with Christ; to be a free individual with Christ" (ibid.). And through what has this possibility been given to human beings today in Anthroposophy? The answer is only and solely through the results that have emerged from the Mystery of Golgotha. ("This new way of looking up to the Divinity has only become possible for humanity through the Mystery of Golgotha," ibid.). And furthermore it says: "We live in an age when we have to realize that what is most holy for us in this present time must be permeated by the Christ-impulse, namely the faculty of grasping pure concepts and the faculty of freedom" (ibid.),[32] for only thereby can these two faculties be so "sanctified" by human beings that they can become the foundation for the future development of humanity as Tenth Hierarchy.

If one now illuminates this inflow of celestial intellectuality and freedom into humankind's evolution with Rudolf Steiner's explanations in the karma lectures – that took place shortly after the Christmas Conference – concerning the Michael-Mystery in conjunction with cosmic intelligence, it becomes evident that one deals here with exactly the same process; illuminated, however, from slightly different viewpoints that nevertheless complement each other in a remarkable way. For it is Michael himself, who in looking up to his paragon [his ideal] – the Christ – offers mankind this "celestial gift", allowing the cosmic intelligence to stream down to the earth, whereby the foundation is prepared for the origin of the human being's true freedom.

Almost in the same manner as earlier, prior to the Christmas Conference, Rudolf Steiner describes the concepts of "intelligence and freedom" in the karma lectures, inasmuch as he connects them together the way they originally were linked with each other and with the Sun-kingdom of Michael. Rudolf Steiner also describes how they then departed from it and continued to live on earth, where Michael was to engage with them in a quite new relationship, now no longer in the cosmos but – following the beginning of his activity as the leading Time-spirit of the present – in the souls of earthly human beings. "Michael descended down to earth. What had in the meantime taken its course so that human beings might attain *to intelligence and to freedom*, he could rediscover only on earth, so that he once more becomes ruler over the intelligence within earth's realm; but now this intelligence is effective within human beings" (GA 237, 28 July 1924). How this can happen in the future becomes evident from Rudolf Steiner's hint that Michael, who from the beginning has been administering the thinking in the spiritual world, "is no longer able to administer it in the cosmos, but in the future wishes to administer it through the hearts of human beings" (GA240, 21 August 1924).

The reality of this process is, however, much more complicated. For, not only has Michael gifted human beings "from above" (meaning from out of the spiritual world) with the gifts of freedom and intelligence (as the modern faculty for abstract thinking), but he has likewise prepared the gradual unfolding of these gifts in humanity "from below", meaning from the corporeal [bodily] side.

Rudolf Steiner speaks of this only one time in an early lecture – which to this day has never been published in the Collected Works. Here he describes how Michael has not only accompanied the earthly path of humanity following the Fall into Sin, but additionally how he has made this possible in the first place by giving the human being a bodily form. As is made clear from later lectures, Michael could do this because he was the servant and mediator of the six Sun Elohim (Spirits of Form) through which the Christ-being as Sun-Logos works (see GA 103, 20 May 1908).

In so doing, Michael shaped the earthly form of man in such a way that in much later times it would represent the predisposition to allow the human being eventually to attain his or her own intellectuality and freedom, or in other words so that human beings would be able to become the bearers of Michael's former cosmic intelligence.

The notes that have remained from this incomplete lecture (unfortunately no shorthand version exists) state the following in this passage: "Christian esotericism calls those 'builders' who are not on our level of consciousness and activity but are entities and Angels at higher levels of consciousness, and that one particular Angel worked who (during the middle of the Lemurian age) shaped the human form. Christian esotericism addresses this higher Angel as the Archangel Michael. Michael is the builder of the human form, subject as it is to birth and death, and subject also to gender. And due to the fact that the human being entered into birth and death, and the Angel of Form, Michael, gave it this form, it came about – just as polarity exists in the world – that the opponent of

Michael made its appearance. This opponent, who is always effective in the course of evolution, is called the dragon or the snake in Christian esotericism" (1 January 1904).

It may at first appear surprising – but will make complete sense as we shall immediately realize – that it was Michael who, at the behest of the higher spirits, implanted the death-forces into the earthly body of human beings as well as causing the separation of mankind into two genders. For, both are connected with the nature and constitution of earthly thinking. This faculty of thinking, however, could only become possible through the separation of the genders. Only due to the fact that since the middle of the Lemurian age the human being could not produce a being similar to itself on its own but required the fructification through a being of the other gender, were the forces freed that were supposed to become the foundation for the origin of earthly thinking in the human body.[33] Thus, as "builder" of the human form, Michael created the first prerequisite for the origination of human thinking.

But so that this thinking would eventually become the site of origin for human freedom, the human brain likewise had to be interpenetrated by death forces. For, only thereby does thinking become shadow-like, meaning bereft of any sort of life. And as mentioned before, such dead shadows of thinking can no longer force the human being to [will, feel or think] anything in his/her consciousness. That alone, however, cannot yet signify freedom per se, it is only its further prerequisite.

At the time, however, when genderality and death became a part of earth evolution in the way described above, the forces of the Ahrimanic dragon likewise found entry into the development of humankind. This is because Ahriman was connected with the nature of death from the very beginning as a result of the separation of the genders.[34] Michael had to wage his battle with him so that human beings would not completely fall prey to Ahriman but, all hindrances notwithstanding, could find the way to freedom and with that to the goal of their evolution.[35]

It is clearly evident from what has already been mentioned in this chapter that it was not Lucifer who once presented humanity with the gifts of intellectuality and freedom, levelling the path for all of us, rather it was still higher beings that provided these gifts; beings who in the supersensible world stand directly under the Christ, yet in front of all the other beings Michael stands as Christ's Sun-countenance. How this is to be understood is something that we can best trace from the phenomenon of freedom with its various forms or stages.

When *Luciferic* freedom (this is only one condition for true freedom as already mentioned before) is merely an emancipation in the sense of leading humankind gradually to the point of complete separation from the spiritual world and its benevolent guidance, then the second kind of freedom, a *general human freedom*, which descended to earth together with cosmic intelligence is of a completely different nature. It is a freedom *for* something and therefore already connected with the increasing responsibility of human beings for their actions in the world.

Nowadays, all human beings possess this general human freedom if they find themselves within modern civilization's social stream of development. This is why Rudolf Steiner states in this regard: "*Freedom* is directly given as fact to every individual who considers him or herself as standing within the contemporary segment of humanity's evolution. Unless one wants to deny an obvious fact, nobody should say 'Freedom is not a given'" (GA 26, Leading Thought 110). And that this can be so nowadays is solely the result of the 'divine gift' by Michael to humanity; it is the direct result of the fact that the cosmic intelligence of Michael descended to the earth and was received by human beings.

When this generally valid freedom is properly comprehended in our present Michael-epoch, we know that it is moreover present in our soul because by our own free will we can increasingly revitalize our thinking that has become abstractly intellectualistic. The path for that is outlined in the first part of *The Philosophy of Freedom*. In this book the direction is pointed out on which human beings should activate the intellectuality available to them, not only in their heads but to develop it so far that it gradually takes hold of their entire nature.[36] In this way we arrive at the experience of the second kind of freedom that makes it feasible for us moreover to carry out such actions in the world as described in the second part of *The Philosophy of Freedom*. There it is a matter of actions undertaken out of pure "love for the object" which alone can be designated as truly free deeds on the part of human beings on earth.

How these two forms of freedom are linked with Michael and his cosmic activity is characterized by Rudolf Steiner as follows: "*When the human being seeks freedom* without any leaning towards selfishness; when freedom becomes for us pure love for the action to be carried out, we have the possibility to draw near Michael" (GA 26, 16 November 1924; italics by Rudolf Steiner). And further: "Inasmuch as the human being feels him or herself in Michael's vicinity, he/she is on the way to carrying the power of intellectuality in his/her entire human nature; we think with the head, but the heart feels the lightness or darkness of thinking" (ibid.). And out of this feeling "of thinking's light or its darkness", the responsibility for his/her action grows in the human being quite in accordance with Michael.

In order to attain to the kind of freedom depicted in the book, *The Philosophy of Freedom*, we furthermore have to transform our thinking as has already been described, that is we have to transform the inner quality of our intelligence in ourselves. For to a higher level of freedom, there must absolutely likewise belong a higher level of thinking-activity. Or put more precisely, only this higher stage of thinking can be the foundation for the corresponding [higher] experiencing of freedom. After all, as we have already seen, freedom and intellectuality arrived together out of the same spiritual world here on earth[37] and therefore cannot be separated from one another.[38] This higher or second kind of thinking is moreover called "pure thinking" in *The Philosophy of Freedom* (GA 4, Chap. IX), for it functions during its use independently from the brain and therefore is free of any sensuality. For here we are concerned primarily with sense-impressions which ordinary thinking is subject to nowadays, and this causes thinking to be "impure" and "sensuous" to a very large extent. This is why Rudolf Steiner writes: "The highest stage of individual life is conceptual thinking without consideration of a specific content of perception (ibid.). Precisely in this context in the same paragraph of this book, the concept of "pure thinking" is introduced.

Yet, before the third stage of intellectuality and the third form of freedom that corresponds to it are dealt with here one more time, the second stage should be mentioned again by means of a particular description concerning the three forms of thinking in the human being that Rudolf Steiner offered in 1921 in a public lecture cycle under the title, *Self-Consciousness; The Spiritual Human Being*, in Kristiania, Oslo (GA 79).

There, he calls the first kind of thinking the "ordinary" or "combining"[39] thinking, and the second kind "organic-morphological" thinking, probably in connection with Goethe. In the course of the lecture, however, he offers further descriptions each of which stresses one particular quality. He thus refers to "sense-free thinking" which takes its course in forms and pictures, and therefore can also be designated as "imaginative" or "formative" thinking. Furthermore, he calls this "an inwardly alive thinking", terminology that refers to the fact that sense-free thinking is primarily connected with the etheric body of the human being, just as ordinary thinking belongs with the physical body, or to put it more precisely, to the human brain. Finally Rudolf Steiner adds: "The old thinking that one requires for ordinary life and ordinary science remains fully intact, but for this thinking a completely new thinking is added" (GA 97, 26 November 1921).

In the same lecture, Rudolf Steiner makes reference to the transition from ordinary thinking to morphological thinking, a transition that results from the inner oath of schooling that is described in his book, *Knowledge of the Higher Worlds and Its Attainment* and in the corresponding final chapter of *Occult Science, an Outline*. In this connection, Rudolf Steiner once more mentions his book, *The Philosophy of Freedom*, and explains why it was so little understood after its publication. The reason for this is supposed to be that this book does not count on ordinary thinking. It can only be truly comprehended with "morphological thinking" – or using the terminology in the above-mentioned book – with "pure thinking".

Furthermore, Rudolf Steiner describes the transition to the third kind of thinking which he designates as "qualitative thinking". We could likewise call this thinking "spiritual thinking" or, as will be seen through the further consideration, "Michaelic thinking".[40] One arrives at this third kind of thinking through a process of *inversion*, which is explained as follows in the lecture: "[It is] a thinking that not only lives in forms that change in themselves [as does the second kind of thinking], it is a thinking that is in a position to turn the 'forming from within' outwards, and in doing so changes its form" (ibid.).

In order to achieve this now, one must ultimately break off every connection not only with space as is done in the first kind of thinking but also with time as one lives in the second kind of thinking. For, "then one comes into a reality that is situated beyond space and time" (ibid.). Only through this mysterious inversion does one come to "qualitative thinking … For it is simply a changing of the entire quality of thought that comes about in this inversion; this turning of what is within to the outside" (ibid.). And for what purpose does one require this third stage of thinking? It is needed in order to enter the spiritual world fully consciously and freely: "And even what I outlined to you as that invigoration of thinking with the inverted thinking, the supra-morphological thinking, even this exists only so that in full awareness one can penetrate into the spiritual worlds. One now actually experiences these higher worlds with a spiritual content" (ibid.).

In order to grasp the essential difference between the second and third kind of thinking, one can more accurately call to mind Goethe's primal plant. Beholding the primal plant in one's own soul belongs among the most beautiful fruits of the second, morphological thinking that Goethe possessed to a marvellous extent. If he had risen to the third kind of thinking, he would have borne the image of the primal plant across the threshold of the spiritual world in his meditation where this image would have experienced a complete inversion. Then in the objective spiritual world, the primal plant would have appeared in a new form to Goethe as a living spiritual entity, namely as the group soul of plants.[41]

In this context *pure thinking* assumes a special position which in Rudolf Steiner's work has two meanings. First of all it is to be equated with sense-free thinking. For, to cause thinking to be "pure" signifies freeing it from any influence from the material world that penetrates to the soul through the senses of the body. (Occupying one's self with mathematical truths and some philosophical problems can already be part of this thinking.) Secondly, it is that thinking which ultimately exits out of the corporeal organisation[42] and proceeds through the gateway of the exceptional state (see GA 4, Chap. III), and is thereby in a position to cross the threshold of the spiritual world. In this second quality, pure thinking is totally imbued with will, something that can only be reached through an intense meditation. In this sense, it represents the transition or the bridge between the second and third kind of thinking, both of which are described in this chapter.

If one wants to imagine the serious results that proceed from such stern meditation even more concretely, we can for once call to mind how Rudolf Steiner himself already in his youth passed through the above-described stages of thinking. Through his intense occupation with the most diverse sciences at the Technical College in Vienna and his study of philosophy that lasted for several years, he could thrust scientific thinking to the highest summit, something that was as yet rarely attained at that time.

Through his later involvement with Goethe's natural-scientific writings, which lasted for several years, he was offered the best opportunity to develop morphological thinking in himself as well. From there, the result for him – likewise because he included the corresponding works by Schiller – was the path to the final version of *The Philosophy of Freedom*, the beginnings of which are to be found already in his book, *The Science of Knowing; Outline of an Epistemology Implicit in the Goethean World View* (GA 2, 1886).[43]

Quite early on, Rudolf Steiner could even take his first probing steps towards the third form of thinking, probably because – at least in rudimentary ways – Rudolf Steiner received systematic instruction in accordance with the modern path of inner schooling through the aid of the Rosicrucian Master, gifted as he was with a certain form of clairvoyance, and whose name remains unmentioned. As he himself states, this Master showed him the directions that later on led to *Occult Science, an Outline*.[44]

Rudolf Steiner described what this signified in reality towards the end of his life – as we already saw in the second chapter – when following the Christmas Conference he happened to mention the origin

of this central work from the esoteric aspect. Thus, Rudolf Steiner –
when he had advanced sufficiently on the Rosicrucian initiation-path in
accordance with the book, *Knowledge of the Higher Worlds and Its
Attainment* – depicts how he himself then took Haeckel's *Anthropogeny*,
transformed its contents in his meditation, and carried them across the
threshold of the spiritual world up towards the gods in order then to
receive from the gods what is pictured in the book *Occult Science, an
Outline* concerning world-evolution.

This method of the three-staged thinking described above was
expanded by Rudolf Steiner step by step in the direction of the other
natural sciences with their materialistic, that is to say naturalistic, form in
which they mostly appeared at that time. He did the same with art turned
naturalistic, and even religion. To begin with, all of this was lifted out of
ordinary thinking as thought-content into morphological thinking, and
subjected to a complete transformation so that in the third kind of
thinking it could assume a shape that could be offered up to the gods on
the other side of the threshold. They handed back what they had received
to Rudolf Steiner who could then hand it back to human beings on
earth as Anthroposophy.[45]

In essence, we concern ourselves here with a marvellous metamorphosis that can only be carried out by a human being in conscious
cooperation with the gods, namely on the basis of the transformation of
human thinking, which through the afore-depicted three stages has risen
into the spiritual world. The actual metamorphosis, however, only
happens along with the attainment of the third stage.

In the already mentioned public lecture cycle, Rudolf Steiner
tries to make the nature of this metamorphosis even more comprehensible to his listeners through the following image. "Now you must
imagine that something happens here like a turning of a glove inside-
out. The inner side is turned to the outside, but at the same time,
however, the elasticity is changed. Another form originates. It is not
only as if one had turned the glove inside out, but after one has done
that it would assume a completely different shape through other forces
of elasticity" (GA 79, 26 November 1921). And then Rudolf Steiner adds,

turning directly to his listeners: "You see, I have to mention something extraordinarily complicated already as the first indication to this third kind of thinking" (ibid.).

How is this comparison to be understood? The key is offered by natural science itself – which confronts us nowadays frequently in revolting materialistic form – but behind natural science an out-and-out high spirituality is concealed that could begin only on earth by way of scientific development.[46]

This spirituality is completely new on earth and still unknown to the gods in the spiritual world. They therefore have a powerful interest in it, and more, they themselves unequivocally need it, but they can receive this new spirituality only from those human beings who like Rudolf Steiner (or the earlier Rosicrucians[47]) can turn natural scientific cognition inside-out in their meditation so as to reach the concealed spirituality contained in there.[48] This spirituality is liberated from its bondage to outward materialistic thought forms and then receives a totally new shape that can be brought up to the gods. But as we have already seen, this is only possible on the level of the third kind of thinking.

Now we come to the decisive point of the entire path. It consists of the facts that in the above-depicted manner one can bring the insights of science (but likewise the results of natural scientific art and so on) up to the gods on the far side of the threshold, meaning, "inasmuch as one bears all that up, one in fact encounters Michael once the faculties have been developed for that" (GA 233a, 13 January 1924).

As quoted above from the *Michael Letters* by Rudolf Steiner, one merely comes "into the vicinity" of Michael through the second kind of thinking in connecting up with *The Philosophy of Freedom*. But on the described path when one has also reached the third kind of thinking, one will encounter Michael *consciously* in the spiritual world. Then one brings the intelligence that has sunk down to earth back to him, however not in its original form – since it has meanwhile passed through the human soul – but in a quite new form as a result of the above-depicted turning around, something that signifies a mighty advancement for the kingdom of Michael.

Now, how is it to be understood that the hierarchies will receive something completely new from human beings through the return of the transformed intelligence? When we consider once more what was already mentioned earlier (namely that cosmic intelligence in actuality brings to expression the ways of interaction amongst the hierarchies themselves) then, in the passing of this intelligence through the souls of human beings, its transformation signifies a quite new possibility as regards the mutual rules of behaviour on the part of the hierarchies. This means that the hierarchies themselves will thereby come into new inter-relationships, which for them are absolutely necessary so that they can start building up the future "Cosmos of Love" out of the present "Cosmos of Wisdom" (see GA 13). The first impetus for this must, however, proceed from human beings, namely from their thrice-transformed thinking.

The above likewise reflects back on human beings themselves. Having once described this new relationship to Michael from the cosmic side, it can further be characterized still more from the human side. As Rudolf Steiner formulated this, the evolution of man is summed up as follows: "Yet, in the beholding of the outward material dimension, the experience of the spiritual and with that the spiritual *beholding* of it can begin to manifest in a new way."[49]

Goethe had already taken the first steps on this new path. This is why Rudolf Steiner could take Goethe's relationship to nature and make it the new basis for the "Goetheanism" which he had created. He himself went much farther, however. For in the manner just described, he took up the entire materialistic science of his age and transformed it in accordance with the Rosicrucian method of schooling into something completely new. He relates this as follows: "What has been acquired under the sign of materialism in the way of natural scientific knowledge can be grasped in a spiritual manner in the inner life of soul" (ibid.). This stage of inner development corresponds exactly to what earlier was designated as the third, or Michaelic, form of thinking.

What sort of tangible consequences this entails for the individual development of the human being and his/her relationship to Michael, is described by Rudolf Steiner following immediately after the above last-quoted words: "Michael, who has spoken from above, can be heard from within [the human being's soul] where he will create his new abode." Speaking more imaginatively, this can moreover be expressed as follows: "The Sun-like element that for long periods of time could only be absorbed by the human being from out of the cosmos into him or herself will become radiant within the human soul. People will learn to speak of an 'inner Sun'. In our life between birth and death we will feel and experience ourselves no less as earthly entities, but we will recognize our own being that moves about on earth to be a *Sun-guided* being" (ibid; italics by Rudolf Steiner).

With this, that stage of inner development is precisely addressed that Rudolf Steiner had attained in Weimar when, around age thirty-three, he had brought the work on *The Philosophy of Freedom* to a conclusion. Accordingly, this book in its entire process of origin is thus likewise a unique example for all that the "Sun-guidance" of Michael signifies for the soul – namely, when the Time-spirit itself begins to speak out of the inner being of the human soul, and this cosmic speech is moreover heard by us.

This is the path in our time on which the encounter with Michael is possible in the spiritual world adjacent to the earth just as it was described already in the second chapter regarding Rudolf Steiner. When it is the Sun-guidance that causes the meditant sooner or later to encounter Michael himself and thereby become a fellow-fighter in Michael's cosmic host, one could go on to say that we deal here with the same process described by Rudolf Steiner from two different sides: The conscious encounter with Michael in the spiritual world adjacent to the earth and the bearing of the Michael-impulse as "inner Sun" in one's own soul.

In the lecture of 13 January 1924, quoted in this book already several times, Rudolf Steiner furthermore mentions that the earlier Rosicrucians tried again and again to encounter Michael in this manner; and that this was possible for them prior to the beginning of Michael's contemporary age (1879) "... only as if in a dream. Since the end of the last third of the nineteenth century, human beings can encounter Michael in the spirit in a conscious way" (ibid.). Thus, Rudolf Steiner is the first

Rosicrucian on this path that encountered Michael in a fully conscious state. In his books, *The Philosophy of Freedom* and *Knowledge of the Higher Worlds and Its Attainment*, he made this path to Michael accessible to human beings of our time. This is why one can rightfully designate the mode of thinking required for this to be a Michaelic one. For we can thereby return our intelligence – that has become terrestrial in changed form – back to Michael, whereby a working together and cooperation with the contemporary Time-spirit as the cosmic countenance of Christ becomes possible. "Human beings must work together with the gods, with Michael himself" (GA 240, 19 July 1924).

Just as the second kind of thinking – that in *The Philosophy of Freedom* is characterized as "pure thinking"[50] – corresponds to the nature of freedom (something that was already described in this book), so the third kind of thinking corresponds to a further form of freedom that Rudolf Steiner characterizes as follows: "For, *The Philosophy of Freedom* emerges out of the purely human forces of cognition [of knowledge] themselves, at which time they can venture into the field of Spirit. Then in order to understand what is recognized here, one does not require "an association with beings of higher worlds. One can however say that *The Philosophy of Freedom* prepares one to recognize what can then be discovered in spiritually 'venturing out' together with Michael."[51]

And what can a modern Rosicrucian discover about freedom; a Rosicrucian who has encountered Michael in the above-described way and from then on has begun to "venture out" with him in spirit? Or formulated more concretely: What has Rudolf Steiner himself experienced in this regard? He found "the possibility to gain enlightenment spiritual-scientifically concerning the cosmic nature of *freedom*" (ibid.; italics by Rudolf Steiner). He likewise describes what this signifies in the last-quoted lecture (GA 240, 19 July 1924). There, he characterizes how Michael works completely differently today than all the other planetary Time-spirits. For, he is the only one that, as representative and guardian of the Sun-intelligence, fully and entirely reckons with human freedom. For that reason in regard to humankind, he becomes "the silent ... spirit closed off within himself" (GA 233a, 13 January 1924). The other

Time-spirits constantly bestow on human beings their impulses, inspirations and incentives for actions. Michael on the other hand, renounces all of this. It is not with the causes that he unites himself, but solely with the consequences of what human beings "create out of the spirit" in their freedom (ibid.). The consequences of such deeds are what Michael evaluates from the viewpoint of the guidance of the entire cosmos. If they are justifiable before the guidance of the universe, he then accepts these consequences of free human deeds and takes them into the spiritual world where they become cosmic deeds, meaning building-blocks of the new Cosmos of Love. Thereby, Michael becomes the "actual spiritual herald of freedom" (ibid.). And it is this sphere of Michaelic freedom that can moreover be designated as Sun-freedom that we as human beings can attain to in this third stage of our transformed thinking and intelligence. From then on, he/she is initiated into "the cosmic nature of *freedom*" (GA 26, 9 November 1924; italics by Rudolf Steiner).

Likewise, the mighty picture of Michael that stands alone in the circle of the other planetary Archangels (as Rudolf Steiner explained it in a lecture – see GA 237, 8 August 1924) belongs to this stage of initiation. And when we ask ourselves where does this tragic opposition have its origin, one discovers among other reasons the following one as well: only Michael steadfastly upholds human freedom in the confidence and hope that human beings on earth will prevail in the great trial of freedom, and that the fire of freedom enkindled on the earth will be carried up into the spiritual world so that gods and men can come together in a new form that never existed before, meaning in full freedom. The strength however, that Michael requires for this lonely quest, he gleans from his original connection with the Sun as the cosmic spring of freedom, but especially through the fact that since the Mystery of Golgotha he has increasingly found himself on the path leading to becoming the cosmic countenance of Christ.

In a lecture, Rudolf Steiner even points out that in our time (more accurately by 1879) Michael had already advanced and fully developed into the countenance of Christ. This is also the reason why Michael represents one single path to the Christ; a path that is suited to the human being of today as described in Anthroposophy. Rudolf Steiner describes this new stage in Michael's development in the following words: "Today Michael is once more the world-regent but mankind is urged to comport itself to him in a new manner. For, Michael *now* is not to be Jahveh's countenance but the countenance of Christ Jesus. We are now supposed to approach the Christ-impulse through Michael" (GA 195, 25 December 1919). And in the same lecture he adds: "One could just as well say 'the Michael-paths' as one could say 'the paths of spiritual-scientific insight'."

If one furthermore considers what Steiner said in the lecture of 2 May 1913 (GA 152) concerning the second supersensible Mystery of Golgotha which began in the second half of the nineteenth century, and the relationship of Michael to this event then it becomes even clearer why Michael has ultimately become the countenance of the Christ in our age, and tells us about His etheric second coming in such a decisive way.

Let us turn back to the path of the initiate. Only now is the initiate prepared truly to learn what was thus formulated at the beginning of this presentation as the goal of the development outlined here: "to think together with Christ and to be free together with Christ" (see also p. 63). For it is Michael himself who now guides one to Christ, the countenance of who he is when the human being has entered the kingdom of Michael in the described manner.

If one at this point recalls that the path on the first stage of thinking begins where Ahriman's forces work most powerfully in modern abstract thinking, one comprehends "how the human being is supposed to be guided in freedom through the image of Michael, in the Ahriman-sphere, away from Ahriman to Christ".[52]

Now, the Christian initiate has fully grasped the secret of the relationship of the human being to the nature of freedom in the Michaelic sense. That the path depicted here is even possible for us today; this is owed to the fact that Christ at the Turning Point of Time, based on pure love and in complete freedom, brought forth His sacrificial deed in the Mystery of Golgotha (without requiring it for Himself). With that, human beings were given the freedom that can allow them to rise up from earth all the way to cosmic dimensions without losing their own human origin.

This in turn has only become feasible because – in Christ as the only godly being that has passed through an entire human incarnation – human and cosmic freedom could unite in a new synthesis so that human beings on this Michaelic path to Christ can bring something quite new into the spiritual world which not even the highest gods were able to do previously.

In deeply moving words, Rudolf Steiner reveals this secret of Christ's connection to human freedom at the conclusion of his main Christological lecture-cycle, *From Jesus to Christ*. Because of their significance, these words shall be quoted in full here: "With the Luciferic influence, the potential for the free human 'I' was developed. This had to be allowed by the Father-God. But after the 'I' – for the sake of freedom – was of necessity entangled in matter, in order now to be liberated once again from this ensnarement, the Son's entire love [compassion] had to lead to the Deed on Golgotha.

"Only through this deed, has complete human dignity become possible. That we can be free beings we owe to a divine deed of love. Thus, as human beings we may feel that we are free beings, but we must never forget that we owe this freedom to God's deed of love... In fact human beings should not be able to grasp the thought of freedom without also thinking of the salvation-thought that is owed to Christ. For, only then is the thought of freedom justified. If we wish to be free, we must offer up the sacrifice to owe our freedom to the Christ! Only then can we truly behold freedom. And people who believe that their human dignity is inhibited if they owe it to Christ, should realize that human opinions count as nothing compared to cosmic facts, and that eventually they should very much want to acknowledge that their freedom was acquired from the Christ" (GA 131, 14 October 1911).[53]

In the light of this primordial image that originated in the Mystery of Golgotha, the freedom of the human being that is meant here becomes the basis of the highest spiritual love, called "agape" in Greek, so that out of these two basic elements of freedom and love there will arise in future times the new Hierarchy – designated by Rudolf Steiner as the Tenth Hierarchy – in the spirit-cosmos. This Hierarchy will bring about something that will be fundamentally new in the entire hierarchical order of the world.  For it will be possible for this Tenth Hierarchy to work world-creatively in the cosmos, not through inspirations from above but based on its own inner power, and the potential for this is already contained in *The Philosophy of Freedom* for today's human evolutionary stage.

Rudolf Steiner describes this tremendous universal perspective in the following words: "Thus we have in the human being a member of the hierarchies, concerning which we see that mankind does indeed distinguish itself from the other hierarchies.  We see that man appears different from the Seraphim, Cherubim, Thrones; the Kyriotetes, Dynamis, Exusiai, and even the Spirits of Personality [Archai], the Fire Spirits [Archangels], and the part of the Angels [that have not fallen into evil].  When we look towards the future we can say to ourselves: I am called upon to seek in the very depths of my inner being for all that gives me the impulses for actions – not by beholding the Godhead [the Trinity] as do the Seraphim, but by beholding it out of my own very deepest inner nature" (GA 110, 18 April 1909-II).  This means that in the future, human beings will reach the stage of an absolute unconditionality in cognition and therefore unconditionality in creative action as well, not only on a human but on a cosmic level.  The human being will then create out of nothing.[54]

What shines forth in these words as the ultimate goal of humanity's evolution can be started on by the human being in a minute germinal way already today as he or she proceeds along the earlier described path of development for our thinking.  Eventually, when a person's thinking will have reached the [yet to be described] fourth and highest stage, the human being sacrifices to Christ the Michaelic freedom ("we must bring the sacrifice") that will have been won through struggle.  Then we can be free together with Christ, and we can think together with Christ.  All this can only happen when, in accordance with the task already mentioned, human beings will also have learned to think in accordance with Christ.

In concluding this first part of the above portrayal, it should however be pointed out clearly just how the highest freedom is achieved as the result of the above-mentioned twofold task – to be free together with Christ and to be able to think with Christ. In his address dealing with the Foundation Stone Laying at the Christmas Conference, Rudolf Steiner offers an unequivocal reply in which he refers to the cosmic warmth and cosmic light of the Christ. With regard to human warmth and human love that dwell as moral forces in the soul, these must also be permeated and strengthened by the cosmic warmth and cosmic light of Christ, so that we human beings can fulfil our destiny on the earth. "And we can best empower that soul-warmth and soul-light which we need, when we enliven them with that warmth and light which radiated forth at the Turning Point of Time as the Christ-light in the world's darkness" (GA 260, 25 December 1923). Then, Rudolf Steiner gave emphasis to these words in the fourth part of the Foundation Stone Meditation in a prayer-like turn towards the Christ who wishes to bestow on us these two cosmic forces which we categorically need for our humanness.

> "Light Divine,
> Christ-Sun.
> Warm thou our hearts,
> Enlighten thou our heads"
> (ibid.)[55]

What this connection of the human soul with the Christ-warmth and the Christ-light signifies, is characterized by Rudolf Steiner a bit later in his essay, *Michael's Mission in the Cosmic Age of Human Freedom* (GA 26, September 1924). Here, he once again goes into the necessity of receiving the spiritual warmth and spiritual light of Christ: "Thus, the human being must live his or her life in regard to the spiritual Sun – the Christ, who has united the Sun's existence with earthly existence – and into his/her soul receives from the Sun in a living manner what corresponds to warmth and light in the spiritual world" (ibid.). He furthermore explains what this signifies. "In the struggle to attain their freedom", human beings had to forfeit the original relationship to the "divine-spiritual existence of primal time". The new connection to the latter is then brought by the Christ to human beings who in the meantime have become free through His warmth. Human freedom thereby reaches a further cosmic dimension.

In order to find this spiritual warmth within oneself, however – that is to accept it into one's own "I" – one must first have an inner relationship to Christ. "Human beings will feel that they are pervaded by 'spiritual warmth' when they experience the 'Christ in themselves'" (ibid.). The well-known words of Paul, "not I but Christ in me"[56] receive their full reality and significance in connection with the "spiritual warmth" that emanates from the Christ.

If human beings are united in this warmth with Christ in their soul, from then on they will experience what is true and genuine manhood. And without feeling in the least that our inner freedom is being restricted or impinged upon, we feel ourselves enfilled by the basic feeling of soul, "Christ bestows on me my humanness" (ibid.). This signifies that human beings, in full possession of their freedom through the Christ-warmth, feel themselves in their soul united consciously with the entire divine-spiritual cosmos. "And once *this* feeling is present, another feeling arises inasmuch as human beings feel themselves lifted up through the Christ beyond mere earth-existence, inasmuch as they experience themselves to be one with the starry surroundings of the earth, and with that the divine-spiritual becomes recognizable in these starry surroundings" (ibid.; italics by Rudolf Steiner). When this is attained, human beings can approach their cosmic future in such a way that in doing so they can "remain faithful to the primordial gifts given by divine spiritual entities, notwithstanding the fact that in their worlds humans have developed into free individualities" (ibid.).

At the Christmas Conference, Rudolf Steiner points to this future perspective of humanity's evolution in the words of the Foundation Stone Meditation at that passage where he describes how the human being "can recognize him or herself as an individually free human being in the reigning working of the gods in the cosmos, as a cosmic being – an individual being in a cosmic being – working as an individual human being in the world-being for the cosmic future" (GA 260, 25 December 1923). Here is the starting-point for the new creative "doing" by the human being's activities that increasingly attain not an earthly but a cosmic dimension.

Rudolf Steiner moreover mentions in the above-quoted article that the possible fear of this [future] perspective (that is prior to the connecting of one's freedom with the Christ-being), could throw people back into the realm of Lucifer. For, any attempt at a return back to the primordial goodness of the past without the full unfolding of individual freedom and its union with Christ leads unavoidably into dependence of Lucifer.

The same thing occurs through accepting spiritual light from the hands of Christ. A thought-activity is always connected with light. The cosmic intelligence radiates so long as it remains in a connection with its origin. It is the spiritual light that fills the cosmos with radiance and glory. Human beings had to separate themselves from this light for the sake of their freedom. After that, they could no longer behold its spiritual power of brilliance coming from outside, but from then on it was beheld only in the form of shadowy thoughts in regard to which they, however, felt themselves as their actual creators which they experienced in their souls. From then on these shadowy thoughts were, however, their absolute property.

With that, human beings lost the original relationship to the "primordial, glorious divine light" that they had possessed prior to achieving their individual freedom of thoughts. This primal light of the world is brought back to human beings by Christ. At this point one must read Rudolf Steiner's words most precisely, because their formulation is extraordinarily delicate and precise. He writes: "In the light that the Christ brings to the human being, primal light is again present" (ibid.). In this sentence, the word "light" relates to the glory, the spiritual brilliance of the cosmic intelligence whereby this intelligence becomes an intermediary for the divine "primal light". To live as a free human being in the primal light signifies, however, to think together with Christ. "In such a dwelling together with Christ, the bliss-bestowing thought can 'like a sun' irradiate the entire soul: The primordial, glorious, divine light is again here" (ibid.), and human beings – while maintaining their individual freedom – can experience this primal light in their "I" in an entirely new way through Christ.

This, however, signifies nothing else than we as human beings begin spreading our "I"-consciousness over ever wider and higher regions of the spiritual world in a cognizing manner, and thus as free individuals unite with the gods of our origin in a completely new manner. "And we will sense the power in this spirit-light that guides us cognitively with an ever higher and wider consciousness to that world in which we will rediscover ourselves as free human beings with the gods of our origin" (ibid.).

If we do not raise our God-given intelligence onto the stage of Michaelic thinking ourselves, sooner or later we will succumb to the temptation "of wanting to experience the use of freedom only in the intellect", and that will lead us "to Ahriman who wishes to take the present world and transform it entirely into a cosmos of an intellectual nature" (ibid.). In this case, we would find ourselves surrounded by an impenetrable darkness in our thinking that will separate us from the spiritual world and its good entities. And thinking itself, instead of lifting itself up into higher worlds, will increasingly connect with subterranean forces and ultimately pull the entire human being down into this abyss.

In the overview [summation] of the above referred-to article, there appears as if in the background the depiction of the sculptural wooden group wherein Lucifer embodies the fear of the individual use of freedom, and Ahriman on the contrary wants to connect this individual use of freedom to the intellect and thus turn man into a slave of his intellect so that he can never again find conscious access to the spiritual world. Between these two polar spirits, who today cooperate frequently against human freedom[57] as well, the middle figure of the Representative of Man stands as the purest revelation of love which alone is in a position to unite all polarity into a higher synthesis. Above the overall sculpture, the words could appear with which Rudolf Steiner concludes the *Third Leading Thought*. There it is a matter of "uniting oneself with Michael where he [the human being] also finds the path to Christ" (GA 26, Leading Thought 120).

Even in Rudolf Steiner's life, we can find clear traces of this path. As depicted above, his encounter with Michael occurs in the spiritual world adjacent to the earth when he was in his 33rd year of life; during that time when he had just concluded the work on his *Philosophy of Freedom*. From then on – having in his soul only the image of Michael that he in his transformed thinking can hold onto – his path leads through the Ahrimanic sphere in order there to liberate the intelligence which already to a large extent has been "occupied" by Ahriman. With the move to Berlin this "journey into hell", with all its dangers and temptations, begins for Rudolf Steiner. Nevertheless pursuing his Michaelic path further, Rudolf Steiner tries to reach the Christ sphere so as to solve the task he is facing.[58]

After the exceedingly dramatic years in Berlin – where everything Rudolf Steiner had attained in the way of inner development up to then and where he had even risked his life – he still succeeded in his break-through at the end of the century. In his autobiography, *The Course of My Life* (GA 28), he describes his mighty victory over the Ahrimanic powers as well as his new Michaelic relationship to Christ and the Mystery of Golgotha as the only source of all the forces through which the Michaelic intelligence had been liberated out of the Ahrimanic realm and thereby could be turned into the basis for the modern science of the spirit. For him, it was a matter of the purely spiritual experiencing of the Mystery of Golgotha that is only feasible through the spiritualization of the human forces of cognition.

For the sake of completeness, *two more aspects* must be added to what was said above; aspects which through the cooperation of intelligence and love on the here-described path lead to the highest love and its source in Christ.

The *first aspect* results from comparing the four above-described stages of thinking's development with the content of the book, *The Threshold of the Spiritual World*, (GA 17). In this book, Rudolf Steiner links the individual members of the human being with the secret of the threefold human "I"[59] as well as with the various spheres of the spiritual world, which (even if to begin with still unconsciously) we as human beings have a connection with during our life on earth. The first stage corresponds to our physical body in its physical-sensory surroundings. Here, human beings develop the first stage of intelligence available to them, which is still completely abstract. We are dealing with the body-bound thinking and the consciousness of the earthly "I" present here in it.

On the second stage, our concern is with the etheric body that has entirely connected itself with the elemental world of the earth. In the etheric body, we develop the second kind of thinking, the morphological one. Then spiritual thinking – the third form – is unfolded in our astral body that stands in a direct relationship to the spiritual world. On this third stage, thinking can be borne across over the threshold into that realm, where it leads to the other self, that is to that higher "I" of man which is effective in the course of the various incarnations – linking all three up into a unity.

Ultimately on the fourth stage, where the human being advances in the depicted way with his/her thinking and freedom into a direct relationship with Christ in order to think and be free with Him, the individual attains a conscious connection to the innermost essence of his/her own being, meaning to his or her own true "I" that is connected with the supra-spiritual world.[60]

In describing this path, however, one may not remain standing merely at thinking and its one-sided unfolding. For then in reality one would not get beyond the first stage, the ordinary thinking. The second stage on this path is already attained by means of the fact that thinking unites with the sphere of human feeling, and thereby consciously perceives the formative forces of nature.[61] One can also say that on this stage we concern ourselves with human intelligence that is completely permeated by feeling which has become conscious. For, feeling that can otherwise only be compared with the condition of dreaming now becomes a conscious, thinking-pervaded, newborn force of cognition in the human being.

The same thing happens on the third stage with willing. In the ordinary human being, this willing is situated in a deep state of sleep. Yet, when the will is penetrated with the transformed thinking of the third kind, willing arrives at the condition of complete awakening. Such a will can be used from then on as an organ of cognition that allows the human being to find his/her higher "I", which at birth had not descended out of the spiritual world into the physical body (see GA 165, 19 December 1915). For, the only soul-force that the higher "I" remains in connection with, even during the earthly incarnation, is the human will. When this will is fully awakened on the path of inner schooling, conscious access to the higher "I" is likewise opened up. And the higher "I" lives in the spiritual world like a spiritual being among other spiritual beings. This is why the hierarchies now become visible for the human being. And because he or she has journeyed on this path into higher worlds quite consciously, meaning in the sign of Michael, the encounter with the Time-spirit becomes possible at this stage.

The sphere of the true "I" on the other hand is located on a still higher level, already beyond the region where thinking, feeling, and willing are effective. This is why Rudolf Steiner characterizes this in the following words: "*The 'true I' is in a supra-spiritual surrounding world. In it the human being finds him or herself as a spiritual entity even when all the experiences of the senses, the elementary, and the spiritual world* [to which the higher self belongs], *hence all experiences of the senses, including thinking, feeling and willing, fall prey to forgetfulness*" (GA 17; italics by Rudolf Steiner). Only on this stage, is a conscious relationship with the supra-spiritual world attainable, and indeed the complete union with the Christ-being. One experiences Him as the World-"I" – with which the true "I" of the human being is related in its very nature since primal times – and oneself as the micro-logos that bears the spiritual forces of the macro- or world-logos in itself. And out of both of these latter elements the human being himself can become creative in the cosmos.

Viewed from the standpoint of modern initiation, the various qualities of time also belong to the here depicted three-fold "I"-being (see the summary on page 73, section: microcosm). Through the physical body, we experience in the earth-"I" everything in a spatial sense, even time. The actual nature of time only reveals itself in experiencing "I"-consciousness in the etheric body (the second kind of thinking). During the transition of "I"-consciousness into the astral body, the human being already arrives on the far side of the threshold with the gradual awakening in his higher "I", which flows towards man from the future and is related not with the earthly but with the "occult-astral" evolution.[62]

This loftier form of evolution can be cognized through the third kind of thinking. If therefore Rudolf Steiner speaks in the already quoted public lecture of 26 November 1921 (GA 79) about the fact that the third form of thinking [belongs] "to a reality that lies beyond space and time", he means by that our ordinary time from which a person now emerges so as to reach the stream of esoteric [occult] time, which viewed from the earthly standpoint does in fact lie beyond space and time.

Ultimately, through the union with his or her true "I", the initiate comes into contact with a still higher kind of time which at the Turning Point of Time was brought through Christ onto earth and "flows from eternity to eternity" (GA 236, 4 June 1924).[63] This means that this stream of time has its origin in eternity (or the realm of "duration") that preceded the evolutionary stage of Old Saturn.[64]

The *second aspect* relates more to the macrocosmic development and its relationship with the spiritual hierarchies guiding it. In order to make human freedom possible on the earth, they have withdrawn stage by stage from the cosmos surrounding mankind. In primal times they were present in it as *definite* beings. On the next stage, only their *revelations* could still unfold. Then after a further withdrawal on the third stage, only their manifold *activities* were left behind, above all in the various regions of nature. But all of this did not suffice to let human beings arrive at their individual freedom. This is why the hierarchies undertook a fourth step. Now they withdrew in their activity so far that for human beings only the results of their *work* remained attainable. And that is our cosmos today in which modern science in all directions does research according to measure, number and weight.[65]

What once ran its course on the macrocosmic level must now be carried out by human beings on the path of inner schooling in the opposite direction in microcosmic form, and in the full possession of their freedom and individual thinking. And this is what is taking place in the sense of the unfolding of human thinking as depicted earlier.

On the stage of ordinary thinking – the thinking that combines – we live and cognize only within the framework of activity that was accomplished by the gods and left behind for us. With the living or morphological thinking, we are in a position gradually to comprehend the living activities of the gods in ourselves and in nature surrounding us. Then on the third stage, already standing on the far side of the threshold and out of our higher "I", we experience revelations by the hierarchies in our thinking. And on the fourth stage we experience these revelations out of our true "I" in their "very own primal being" (ibid.).

Here we recognize that the highest love belongs inseparably to our true "I". For this love in reality is not only a mere feeling – the way it is frequently experienced by human beings on earth – but a force that extends far beyond thinking, feeling and willing,[66] and that can become a bridge,[67] which alone can connect us with the Christ-being.

Then, through the connection with Christ in the fourth stage, the power of love turns into the highest creative power. One now gains access to the surroundings of the gods (hierarchies) as a free (self-determining) and intelligent (independently-thinking) being that carries up from the earth towards the hierarchies freedom and love with a completely new quality; a quality which up until then had been completely unknown to them, and that now enriches their world enormously. Or in other words, we bring to the hierarchies the basic qualities of humanity as the future Tenth Hierarchy, namely freedom and love.

In this way, we human beings attain that stage of initiation on the Michaelic path to Christ, which Rudolf Steiner in regard to Benedictus indicates in the third scene of the *First Mystery-Drama, The Portal of Initiation*:

> "When on the pilgrimage of soul
> I had attained that stage
> Which granted me the honour
> Of serving with my counsel in spirit-spheres ..."
> (GA 14)

Only an initiate who can think together with Christ and be free together with Him is in a position to bring to the higher hierarchies something from the earth that they otherwise do not possess in the higher worlds, yet require unconditionally in order to guide humankind further in accord with their true destination.

| Macrocosm | | *Intelligence* | *Freedom* | Microcosm |
|---|---|---|---|---|
| Being | **4. Thinking with Christ** | **Being free with Christ** | **The True "I"** (Duration) | |
| Revelation | **3. Qualitative Thinking** – Supra-morphological Thinking – Spiritual Thinking | **Michaelic Freedom** | **The Higher "I"** in Astral Body (Spiritual-time) | Anthroposophy |
| | | | **Threshold** | 'Philosophy of Freedom' as Book of Inner Schooling |
| | —Pure Thinking———— | | —Exceptional Condition | |
| Activity | **2. Organic-Morphological Thinking** – Forming Thinking – Living Thinking – Sense free Thinking – Body free Thinking | **Concept of Freedom in Book, 'The Philosophy of Freedom'** | **Etheric Body** (Time) | Goetheanum |
| Work | **1. Intellectual Thinking** – Abstract Thinking – Deductive Thinking – Natural-scientific Thinking | **General Human Freedom** | **Physical Body** The Earth-"I" (Space) | Outer World |

**Fall into Sin**
The Luciferic Supposition of Freedom
and Individual Intelligence (of the Intellect)

Such an initiate will also enrich Michael; and more, if he or she acts on the lofty behalf of the Christ out of His spiritual sphere on earth (pervaded by the power of the Mystery of Golgotha) – the full understanding of which is actually only accessible to earthly human beings – then it is also the hierarchies and Michael himself who *serve* such an initiate. Rudolf Steiner described such a state of affairs once towards the end of his life in a personal conversation with Ita Wegman. She recalled this later as follows: "And in this way the mystery originated that extended further across Rudolf Steiner's life and activity up to the time of his final ailment. Not only Michael expressed himself through him; far higher powers also expressed themselves through Rudolf Steiner; Michael became the servant of his spirit" (*An die Freunde* [To the Friends], Article of 20 September 1925, Arlesheim, 2ⁿᵈ Edition, 1968).

This moreover refers to the stage of initiation that Rudolf Steiner had attained above all after the Christmas Conference. Among other things, this stage consisted of the fact that he could think with Christ, and he could be free with Him.

At this point, the quite justified questions can arise in the reader regarding the here outlined perspective: How can this here-depicted ideal ever be attained, and aren't we infinitely far distant from it? Or is this goal only reserved for initiates of the rank of Rudolf Steiner? The circumference of all that Rudolf Steiner had reached on this path is obviously open to a non-initiated individual, but in an as yet far distant future. However, an actual working-alongside in the here-described processes can already become possible for one who in this incarnation has prepared him or herself already for the next incarnation, thus enabling progress on the spiritual path, to a far greater extent than can be imagined presently. For, the solution of the riddle to a faster advance is based on the law of reincarnation and karma.

It is obvious therefore, that hardly anybody can attain this goal during one incarnation; nonetheless through Anthroposophy, even now decisive preparatory stages can be undertaken on this path. And more, during incarnations in the present age conditions for this preparation are especially favourable. Already in a thousand years conditions will be significantly more difficult. So, today it is initially a matter of cultivating in our ordinary logical thinking a most solid and consistent character. And then, by way of Rudolf Steiner's early book – above all the intense study of *The Philosophy of Freedom* – the basis for the second kind of thinking and even the first beginnings of third kind should be acquired. In the same way, a deeper comprehension of the Goethean views of nature, and a spiritual consideration of art in accordance with the forms of the First and Second Goetheanum lead to this goal.

Added to these two stages, there moreover belongs the abundant study of anthroposophical contents themselves, for the pursuit of which conditions are particularly favourable in this Michaelic age at the present time. Rudolf Steiner states in this regard: "Human beings must become accustomed to think of interconnections in the world that are in accord with great unselfish viewpoints. The best way for that is when as a simple individual one is willing to pursue this Rosicrucian path,[68] which means the study of the basic teachings of spiritual science... For occupying oneself with these truths purifies thinking and disciplines it in such a way that one becomes mature enough for the other measures that lead to the occult path" (GA 96, 20 October 1906).

In order to activate the third form of thinking in the soul, one must already carry out the first steps on the modern path of [inner] schooling. To do so, it takes not only a thorough study of spiritual science and the strict development of moral qualities; it furthermore requires an intense meditative life in accordance with Anthroposophy. We are guided still further on this path through the inner work with the mantras from the First Class of the School for Spiritual Science in which the third form of Michaelic thinking in its actual form emerges and is schooled. That is why the mantras are suitable to aid one in the initial experiences within the realm of the fourth kind of thinking.

Again and again, Rudolf Steiner points out that the central point, and at the same time the heart, of the totality of Anthroposophy is the communications of the spiritual research concerning the nature of the Christ, whose deed occurred during the Mystery of Golgotha and the present appearance of Christ in the etheric region. Students of spiritual science must take all this in with special intensity and endurance, and make it the essential content of their soul. For today on this basis – meaning through one's thinking about the spiritual world – it is a matter of creating a completely new relationship to the Christ.[69] For in this the first real beginnings are found for being able in future times to think with Christ and to be active in the sphere of Christian freedom as His servant and co-worker. For Anthroposophy – as the message to humanity by the contemporary Christ-being – is given us so that the opening first few steps can be taken already now freely and consciously towards this fourth stage of the above-outlined development.

The spiritual fruits of this inner schooling – which may be started by everyone during the present incarnation, although in the framework of a single earth-life he or she might not progress very far on this path – are taken with us into life after death without any loss, where they are transformed into new higher faculties between the time-interval of two incarnations and corresponding to the laws of the spiritual world. Thus, such a person returns to the earth already in his or her next incarnation with a special gift regarding all the here-described stages of inner development, and in this way he or she will attain even greater successes and perhaps come very close to the ultimate goal outlined here, in order then – to the extent that one remains faithful to one's inner path – surely to attain the ultimate goal in the third incarnation.

The optimal path of inner development outlined here can naturally be more difficult due to certain conditions of personal karma, and therefore may not lead so directly to the goal. Nevertheless, we are concerned here not with dozens but with only a few incarnations. The decisive point is that we *begin* the Michaelic path to Christ during *this* present life on earth with full energy and good will. To catch up with that later on will be incomparably more difficult than in the present time. For, the beginning of this path is available now as part of this epoch, in which Michael himself reigns as Time-spirit *and* leader of humanity. And in this lies the reason – in accordance with the law of karma – that everything one sows in the life of soul as justified seed (in harmony with the spiritual world in the Michaelic sense) brings that many more fruits in the coming earth life.

Presently, it is not only a matter of tangible successes that one attains on the path of schooling in *this* earthly life. Rather, it is a matter of all the efforts one undertakes based on one's own freedom in this regard. And if in one's inner development one does not only remain just on the thinking level, but invigorates one's efforts to such an extent that feeling, and in an initial way even willing becomes involved, one then already now begins creating a solid foundation for new spiritual faculties that in the spiritual life between incarnations are developed further. And in an individual's next earth-existence, he or she will already be prepared inwardly in such a way that it becomes possible even today to progress on the inner path infinitely more quickly. For, every will-imbued effort of soul that is directed to the reality of and conscious connection with the spirit will turn into a golden thread reaching beyond a single incarnation; a thread that leads from life to life and allows human beings to reach what they set out to do at the beginning of their path as the goal of inner evolution.

*

Inasmuch as we now return to the most significant aspect of the Michael-Mystery of the present age – that is to the destiny of the once cosmic, celestial intelligence that has now become "human" on earth – we must direct our inner sight to the mighty battle that Michael and Ahriman wage with one another for the future of earth and mankind. For, after the Michaelic intelligence had separated from its own cosmic origin and henceforth dwelled in human souls, the Ahrimanic spirits have above all been the ones who engage in battle with Michael for this intelligence throughout all future times. Rudolf Steiner describes it like this: "For at the same time when intelligence sank from the cosmos to the earth, there the aspiration of the Ahrimanic powers rose more and more – inasmuch as it became terrestrial – to tear this cosmic intelligence away from Michael and, free of him, to make it suitable for the earth only. This was the great crisis from the beginning of the 15th century[70] until today. It is the crisis we find ourselves in now, the one that is expressed in Ahriman's battle against Michael. Ahriman is making every effort to wrest away from Michael his rule over this intelligence which has now become terrestrial. Michael conversely tries with all the impulses he has – now that the rule he once had over this intelligence has fallen away from him – once again to take hold of it at the beginning of his earthly rule since the year 1879 here on earth" (GA 237, 28 July 1924). The decisive part in this cosmic-telluric battle, however, is assigned to the free human beings of the present age.

With this, the tremendous danger for the future of earth-evolution is indicated, namely, that the general intelligence possessed by all human beings can be utilized today not in the Michaelic sense but in the Ahrimanic manner and direction. And since – along with intellectuality – freedom came to the earth as well, every one of us is completely at liberty to decide whom he or she wants to surrender to; meaning with whom we wish to share this intelligence that has become our own.

The entire dramatic nature of Michael's cosmic situation in our epoch is here outlined. On the one side, humanity increasingly has the tendency to give up this Michaelic intelligence, which has become terrestrial, to Ahriman. On the other side, Michael, who began his guidance of humankind in 1879, restrains himself because (as we have seen already) he is the only Archangel who totally respects human freedom in contrast to the other spirits of his hierarchy.

This is why Michael must above all wait in the spiritual world to see what human beings will do with what he has bestowed on them as his very own gift – Anthroposophy[71] as the wellspring of the new spirituality. As already described in this chapter, he has to wait and see if we will take hold of Anthroposophy as the path of transforming intelligence in such a manner that Michael can thereby assume its administration once again but this time in our hearts; or whether, under the influence of Ahrimanic powers, we turn downwards in the opposite direction which would lead earth's entire civilization into the abyss.

This is indeed the decisive battle of the present age. "And more than any other struggle, this battle is laid into the human heart." For, "in the course of this twentieth century, when the first century following the end of the Kali Yuga [1899] will have passed, humankind will either stand at the grave of all civilization or at the beginning of that epoch when in the souls of human beings – who in their hearts combine intelligence with spirituality – the Michael-struggle will be fought out in favour of Michael's impulse" (GA 240, 19 July 1924).

Since the path to a positive ending of this struggle is outlined in detail in this chapter, now the likewise negative development will be dealt with even if only briefly. For in the contemporary epoch of freedom, everything is given into the hands of human beings; this also refers to what Ahriman and his cohorts want to achieve. Furthermore, if the Michaelic path leads to spiritual heights where the inner being of women and men increasingly assumes divine traits – in accord with the words in the Gospel of John, "Thou art gods", (10:34) – the second path that must more readily be called a fall, leads into the world-abyss where we humans are ultimately threatened with the complete loss of our humanness.

This fall too has various stages that appear like negative mirror-images of those previously depicted stages above that lead into spiritual heights. While on the path upwards, humankind's freedom assumes ever more cosmic dimensions, in the fall into the world-abyss we are threatened with the ultimate loss of our freedom; a loss that can be observed even now in its initial stages inasmuch as an ever-increasing possession by the Ahrimanic beings takes place. "For all sorts of demonic Ahrimanic forces cause human beings to become possessed [in our time] with them" (GA 240, 19 July 1924). Here too it is most of all a matter of the further fate of human intelligence which, corrupted through Ahriman, is pressed into the service of evil in this case.

Thus, corresponding to the upward path, four stages can also be discovered on the downward path below. The first stage becomes more comprehensible when we contrast it to ordinary thinking. As a basis for our earthly ego-consciousness, this thinking is at the same time the point where our first contact with the sphere of freedom begins, and our thinking thus remains *morally neutral*. One can even say that – in accordance with its moral neutrality – earthly thinking is an inevitable presupposition for human freedom. And so it has to be possible for humankind to take hold of freedom unhindered. Above all, today's science which supports itself on this thinking highly values this fact. Any form of morality must be kept at a distance from the intentions of scientists regarding research for natural scientific thinking, which only occupies itself with objective reality that is accessible to the corporeal senses, against which all moral elements must be rejected as a subjective conditionality of the human soul. One can even say that in this moral neutrality there lies the greatness of natural science attributable to it.

Since, however, the Ahrimanic powers in our thinking are "allowed to be present", intelligence readily loses its neutral character and becomes evil – that which is amoral. On the first stage downwards this amorality remains only in abstract thinking and as yet does not attain to the deeper strata of the human soul. Yet, Ahriman does "work" in this form of thinking. Rudolf Steiner offers a shattering example for this. The last works by Friedrich Nietzsche were no longer written by him (by his human "I"), but by Ahriman himself who in the bodily sheath of Nietzsche appeared as a brilliant but certainly devilish author (see GA 240, 20 July 1924). Because Nietzsche was a strong and deeply spiritual personality, he inwardly became ensnared in a great and for him unsolvable conflict with the Ahrimanic power that had taken possession of his body. The consequence of this was a spiritual darkening in the last years of his life which, however, signified to a certain degree his soul's salvation in regard to the latter's existence after death. If Nietzsche had not been so strong, Ahriman could have taken full possession of his thinking and Nietzsche would have had to serve the former as a medium for Ahriman's aims without being "psychically ill" in so doing. Individuals such as this do exist already today worldwide in large numbers, for, since Nietzsche's death, Ahriman has in countless cases appeared in the most diverse areas of general human culture as an author.[72]

To this and all following stages of intelligence that have fallen prey to evil, there moreover belongs what Rudolf Steiner depicts as a "counter-school" to Michael's supersensible school. He recounts this as follows: "While Michael taught his hosts above, a kind of subterranean Ahrimanic school was established directly below the surface of the earth (ibid.). This counter-school had as its task to work on certain human souls which were predestined for this already due to former incarnations, in such a way that they would become outstanding instruments now of the Ahrimanic spirits. It means that they would become individuals who would most easily be brought into a state of possession for a shorter or longer period of time.

And the incarnation of Ahriman,[73] which is soon to occur in our time, will bring about an additional impulse for the further deterioration of human intelligence and make use of human beings in particular who are possessed by Ahrimanic spirits. They will then be gifted with a powerful intelligence, but one that will bear a purely Ahrimanic character, which will adjust quite well to today's artificial intelligence, whereby these individuals will bestow on artificial intelligence an extraordinarily further advanced development. After that it will become even more difficult for human beings to unite their personal intelligence with Michael's spiritual sphere.

Achieving a greater spiritualization of human thinking will today and in the near future represent a huge problem for humankind, because the Ahrimanic intelligence will presently attain powerful dimensions and great power. Therefore it is necessary to work on building-up a most serious relationship to the Michael-Mysteries – as they are today revealed through Anthroposophy – so that contemporary earth civilization becomes able to advance in the Michaelic and likewise a Christian sense.

Now, however, it becomes far worse when the amoral and Ahrimanically occupied intelligence reaches the sphere of feeling which will then also assume an evil tendency. On the second downward stage which is connected with feeling, human intelligence is placed in the service of the lowest and most perverse instincts of humanity. So as to satisfy these instincts, consider that a world-wide industry of amusement exists already today that works only in this direction. It is paired with an immense financial engagement, social correlations, and a turn-over of billions of dollars. With cunning cleverness, all this is made available to the Ahrimanic corrupt feeling through the medium of money.

On this level, the Ahrimanic spirits already work together with the Azuric spirits. The Azuras produce the lowest animalistic instincts in human beings; the Ahrimanic spirits with their cunning intelligence produce for the Azuric spirits the entire above-mentioned industry of amusement. Rudolf Steiner spoke of the Azuras already at a time when their activity was still essentially more limited than in our age today: "And in some areas which need not now be characterized in detail further – namely in certain locations in big cities where wild orgies of pointless sensuousness can be found – we already see the grotesque hellish lightning flashes of those spirits we designate as the Azuric ones" (GA 107, 22 March 1909). How intensely the Azuric spirits are linked here *on this level* with the Ahrimanic ones becomes clear through Rudolf Steiner's following comment: "Certain occult teachings furthermore call Ahriman's hoards the shadows of the Azuras" (GA 107, 1 January 1909).

In front of this "journey into hell", the realm of the Azuras, having as its origin the corruption of intelligence, then opens up in us all the abysses of sensuousness and brings to the surface our animalistic nature. We can only experience protection from these forces through the conscious connection with the Michael Mysteries. For these mysteries lead nowadays, as we have already seen, up into the very heights of the Christ-Mystery, which alone will be able to put a hold on the contemporary and future confrontations with Ahriman.[74] "Less and less will there be protection in the world against Ahriman's influence outside the forces that stream out from the Christ-Mystery"[75] (ibid.). This is why the path to Christ under Michael's guidance is of such decisive significance. If mankind does not enter upon this path, human beings will not float in some sort of "in-between" condition, but will unavoidably continue to slide down into the abyss, concerning which today more and more threatening symptoms are recognizable.

On the third downward stage, the intelligence that has become evil even takes hold of the realm of willing. A symbiosis will thus originate between cold-blooded intellect and criminal will. Above all one can see here that the twentieth and twenty-first centuries offer the most terrible examples of humanity's depravity. To this stage belongs such phenomena as Bolshevism, National Socialism, and in our present days principally terrorism. People who are possessed in this way can without the slightest stirring of their conscience become so fanatical over a completely abstract idea (which will lead to possession) that they destroy any number of innocent human lives.

At the latest on this third downward level it can be determined that for the execution of these monstrous crimes the mere Ahrimanic (and even the Azuric power) does not suffice. For on this third stage, Ahriman, who is further and further descending into the world-abyss, is met by the force of the Sun-demon [Sorat], who in the Apocalypse is designated by the number 666. In it this being is likewise described as the beast with the two horns that is the actual opponent of the Christ in the spiritual world (see GA 104, 29 June 1908). Thus, Ahriman and Sorat work together on this level; that is the Ahrimanic spirits are pervaded on this level by Sorat and used by him in accordance with this being's anti-Christian aims.[75]

The specific characteristic of this stage moreover consists of the following: The human being is here increasingly being cut off from his or her higher "I", which to an extent explains the special cruelty of the actions carried out previously by the terror-regimes of Bolshevism and National Socialism.

On the fourth downward level, human beings increasingly lose their human nature altogether. They cease to be human. They themselves become the apocalyptic beast with the seven heads and ten horns, and as such join the ranks of Sorat. Now, they are separated from their true "I", and in that way they lose any connection to Christ. They are on their way into the abyss. Even the power of Ahriman does not reach down into these depths. For the human being is here on the way of completely "falling out" and away from human evolution.[76]

It is significant for this last and lowest level that the intelligence, here completely corrupted by Sorat, continues furthermore to play a decisive role: "It will ultimately be nothing else than what restrains the human being and thoroughly prevents him from coming to the Christ principal. That would then be this corrupted reasoning power, this corrupted intelligence. And if those who are taken in by and fall for the two-horned beast [Sorat], could look back to what had actually played the most evil trick on them, such individuals would then say that the predisposition for the abyss actually came later, but first what darkened for them the Christ principal, that was the intellect" (GA 104, 30 June 1908).[77]

From what has been depicted here, the entire significance of human intelligence for the present and future becomes very clear one more time. Whether we hand over this intelligence to Michael and with that to Christ, or give it to Ahriman and thereby to Sorat through its further decline – on this depends the further destiny of the human "I", and with that the entire development of humanity and the earth. Based on what has just been said, one can now well understand why Rudolf Steiner expressed himself so radically: "It is a matter of great – of gigantic – implications!" (GA 240, 19 July 1924).

What has been described here can be summarized as follows for a better overview (see opposite page):

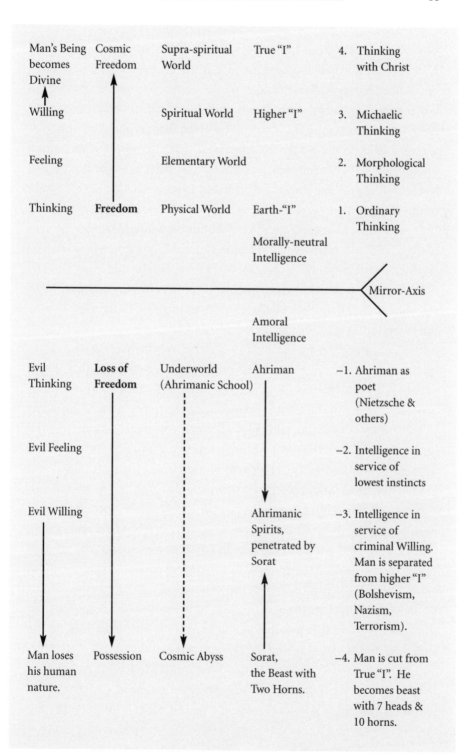

| | | | | |
|---|---|---|---|---|
| Man's Being becomes Divine | Cosmic Freedom | Supra-spiritual World | True "I" | 4. Thinking with Christ |
| Willing | | Spiritual World | Higher "I" | 3. Michaelic Thinking |
| Feeling | | Elementary World | | 2. Morphological Thinking |
| Thinking | **Freedom** | Physical World | Earth-"I" | 1. Ordinary Thinking |
| | | | Morally-neutral Intelligence | |

Mirror-Axis

Amoral Intelligence

| | | | | |
|---|---|---|---|---|
| Evil Thinking | **Loss of Freedom** | Underworld (Ahrimanic School) | Ahriman | −1. Ahriman as poet (Nietzsche & others) |
| Evil Feeling | | | | −2. Intelligence in service of lowest instincts |
| Evil Willing | | | Ahrimanic Spirits, penetrated by Sorat | −3. Intelligence in service of criminal Willing. Man is separated from higher "I" (Bolshevism, Nazism, Terrorism). |
| Man loses his human nature. | Possession | Cosmic Abyss | Sorat, the Beast with Two Horns. | −4. Man is cut from True "I". He becomes beast with 7 heads & 10 horns. |

When we look around in the world outside us today or in the Anthroposophical Society and movement (in its practical initiatives), a great concern may well take hold of us. In many areas, one can experience a withdrawal of Anthroposophy and moreover with that a retreat of the Michaelic substance. In this struggle, however, there is no neutral middle-ground. Where the Michaelic substance that is connected to human intelligence is not taken hold of actively and then brought back up to Michael, it slips down into the Ahrimanic regions whether we are aware of this or not. Michael is fully conscious of it. He knows that already for many centuries his intelligence lives without his guidance among human beings, and increasingly is "occupied" in the contemporary age by Ahriman, since up until the present Michael-epoch he no longer had any direct link to it on earth. "Thus, Ahrimanic powers in some human bodies were already jubilant that Michael could no longer maintain his cosmic intelligence that has fallen to the earth" (ibid.).

On the other hand, Michael is an actively busy spirit who is not inclined merely to watch how his intelligence in human souls is being occupied by Ahriman on earth. While Michael cannot influence this process from out of the spiritual world, he strives to begin a turning-point in this process, where he still rules fully and completely, namely in the Sun-sphere. What he has undertaken in this regard as a first stage of development is well-known in anthroposophical circles, for he founded and guided the great Michael-School from the fifteenth to the eighteenth century. In this school he taught how in all Mysteries since the primal beginning of earth-evolution human souls were prepared to comprehend the "Cosmic-will" and its intentions and to follow it consciously. Human beings were supposed to become free co-workers of this "Cosmic-will" on earth; the will which at the same time is the will of Christ.[78] In the cosmos on the other hand, in the Sun-realm, the "Cosmic-will" is represented through Michael. It is possible to summarize the entire teaching in the supersensible Michael-School in regard to this central point.

Then the second stage in this development followed. Around the turn from the 18th to the 19th century, Michael arranged a supersensible cultus in the spiritual world adjacent to the earth. Initially, he had introduced this cultus but later allowed it freely to evolve further. For at that time, Michael himself had as yet not descended to the surroundings of the earth himself where this cultus now unfolded, but remained behind in the Sun-sphere. And what was the content of this cultus?

Rudolf Steiner offers us an essential communication about this. He repeats frequently that what had been evoked out of the Michaelic substance in the supersensible Michael-School was then established in this cultus as the *new Christendom.* And what is this new Christendom? It contains what guides human beings to a conscious and new relationship to Christ as basis for the spiritualized Michaelic intelligence so that human beings can hear the "Christ-word" directly today.[79] And in hearing, comprehending, and recognizing the Christ-word, human beings attain to the experience that Christ Himself as Logos is present in this Christ-word and wants to unite Himself initially with the forces of cognition, then the forces of the heart, and ultimately with all will-forces, meaning with the entire human being.

We must now examine the supersensible stages of preparation in the spiritual world for Anthroposophy somewhat more closely. Yet one question must still be posed beforehand: Why does Rudolf Steiner in his later karma lectures speak so carefully and in such an obviously forceful yet restrained way about the actual contents of the Michael-School and the cultus following from them? Why does he resort only to indications? The reason seems to be that the karma lectures were above all intended to accompany his work on the First Class of the School for Spiritual Science.

He announced at the end of the Nineteenth Class Lesson given in August 1924, that he planned to begin with the further elaboration of the School that following September, and would have approached the direct communications of the contents of the supersensible Michael-School more closely, as well as beginning with an immediate description of the Imaginations from the cosmic cultus which would have then followed.

It is quite obvious that, parallel with the esoteric contents in the framework of a Second and Third Class of the school, further karma lectures – just as before, so afterwards – would have accompanied the corresponding reports about the heavenly preparation of Anthroposophy.

The earlier indications would have been essentially deepened and elaborated upon by Rudolf Steiner. This became impossible, however, because due to his illness the further build-up of the Class did not come about. Likewise, because of the presence of many new members in September 1924, he had to limit himself to repeat what had already been given in shortened form, as opposed to the intended beginning of the Second Class. (Here, we interest ourselves with the so-called Recapitulation Lessons.)

Corresponding to the karma lectures that accompanied the Class Lessons, Rudolf Steiner recounted to a large extent the themes dealt with already earlier. Although many new points were discussed then, this changes nothing concerning the basic fact that a pause was made in regard to the description of the celestial "pre-history" of Anthroposophy in connection with the supersensible Michael stream.

So as to understand these already described matters even better, one must add to the two above-mentioned heavenly pre-stages of Anthroposophy a third stage. In the time sequence, however, the first pre-stage (of which Rudolf Steiner spoke only once) is to be found in the lecture of 28 July 1924 in Dornach. There, it is a matter of concerning ourselves with a "mighty event" (GA 237) within the spiritual worlds preceding the actual instruction in the supersensible Michael-School of the 15th century. Rudolf Steiner depicts this mighty event as a kind of "cosmic thunderstorm", the origin of which lies in the activity of the Seraphim, Cherubim and Thrones. These entities transferred the substance of the Sun-intelligence which belonged to the realm of the Second Hierarchy, the Kyriotetes, Dynamis and Exusiai, to the earth into the kingdom of humanity, whereby the human being was constitutionally transformed, which means a transformation that even reached into the spiritual foundations of our physical body. What was then called forth in human nature as a fundamental change is formulated by Rudolf Steiner in a brief emphatic sentence as follows: "Human beings earlier were beings of heart. Afterwards we became head-beings. Intelligence becomes our own intelligence. Viewed from the supersensible dimension this is something exceptionally significant" (ibid.).

All this was necessary back then so that – at the beginning of what would be the new epoch of the consciousness-soul – we could receive the bodily and psychological foundations not only to begin working with the newly acquired consciousness-soul on sense-perceptions transmitted to us by the body; but also so that we could consciously receive spiritual thoughts into ourselves in order with these thoughts to create the basis for a new spiritual culture on the earth.

This cosmic thunderstorm was carefully observed at that time in the supersensible Michael-School by Michael and his human disciples from the Sun-realm. They understood in its full significance that the Michael-School pointed to future Anthroposophy and its activities on the earth. This is why Rudolf Steiner says that recollection of this event – to the extent that Anthroposophists today discover it in the depth of their souls – can lead to authentic enthusiasm in their hearts and minds for Anthroposophy and the new spiritual culture connected with it (ibid.).

Furthermore, this world-encompassing activity by the First Hierarchy was followed by the activity of the Michael-School that unfolded on the Sun, meaning in the realm of the Second Hierarchy, the substance of which had been impressed through the cosmic thunderstorm onto human beings on the earth. Aside from Michael as their leader, numerous human souls and various elemental beings took part in the supersensible Michael-School, as well as beings of the Third Hierarchy, Angels, Archangels and even Archai, who belong to the Michael-stream in the spiritual world (see GA 240, 27 August 1924).

Later, this encompassing activity of the Michael-School was continued in the Moon-sphere, which in the spiritual world is directly adjacent to the earth. Rudolf Steiner states verbatim that in the supersensible cultus nothing other than the contents of the Michael-School were further worked upon, "where in mighty imaginative images what the Michael-disciples had learned at that time in the supersensible 'school of teachings' was perfected" (GA 237, 28 July 1924). Since the Third Hierarchy is connected with the Moon-sphere, one may well assume that those [higher] entities in particular who earlier had already participated in the instruction of the Michael-School also participated in this supersensible cultus, along with the human souls belonging to them.[80]

All of the above when taken together allows a mighty image to arise regarding the participation on the part of all nine hierarchies in the cosmic preparation of Anthroposophy. If to this the fact is added that, according to the Foundation Stone Meditation, the Father-forces work chiefly through the First Hierarchy, the forces of the Son through the Second, and those of the Holy Spirit through the Third Hierarchy, we can take a further step in cognition of the Michael-stream, whose spiritual roots lie in the activity of the Father-forces in our cosmos. For, Rudolf Steiner reports that events such as the cosmic tempest at the beginning of the 15th century emerge from the region of the First Hierarchy, and are repeated only after the course of very great cosmic spans of time.[81] Nevertheless, however, they all have a direct relationship to the Michael-stream in the spiritual world (and especially the last event), for then it became a matter of the effectiveness of cosmic intelligence that Michael himself is deeply connected with.[82]

Then in his supersensible "Sun-School", we deal with the transformation of the ancient still pre-Christian Mystery endeavours – likewise rooted in the primal revelation of the Father – into the new Mystery activity that became possible only after the Mystery of Golgotha, and which fully and completely depends on the free intelligence of human beings. "Then, however, the future was taken into consideration [in the Michael-School] as to what was supposed *to become new Mystery activity*. We must now begin to understand this new mystery activity on an anthroposophical level, unlike the ancient Mystery activities that entered human beings who did not yet have today's intelligence and who therefore could only experience the supersensible worlds in a dreamlike manner. This new Mystery activity that we must begin to understand in our time is fully compatible with clear light-filled intelligence" (GA 237, 1 August 1924). In the Michael-School, it was in the first place always a matter of developing the New Mysteries, which later were established by Rudolf Steiner on earth through the Christmas Conference and its consequences.

From his words that follow – which describe in human speech the mighty speech of Michael in his supersensible school – this can be experienced even more clearly: "Consider the *mighty initiate-teaching* which once in ancient form streamed down to earth through the Mysteries, let us consider it before the souls of those who now in an intelligent way were connected with Michael" (GA 240, 20 July 1924). We concern ourselves here with the purely supersensible founding of the new Mysteries in which the old initiate-teaching had to be totally renewed out of the fount of the Mystery of Golgotha in order then "in a new way" (ibid.) to blossom forth in the souls of human beings, initially in the spiritual world and then later on the earth. At the same time it was also a matter of the new initiation-path that was supposed to guide human beings to the cosmic Christ as the creative Sun-Logos, as Rudolf Steiner depicted it later first in his basic books, *Theosophy*, *Knowledge of the Higher Worlds and Its Attainment*, and *Occult Science, an Outline*, and further in the nineteen esoteric lessons of the School for Spiritual Science.

How did this transformation of the ancient Father-Mysteries into the new Christian or Son-Mysteries even become possible – at first only in the realm of the Sun and under the direct guidance by Michael? As already mentioned earlier, this could only happen as a result of the Mystery of Golgotha, and this means only by means of the fact that Michael himself with his entire cosmic activity could link up with the Mystery of Golgotha and its consequences. "He attains this by bringing his activity into the most perfect harmony with the Mystery of Golgotha."[83]

Only in this way did the step from the Old to the New Mysteries become possible; meaning the transition from the ancient Father-wisdom to the new Son-wisdom. And Michael was only able to carry out this transformation of the Mysteries in the realm of the Sun because, in pursuance of the Mystery of Golgotha, he himself had experienced a decisive transformation in his entire being as well. Rudolf Steiner characterizes it like this: "For him [Michael], the Mystery of Golgotha signifies the transformation from a night-spirit into a day-spirit" (GA 194, 22 November 1919).

"Night-spirit" signifies that up until the Mystery of Golgotha Michael influenced the subconscious of human beings primarily, something that the hierarchical beings do only while human beings are asleep. Since the Turning Point of Time and particularly since the descent of the cosmic intelligence to earth, Michael has been allowed to appear more and more consciously to human beings; a process that will reach its culmination in our time. For in our Michael-epoch – for Michael it is the first epoch since his previous rulership prior to the Mystery of Golgotha – the human being, as we already heard, can enter into a completely new relationship with Michael and the spiritual world in a quite conscious form. And this takes place above all on the path of the transformation of human thinking that is now in a position to bring the Michaelic intelligence, which has become earthly, back to Michael so that a new and fully conscious relationship between human beings and the gods is possible beginning in our age.

That the secret of the Christ as a lofty Sun-being stood in the centre of the teachings given in the celestial Michael-School likewise follows from many statements by Rudolf Steiner. In them he always points out again and again that it was, and continues to be, a part of Michael's special tasks to bring to human beings on earth the closer insight that Christ is a lofty Sun-being.[84] It is in this regard quite important that as early as 1910 when the book *Occult Science, an Outline* was published, the "Sun-secret" of the Christ stands in the centre. This speaks for the fact that this book was written based also on the direct inspiration of the supersensible Michael-School.

On the earth, through His deed on the hill of Golgotha, Christ has brought about the liberation of mankind from the "fall into sin" that still had been allowed by the Father in Paradise.[85] Thus, as if in line with the Imitation of Christ, the foundations have been laid by Michael so that human beings on earth can begin with something similar, but now not just on the level of *existence* but on that of *consciousness*, namely through the overcoming of the intellectual "fall into sin" in the realm of cognition that followed the original biblical "Fall".[86] Already during the age of Aristotle, which simultaneously was the age of the progressive deterioration of the ancient Mysteries, there rang forth Michael's mighty voice in the spiritual world from the Sun: "These were then Michael's words: 'Man must come to the pan-intelligence, to a grasp of the Divine on the earth in sin-less form'" (GA 237, 1 August 1924).

This is why Rudolf Steiner reports that the secret of the fall into sin plays a special part in the Michael-School. For it was Michael's task to guide human beings on the path of overcoming that fall out of the forces of the Mystery of Golgotha. For this path begins on the level of consciousness and continues on to the level of existence in the future, a process which will find its conclusion along with the renewed union of earth and Sun. Thus, according to Rudolf Steiner, to the "intimate teachings of that supersensible school" there moreover belongs the following: "It is the teaching of sin, of sinful human beings that at the very beginning of human evolution were not meant to descend so deeply into the material element, but into which we have now descended" (GA 237, 1 August 1924). And the first step upwards and away from sin – to begin with only on the level of consciousness or thinking – is entering the Michaelic path which ultimately leads to the penetration of human thinking with the substance of the Christ – "to think with Christ".

This became possible for Michael because, together with the human souls connected to him in his Sun-realm, he could open the paths so that the Christ-impulse could penetrate into human thinking, meaning to Christianize human intelligence. With that, an answer was given in the Michael-School to the question that Thomas Aquinas died with in 1274: "How does the Christ enter into human thinking?" (GA 74, 23 May 1920.)

What Michael had in this manner set in motion in the spiritual world was then guided onto earth in Anthroposophy, or spiritual science, to full reality by Rudolf Steiner. For in his early principal book, *The Philosophy of Freedom*, the ways are indicated that lead to the overcoming of the fall into sin in thinking (see ibid.). How this path for prevailing over the intellectual fall into sin – which is connected with the here-outlined cosmic Mysteries of Michael – was described by Rudolf Steiner at the end of his life in the so-called *Michael Letters* (GA 26).

An exceptional correlation of the Michael-School to the Sun-secret of the Christ consists of a later spiritual-research insight on the part of Rudolf Steiner, which reveals that on His journey to the earth Christ left His cosmic "Spirit-Human sheath" on the Sun (see GA 240, 27 August 1924). But since it was Michael and his host who joined in experiencing the profound drama of Christ's farewell from the Sun, it is quite likely that it was Michael who, like a kind of "last will and testament", was connected with what Christ had left behind on the Sun. Some points by Rudolf Steiner speak of the fact that, as regent of the Sun, Michael moreover became guardian of this Christ-imbued "Spirit-Human".[87]

As was indicated elsewhere,[88] with the spiritual inspirations of this cosmic Spirit-Human on the Sun, one particular individual was closely connected and deeply linked with Michael and the destiny of cosmic intelligence from the beginning. This was the individuality of Aristotle.[89] In the same lecture Rudolf Steiner tells us that on the further descent to earth, Christ left His cosmic life-body behind in the direct vicinity of the earth. The effectiveness of this life-body later served the Arthurian knights as their main fount of inspiration. This life-body then arrived on the earth with His Spirit-Self, the forces of which were effective in the Grail Mysteries (see ibid.). If one furthermore considers these above communications by Rudolf Steiner, the following statement by him concerning the contents of the celestial Michael-School becomes comprehensible in its entire implication. "A Michael-host formed [in the Michael-School], which in supersensible regions of the spiritual world absorbed those teachings by the Michael-School teachers from the ancient Alexandrian time [the earlier teachings by Aristotle that Alexander spread out far and wide in the world during that time]; the Michael-School teachers from the time of the Grail-tradition; and the Michael-School teachers who also were present in such impulses as the Arthur-impulse" (GA 240, 21 August 1924).

If we moreover consider that regarding these three streams in the Michael-School it was a matter of their cosmic backgrounds – Rudolf Steiner calls them "a cosmic Christendom" in the same lecture – for it becomes understandable that in addition to the essential teachings in the Michael- School there must also be added the further destinies of the Spirit-Human, Life-Spirit and Spirit-Self of the Christ. In their further relationship they belong to the earthly activity of the Aristotelian, the Arthur and the Grail-streams.

The Aristotelian impulse above all played a central role in the Michael-School. For as early as in the 4th pre-Christian century, through the founding of the science of thinking, of logic, Aristotle had shaped as if into a spiritual chalice what let the Michaelic intelligence flow into the souls of human beings on earth more than a thousand years later.[90] This was the reason why Aristotle became the precursor of the coming consciousness-soul development. Until today and far into the future, the thinking of human beings is shaped in the way it was described by Aristotle in his logical writings already more than two-thousand years ago.[91]

At the beginning of the period of the intellectual or mind-soul, it was also Aristotle who – through his commitment to the pure observation of nature – conceived the coming of the consciousness-soul from this side like no other human being of his time. These two directions – the logical and the scientific one, founded as they were by Aristotle and further culti-vated through his two significant disciples, Theophrast and Alexander the Great – played an extraordinary role in the Michael-School. For on one side, "in this school we dealt with the supersensible world; in a new way lifting *up* the ancient initiate-wisdom into intelligence-filled consciousness – the *consciousness-soul* – in human souls predestined for this between death and a new birth; summing up what in earlier ancient times had been man's treasury of wisdom, his 'wisdom-property', in the intellectual-soul, mind soul, and so on" (GA 240, 20 July 1924).

In other words, within the Michael-School there was something that long ago had already been pre-planned on earth by Aristotle, but further evolved in a cosmic sense and brought to a certain culmination. Furthermore, there can be no doubt that the individuality of Aristotle played a central part in this context. The same can be said in regard to a second side of Aristotelian teaching in connection with the Michael-School. Rudolf Steiner affirms this in the following words: "Then, everything assumed life again in supersensible worlds; something that once had been alive in the Sun-mysteries as Michael-wisdom. In a momentous manner, what was then summarized and brought forth was Platonism transformed into an Aristotelian continuation. Through Alexander the Great, this was brought across to Asia and down to Egypt" (GA 237, 28 July 1924).

One can therefore say that the individuality of Aristotle likewise assumed a leading part in the activity of the Michael-School. This is moreover affirmed by Rudolf Steiner in that these words, despite their simplicity, must be grasped in their full significance. What is meant here is the brief comment by him which states that "During the illumination by Aristotelianism in the supersensible world during the time of the Michael-School-activities of the 14th, 15th, 16th and 17th centuries etc., Christendom went through its most important development" (GA 240, 27 August 1924).

Everything that has been stated represents the essential building blocks for what Rudolf Steiner designates as the central task of the Michael-School: The establishment of cosmic Christendom – initially still in the spiritual world – through the transformation of the old Mysteries into the new by means of the Christ-impulse, the way it works in the world after the Mystery of Golgotha. Thus, this supersensible Michael-School in the Sun-sphere was the fount for true comprehension of the cosmic being of Christ and His deed at the Mystery of Golgotha. For His death and resurrection in a newly transformed body were the highest fulfilments of all true Sun-mysteries in the past. What in the ancient Sun-mysteries, inspired as they were through millennia by Michael and only carried out symbolically, will attain their full reality as the loftiest union [in German 'Vermählung'!] of earth and Sun; as the flowing of the Sun-evolution into the entire earthly evolution. This union of the Michael-School with the Sun-secret of the Christ and His deed in the Mystery of Golgotha, were among other matters to represent the content of the further karma lectures that would have accompanied the founding of the Second and Third Classes of the School for Spiritual Science.

The next and third pre-stage in the heavenly development of Anthroposophy consisted in the supersensible cultus into which, according to Rudolf Steiner, the foundations of the "new Christendom" were placed (GA 240, 18 July 1924). Moreover, aside from the excarnate human souls, numerous elemental spirits and various entities of the higher hierarchies participated in this cultus. Above all there were beings from the Third Hierarchy that participated, meaning those Angels,

Archangels and Archai who from the beginning belonged to the Michael-School in the spiritual world.[92] Yet, unlike the Michael-School where, aside from the most advanced ones human souls were merely listeners – although "hearing" is definitely something most active in the spiritual world – human souls themselves then became creative in the supersensible cultus.[93] Together with the higher hierarchies they worked on the "mighty cosmic imaginations" (ibid.) that profoundly marked their entire being all the way into the base of their will.

And here lies the second transition, namely the transformation from the Sun-Mysteries to those of the Holy Spirit. In the New Testament, this corresponds to the life of the Apostles *after* the Whitsun event. After they had been Disciples of Christ Jesus for three years and above all had received His teachings, which were now filled by His spirit, the disciples subsequently were allowed to be active on earth through their own initiative based on the Christ-impulse.

In this way, human souls who were connected with Michael – initially still in the spiritual world – could change from "listeners" to "co-active" men and women; human beings who were given the task of working in their further incarnations on earth in accord with Michael-Christ.

That is also why Anthroposophy is called "spiritual science." This is for the reason that spiritual science undertakes doing research in the spiritual world by strictly scientific methodology. Therefore Anthroposophy is indeed a *science of the spirit* that leads to Christ on the Michaelic path.

Due to the reasons mentioned above, Rudolf Steiner initially speaks very little about the actual content of the supersensible cultus in the karma lectures. But in this connection he does make one essential reference to a far more tangible image regarding what he designates as the "new Christendom". We are concerned here with the content of the fairytale by Goethe, *The Green Snake and the Beautiful Lily*. When Goethe wrote this fairytale, something seeped down, as it were, into Goethe's soul regarding the cultus-content from the spiritual world adjacent to the earth. "Goethe was not familiar with the great, mighty images that took their course up above" but "they came through to him in miniature pictures" and "he created these little images in his 'Fairytale'" (GA 240, 19 July 1924).

Now, if we recall the teachings of the Michael-School and their continuation in the supersensible cultus, then the main motifs of the *Fairytale* can become the very first indications of this content in the supersensible cultus. Thus we see in the transformation of the temple and its arising, with all its symbolism, out of concealment into a public activity, the already mentioned metamorphosis of the ancient Mysteries into the new Mysteries. The primordial wisdom of humanity that was preserved in the temple is thus renewed so that it becomes accessible to all people of good will. The striving of the youth for his higher nature (the Lily) and the death and resurrection which follows, are woven into the *Fairytale* as central motifs. The awakening of the youth to new life does, however, become possible only through the sacrifice of the green snake that knows the fourth secret, that of love. Thus, through the serpent's love of sacrifice, the new Christian epoch in humanity's evolution is thereby proclaimed "It is timely!"

Out of this central motif of the *Fairytale*, one can receive a hint that in the supersensible cultus it was moreover a matter of the nature of Christ's resurrection forces, forces that must penetrate from the beginning of the present Michael-age ever more into the consciousness of human beings so that the future transformation of humankind can begin.[94]

In this way, the transition takes place from the world of the Father into that of the Son. Yet, the next transition – the one that is called forth through the working of the Spirit – is likewise indicated in the *Fairytale*. There we are concerned with something like a minute Whitsun-event that Goethe describes in the following words: "The old man looked up to the stars and then began to speak: We are gathered here at an auspicious hour; everyone carries out his task, everybody does his duty and a general good fortune shall dissolve the individual sorrows into themselves in the same way as a general misfortune consumes various pleasures. After these words a wondrous sound arose; for all the persons who were present spoke to themselves and loudly expressed what they would have to do."[95] And at the end of this *Fairytale* we experience the initiation of the youth and his marriage to the beautiful Lily from out of the power of the spirit.

In regard to the cultus, Rudolf Steiner moreover indicates that what was acquired in the Michael-School by the participants in a more cognitional way, henceforth united in a cultic activity with their will, meaning that the cultus became the source of their spiritual initiative. From then on, as Michael-disciples, they not only wanted to acquire super-sensible insights, but based on them to be active on the earth, in accordance with the renewed event of Whitsun. This striving for their own deeds, which then seeks the connection to the other person's deeds ensouls and enfires all protagonists of Goethe's *Fairytale*. The same propensity can be found in Anthroposophists to the extent that through their mutual participation in the supersensible Michael-cultus they inwardly link up with one another in their earthly endeavours.⁹⁶

Yet another motif that points to the content of the supersensible cultus is to be found in the *Fairytale's* history of origin. Initially, Goethe had intended it as an artistic and poetic reply to the more intellectually styled letters, *Concerning the Aesthetic Education of Man* by his friend, Friedrich Schiller. One can gather from this that something like an original inspiration from the supersensible cultus indwelled this work by Schiller. How can this be comprehended even more precisely? The key is found at the end of the short lecture-cycle with the title, *Der Zusammenhang des Menschen mit der elementarischen Welt* [The Connection between Human Beings and the Elemental World] (GA 158). There in the lecture of 22 November 1914, Rudolf Steiner happens to refer to Schiller and his philosophical letters from the standpoint of man's twofold relationship to duty. For, we can either become slaves of duty or reject it due to love of self. Nevertheless, both behaviours lead us past our actual earth-task and deliver us either into the hands of Ahriman or Lucifer.

Schiller himself discovered by means of his confrontation with Kant, and the overcoming of that philosopher's thinking, the only correct solution of the problem, which at the same time signifies the inner balance between Lucifer and Ahriman in this sphere. For Schiller it meant the *love* for duty, something that according to Rudolf Steiner is a quality of humankind that will only unfold in the most distant future of evolution. But because Schiller could solve this problem in his work inasmuch as he brought both polarities into balance, in *this* solution even the Christ-impulse came to be effective in Schiller's own soul. Simultaneously, he thereby formed a bridge into the central Christological content of the later Anthroposophy. Rudolf Steiner points to this with the following words: "The only thing was that Schiller did not use the expressions Lucifer and Ahriman, because he did not think of the matter in a cosmic sense. But these wonderful letters by Schiller, *Concerning the Aesthetic Education of Man*, are directly translatable into spiritual science."

When we translate the content of this work of Schiller's into the cosmic domain, what is the result? That would be the depiction of the Representative of Man, creating balance between Lucifer and Ahriman as shown by Rudolf Steiner's wooden sculptural group. It follows from this that he took his inspiration for creating the wooden group out of his own prenatal participation in the Michael-cultus, and then transformed it into a remarkable work of art. Here the main inspiration of Schiller's *Letters* is probably found which shone from the supersensible Michael-cultus into his soul.

One can therefore say that the being of what on earth became the wooden sculptural group stood initially as an "imagination" in the centre of the supersensible cultus. And when one adds to this that the sculpture brings to expression the secret of evil, there follows that the cognition of this secret also belonged to the fundamental experiences of the supersensible cultus.

It is furthermore significant that Rudolf Steiner pointed out relatively early (1909) that in future times an image would have to arise in mankind that would be created purely out of the impulse of the spirit:[97] "What is to come into being through the spirit and sent by the Christ, will dispose of its sheaths and then be expressed in the image which as a mighty ideal can stand before the soul of every Anthroposophist"[98] (GA 284, 5 May 1909).

With this image Rudolf Steiner refers to the central motif of the paintings of the small cupola in the First Goetheanum which later also found expression in the sculptural wooden group (see on this GA 171, 16 September 1916). Both were created by Rudolf Steiner based on the direct impulse of the spirit.

Concerning this spirit-motif, Rudolf Steiner furthermore stated that the decisive step from twofoldness to threefoldness in him was taken as a world-principle. For, the mere twofoldness can only lead away from Christ. "And if the Christ-impulse is to be indicated once again in a true sense, then it is necessary that next to the twofold number the threefold one is added" (GA 194, 21 November 1919), something that the sculptural group (and likewise the central motif of the Goetheanum paintings) brings to expression.

All this in turn is connected with the contemporary activity by Michael as well as Michael's relationship to still higher hierarchies. "Everything hangs together with the mission of Michael as regards those entities of the higher hierarchies with whom he likewise stands in a connection again" (ibid.). It follows thus from what was said that in the way the transition from the epoch of the Father to that of the Son was carried out in the Michael-School, so in the supersensible cultus the further transition from the Son to the Spirit was instituted,[99] and with that the ability to be able to work on earth out of the spirit-impulse.

In today's Michael-epoch (with him as Time-spirit), this new spirit-impulse was borne to the earth and revealed there through the endeavours by Rudolf Steiner as Anthroposophy, or the science of the spirit. For in the present time, Anthroposophy is the only spiritual movement, or stream, that can transform earth's entire civilization in the Michaelic sense, inasmuch as the spirit works its way into various practical activities of human beings, something that in the past one-hundred years has found validity in many initiatives that have originated out of Anthroposophy.

Here a further reason is found as to why one can designate Anthroposophy as a spiritual science or "science of the spirit". For in it, as the fourth pre-stage of the above-described celestial-earthly development of Anthroposophy, the revelation of the Holy Spirit comes to earth just as was proclaimed by Christ in His farewell-discourses in the Gospel of St. John. For this reason, Anthroposophy is today the great Michaelic message of Whitsun to humankind.[100]

The founding of Anthroposophy on earth is, however, preceded by a decisive change in Michael's Sun-kingdom. Michael descends from the Sun to the earth so that beginning in 1879 he can take hold of the guidance of humanity in the contemporary Michael-epoch, no longer from the cosmic but from the earthly standpoint, meaning from the direct surroundings of the earth; and that implies from where the supersensible cultus had previously occurred. As we have already seen, it is the same path from the Sun to earth that Christ earlier chose. In the imitation of Christ, Michael likewise chooses this path down to earth, although not into physical incarnation but so that spiritually he comes as close to earth as possible in that sphere where Rudolf Steiner encountered him during his stay in Weimar.

Thus, the cosmic-telluric presupposition was fulfilled so that Anthroposophy in the fourth pre-stage of its development could "incarnate on earth", for as mentioned above, it is "the gift of Michael to humankind of the present age" (GA 152, 2 May 1913). It follows from this that from the beginning everything that was given by Rudolf Steiner in written or in oral form as Anthroposophy originated from the same source. In this regard during his description of the supersensible Michael-School, he already spoke about the "heavenly Anthroposophy ... which preceded the earthly one. For, the teachings that Michael offered in his supersensible school were of a kind which at that point of time prepared what was to become Anthroposophy on earth" (GA 237, 28 July 1924). And in a different passage, Rudolf Steiner adds further that all the human souls who participated in this "heavenly school" were instructed by Michael himself, and that his teachings were supposed to be "borne downwards to the earth at the beginning of the new Michael-epoch" (GA 240, 21 August, 1924).

This Michael-teaching that was borne downwards to the earth is Anthroposophy![101] About the instruction in this school itself, Rudolf Steiner speaks as follows: "The way in which one can speak about the inner word, something that is difficult to do in many regards, Michael explained to his listeners, both human beings and higher hierarchical entities, the world-relationships, cosmic relationships and anthroposophical relationships. These souls that participated in the school received teachings that unveiled cosmic secrets" (GA 240, 20 July 1924). Rudolf Steiner expressed himself quite similarly about the "mighty Imaginative-cultus", for in it human souls united who were karmicly predestined for it "so as to prepare Anthroposophy in super-earthly regions" (GA 240, 19 July 1924).

But what are the above-mentioned "anthroposophical relationships" in particular that were contemplated in the supersensible school of Michael, and transformed into mighty imaginations in the cultus that followed? They are none other than what comprises anthroposophical cognition; insight concerning the nature of the human being; the development of the cosmos; the working of the hierarchies and forming of karma in individual human destinies and the entire history of humanity; briefly put, all the themes that Rudolf Steiner summed up and depicted in his book, *Occult Science, an Outline*. It was not for naught that he later stated concerning this work that it "contained the outlines of Anthroposophy as an entirety".[102]

Subsequently when Rudolf Steiner brings the imaginations of the supersensible cultus into connection with the founding of the "new Christendom" in the spiritual world, what is meant by this is that the entire imaginative material or tableau that was woven there by human souls – together with the hierarchical entities out of the teachings of the Michael-School – contains a central figure that bestows its meaning on the totality. Thus, the following words by Rudolf Steiner illuminate the essential element of this Imaginative-cultus. For they attest to the fact that it was truly a matter of the founding of a new cosmic Christendom. "Thus, like the very midpoint, the Christ-being places Himself into the entire tableau of reincarnation, the nature of humanity, the contemplation of the cosmos, and so on. And if we consider this anthroposophical world-view in the proper sense, we can say to ourselves: I can look at it all, but I can only comprehend it when the entire picture indicates for me the mighty centre, the Christ. I have portrayed the teaching of reincarnation through different images; the teaching concerning the human races, the planets' evolution, and so on; but here from one point I have painted the nature of the Christ, and in that way light spreads out over all else. It is a picture containing a main figure with everything else relating to it, and I only understand the significance and expression of the other figures when I understand the main figure. This is how it is with the anthroposophical world-view. We design a huge picture concerning the various sets of facts regarding the spiritual world; but then we look at the main figure – at the Christ – and only then do we understand all the details of the picture" (GA 112, 30 June 1909).

Approximately something like what follows – translated into human language – is what every individual who participated in Michael's supersensible cultus at the turn from the 18th to the 19th century in the spiritual world adjacent to the earth could say to himself: The entire tapestry of great cosmic imaginations that were woven together as celestial Anthroposophy by human beings and gods has one central figure which alone bestows on the totality its true and future-oriented meaning and implication.

In the karma lectures, with which Rudolf Steiner accompanied the founding of the First Class of the Michael-School on earth, he could not yet directly point this out. For, this secret was supposed to be partially revealed in the Second and above all in the Third Class. Rudolf Steiner points this out in his brief communication to Ludwig Polzer-Hoditz in regard to the structure of the three classes of the Michael-School. In regard to the Third Class, he tells Polzer-Hoditz: "Class III: 12 members. These would then be the Esoteric Council. This Class III, the so-called Master-Class, will have a purely cultic character where, simultaneously at three altars, rituals will be conducted. While in Class II we turn to the corresponding Archangel-entities, above all to those who serve Michael, so in Class III we turn directly to the Spirit of the earth, to the Christ-entity."[103]

That at the very beginning of his anthroposophical endeavours, Rudolf Steiner himself wanted to link up with the reality of the supersensible cultus – albeit at the outset in a quite guarded way – is vouchsafed by the fact that he devoted his first purely anthroposophical lecture, that he gave interestingly enough on Michaelmas Day of 1900, to the esoteric content of Goethe's *Fairytale*. Later he recalled in his biography, *The Course of My Life*, how significant it was for him then to speak based on the spiritual founts of Anthroposophy for the first time in a direct manner. "Now I noticed that, amongst the audience [in the Theosophical salon of Count Brockdorff] in Berlin, there were individuals who had great interest in the spirit-world. Therefore, when invited to give a second lecture,[104] I suggested speaking on the theme of *Goethe's Secret Revelation*. And in the context of *this* lecture, I became completely esoteric. It was quite an experience for me to be able to speak in words that were shaped from out of the spiritual world" (GA 28, Chap. XXX; italics by Rudolf Steiner).

Thus, the beginning of Anthroposophy's incarnation on the earth was carried out,[105] although still connecting with Goethe, but nevertheless in the esoteric sense directly based on the supersensible Michael-cultus. With that, a direction was chosen for the ongoing development of Anthroposophy, the occult backgrounds of which could be revealed by Rudolf Steiner only after the Christmas Conference.

Before Rudolf Steiner's sacrificial deed is considered in connection with the re-founding of the Anthroposophical Society at the Christmas Conference, it should at least not remain unmentioned here that the promulgation of Anthroposophy as the essential Christian message of the contemporary Time-spirit occurred, and continues to occur, not without vehement opposition on the part of the Ahrimanic counter-forces. This has happened and continues further even now. These forces utilize human beings for this; individuals whom they have misled and who have succumbed to their power. So as to prepare human beings, meaning to make them receptive for Ahrimanic inspirations on earth for their anti-Michaelic task – something that can even extend into a temporary incorporation of Ahrimanic spirits in these people[106] – the following also took place. At the same time when the Michael-School in the Sun-region was being conducted, directly under the surface of the earth an Ahrimanic opposing school was set up.

This is probably the actual reason for the otherwise almost incomprehensible enmity, which does not desist from any lie, slander and distortion that accompanied Rudolf Steiner and his work from the start and, along with the spreading of Anthroposophy, only continued to get worse. In the destruction of the First Goetheanum through the enemies

of Anthroposophy, it found its interim culmination.[107]  In this regard
Rudolf Steiner spoke of human beings who nowadays are increasingly
possessed by Ahrimanic spirits. (See GA 346.)

So it is obvious – even though not in all cases but often enough –
where such completely unfounded and truly evil-willed hostilities appear
in people, that they stand under Ahrimanic inspirations to which they were
conditioned during their prenatal participation in the above-mentioned
subterranean anti-Michaelic school.[108] And we can assume, and it is to be
expected, that in future times more and more individuals will participate
in such campaigns of hatred and agitation.  However, in these confrontations the knowledge of the spiritual background-motifs for today's slander
of Anthroposophy and its founder can be an essential help.

\*

Within the limited framework applied to this presentation, it is not an easy
undertaking to delve into the spiritual nature of the Christmas Conference
in the light of the Michael-Mystery standing behind it.  To this event that
initially led to the founding of the new Michaelic-Christian Mysteries upon
the earth, the greatest *sacrifice* in the life of Rudolf Steiner is to be found
which he brought in full freedom and in the stern imitation of Christ.  This
deed of sacrifice was probably the most powerful revelation of the
Manichaean impulse in Rudolf Steiner's life.  For, the greatest calamity that
ever befell his work as well as he himself was the destruction of the First
Goetheanum.  Yet, in the course of the years that followed, he took this deed
of evil completely into himself and transformed it in such a way that the
greatest good could arise in the earthly history of the anthroposophical
movement, namely the Christmas Conference of 1923/1924.[109]

Two of his closest and in many respects most advanced co-
workers, Marie Steiner and Ita Wegman, have reported independently of
each other on the kind of sacrifice that was at the basis of this deed by
Rudolf Steiner.  Their testimonies, which exist in writing, are of such
decisive importance because from these two personalities Rudolf Steiner
received questions without which the above-described fourth stage of
Anthroposophy's development, its incarnation on earth, could not have

taken place. So it was Marie Steiner, quite at the beginning of his public activity, who posed the question to Rudolf Steiner regarding whether a possibility existed for the establishment of Anthroposophy on earth. In the late summer of 1923 it was Ita Wegman who asked Rudolf Steiner about the possibility of founding the new Mysteries on earth.[110]

In view of these two questions, one can hardly do other than think of the two best known disciples of Aristotle; of Theophrast who had to maintain and cultivate all the logical and philosophical works,[111] and Alexander the Great, who promulgated the natural scientific writings of Aristotle from Hellas across the entire then-known civilized world far into the Orient. The ongoing impulse from the period of Michael's regency at that earlier time in human history obviously underlies the basis of these two deeds.

The two above-mentioned testimonies follow here verbatim. In her so-called *Appeal to Reconciliation* on 12 December 1942, Marie Steiner wrote: "In view of this sacrifice and this death in which, as individuals and as a society, we certainly all bear our share of guilt – for he assumed *our* karma – can we not forget, reconcile, and open our portals wide to those who seek?"[112]

Much earlier, Ita Wegman had expressed herself in this regard: "Did every member then [during the Christmas Conference] properly comprehend that henceforth he or she would have to bear new and weighty responsibilities? Has such a person understood what kind of sacrificial deed was undertaken? Rudolf Steiner assumed the karma of the Anthroposophical Society into his own karma. It was an unheard of risk; a deed through which, when it occurred, the shock of the entire cosmos could almost be sensed and felt."[113]

Even Rudolf Steiner spoke after the Christmas Conference in various locations of the great danger and risk that was connected with his sacrifice. The risk consisted of the possibility that he could not know beforehand how the spiritual world, that is the spiritual powers that are associated with Michael and which had guided the anthroposophical movement up to then,[114] would react to his sacrificial action; above all to the fact that through assuming leadership of the Society he had at the same time connected himself to it even into his own karma.

After a period of time that Rudolf Steiner designated as a nightmare[115], the spiritual world responded; and taking the lead, Michael himself. In addition to that, revelations from the Michael-sphere flowed much more generously into his research-work,[116] and he could even begin speaking in a public lecture about the *founding of the new Mysteries* as an achieved fact. Thus, he stated on 26 May 1924 at the end of his public lecture in Paris: "One who is honest about the spiritual world, beholds a will in human beings that quite certainly will be born following the new Mysteries, for spirituality will only return to humankind, when new Mysteries will originate in which human beings will find the spirit in a more contemplative Sun-radiant way than was the case in the old Mysteries" (GA 84).

If one wants to understand this sacrificial deed on Rudolf Steiner's part even better, further words by Ita Wegman must be added in which she compares this sacrifice with the Christ-deed at the Turning Point of Time: "Just as the Christ-entity united Himself with the earth for the wellbeing of humanity, so Rudolf Steiner identified himself with the Anthroposophical Society. It was a Christ-deed."[117] And this signifies for our age that Rudolf Steiner carried out this step in the light of the Christ as Lord of Karma.

This moreover makes it comprehensible why, already during the Christmas Conference – in the evening lectures and subsequently in the mighty karma lecture cycles – Rudolf Steiner revealed to the members the newly established Anthroposophical Society and their Michaelic karma in connection with his own. For just as Christ, since the beginning of His activities as Lord of Karma, connects the karma patterns of human beings in such a way that in a karma-neutralization amongst themselves the very greatest good results for the entire evolution of humankind,[118] so has Rudolf Steiner also made known to the members their Michaelic karma in order that in light of the Michael-Mystery on the basis of this cognitive insight, they can turn the equalization, or neutralization, of their karma amongst themselves into the good, not only for themselves but for the world. In other words, what Christ does today macrocosmically as Lord of Karma, His servant and disciple Rudolf Steiner started within the framework of an Anthroposophical Society on earth; a society actually existing so that the execution of this task might then be left to its members' freedom and initiative.

From this it follows that if only human beings within the Anthroposophical Society will work with each other in a selfless manner, meaning to work on their Michaelic karma based on what has been revealed to them,[119] and on this foundation to try, out of the power of this Sun-karma, to purify and change their Moon-karma which holds back their inner development and their social relations,[120] then such individuals work in accord with the Lord of Karma, and even today are already on the way, more and more stalwartly, toward being His co-workers in the "field of karma".

If we wish to deepen the comprehension of the Christmas Conference still farther in its connection with the Michael-mysteries, then the key for that can be found in Rudolf Steiner's lecture of 13 January 1924, the content of which quite obviously bears autobiographical traits. It is also of significance that he gave this lecture exactly twelve days after the conclusion of the Christmas Conference and, as it happened, on the same day when the entire text of the Foundation Stone Meditation was published for the first time in the Newsletter, thus becoming accessible to all the members of the Anthroposophical Society. Among other issues in this lecture, Rudolf Steiner describes how Michael – in contrast to the other Time-spirits who ruled before him – is mindful of human freedom to the full extent and therefore does not direct his attention to human motives but to the results of their actions. This in turn brings it about that when an individual carries out an action in his or her life based on freedom, and spiritually appears before Michael, whether during the night in sleep, during initiation or following death, then he or she experiences and finds out from Michael his cosmic judgment concerning this action. This occurs especially when an individual was motivated to his or her action by reading in the astral light.

This comes within reach for us either through directly "looking into" the spiritual world, or through the study of spiritual science because the facts of that science have emerged in the process of Rudolf Steiner's own spiritual research out of reading in the astral light. For such an encounter with Michael, it is not of decisive importance in what way we transpose the content of the spiritual facts we have beheld in the astral light into our consciousness as a basis for our free deeds. The only difference is that in one case an individual must take what has been seen into his or her earthly thoughts so that they become *conscious* stimuli for his or her deed. In the other case, the "translation-work" has been assumed for us by an initiate – in this case Rudolf Steiner.[121]

When in this way access to the astral light has become possible, then the following happens in the above-described spiritual encounter with Michael: "Now, this is what one has to strive for more and more; to ponder, as it were, in order to push through all the way to the astral light; to behold the secrets of existence[122], and then to approach and stand before Michael and receive the approving glance that tells one: That is correct [right], that is justified in the presence of the guidance of the cosmos" (GA 233a, 13 January 1924).

Moreover, if one considers that in the very centre of the Christmas Conference – viewed esoterically – there does not stand a new wisdom but the *actual spiritual deed* by Rudolf Steiner, namely the creation of the supersensible Foundation Stone of Love, then in the sense of the last quoted words, one understands that here Rudolf Steiner had in the main stepped up to Michael in consequence of his free creation, in order to find out from Michael whether his action, deed, was seen to be "correct", indeed "justified" as far as the Guidance of the Cosmos was concerned. If, moreover, one adds to this sequence of thoughts that the Foundation Stone of Love was created by Rudolf Steiner from the loftiest forces in the spiritual world, those of the Trinity,[123] one begins to fathom the entire significance of this occurrence, not only for humankind but likewise for the gods and most of all for Michael himself.

Rudolf Steiner describes what happened further in the same lecture mentioned above: "But when, based on our freedom and stimulated through reading in the astral light, we consciously or unconsciously do this or that, Michael carries what is human earthly deed out into the cosmos *so that it becomes cosmic deed*. He cares about the consequences;

other spirits care more about the causes" (ibid.). Then, the free creation of human beings becomes cosmic deed; the basis for the new cosmos that will arise through actions of human beings out of the present cosmos. At the end of his book, *Occult Science, an Outline* Rudolf Steiner describes this spiritual transformation of the present cosmos into the future cosmos of love which, in accordance with Anthroposophical-Michaelic cosmology, he also refers to as New Jupiter. This is why the Foundation Stone for this future cosmos consists of the substance of "World-Human-Love", which Rudolf Steiner speaks of during the cultic act of the foundation-stone laying on 25 December 1923.

Furthermore, it becomes understandable from what has been stated why it was a matter of the creation of the "Stone of *Love*" during the inauguration of the new Mysteries. For, one has to do here with the "foundation stone" of the future Cosmos of Love that eventually will be created out of the free deeds by human beings; deeds that will then be "lifted up" by Michael to cosmic facts. In Biblical terms of the Apocalypse, we concern ourselves here with the foundation stone of the New Jerusalem. It is in this extraordinary perspective that one must behold Rudolf Steiner's deed and at the same time the founding of the new Mysteries. And in these Mysteries, every contemporary human being of good will can become a fellow-builder of that future cosmos by implanting the spiritual "Foundation Stone of Love" into the ground of his or her heart.

During a night-time automobile drive from Dornach to Stuttgart, Rudolf Steiner entrusted the following words to the two young anthroposophists, Guenther Wachsmuth and Ernst Lehrs, concerning such a cosmic dimension of Anthroposophy that at the same time reveals the communal cooperation of human beings with Michael: "*With the Christmas Conference, Anthroposophy has changed from an up-until-now earthly affair into a cosmic one.*"[124]

Michael himself responded as an active and creative spirit to this deed by the Michaelic individual Rudolf Steiner, not only with a flood of further and still higher revelations that were recounted by Rudolf Steiner in the karma lectures, but likewise with an actual deed — with the founding of the Michael-School on earth. For this school was not established by Rudolf Steiner but through Michael himself among human beings. Thus, the establishing of the Free School for Spiritual Science is nothing less than Michael's reply to Rudolf Steiner's deed.

Likewise the third consequence of the Christmas Conference, which Rudolf Steiner continued to work on until his death, goes back to a direct inspiration by Michael. It is the setting up of the model for the Second Goetheanum.[125] Ita Wegman, who experienced the process of the origination of the model as an eye-witness, noted down the following words by Rudolf Steiner concerning this: "The new Goetheanum will be constructed like a fortress, for the protection of all those who belong to it." And she added to this: "When the model was finished, he [Rudolf Steiner] said of it: '*Michael* has indicated the forms.' And thus the new Goetheanum is a Michael-castle."[126]

What was said can be summed up as follows: The three most important Michaelic consequences of the Christmas Conference are:

1.   The creation of the Foundation Stone of Love as centre of the new Mysteries.
2.   The karma lectures with their culmination in unveiling the Michael-Mysteries in connection with the Sun-karma of anthroposophists. The establishment of the Michael-School on earth.
3.   The creation of the model for the Second Goetheanum.

This makes it obvious that the Christmas Conference itself and all additional deeds by Rudolf Steiner originated – as the consequences of that conference – by means of his working together with Michael. Out of this sphere emerged the great karma revelations, which increasingly became richer and grander as well as their very heart-centre; the opening of the Michael-Mystery, the description of the supersensible Michael-School, and the Michael-cultus. All this is part of the Sun-karma of anthroposophists, which speaks of their original connection with Michael and his celestial deeds. And as is evident from the later *Michael Letters* (GA 26), this ultimately speaks also of the connection with Christ, as whose countenance Michael works today.

For, in his description of the Michael-Mystery, Rudolf Steiner speaks repeatedly of "Michael-Christ" as *one* entity. And concerning the contents of his *Michael Letters*, he himself says that in them the cosmic facts are recounted the way they reveal themselves to the initiate, not from the human viewpoint but from the "standpoint" of Michael.[127] And in the mantric path of inner schooling in the First Class, Rudolf Steiner has given to the members what is for our time the only correct "Michael-path that finds its continuation in the Christ-path" (GA 194, 23 November 1919).

Thus, after the Christmas Conference, the Michael-Mystery is "unfolded" more and more by Rudolf Steiner up until his last days on earth. The actual culmination of these revelations is, however, *The Last Address*; the final testamentary turn by Rudolf Steiner to his disciples who are at the same time *Michael-disciples* – a wondrous radiant saying that we may not light-heartedly apply to ourselves but should place before ourselves as our ideal that we wish to follow like a spiritual load-star. For as Anthroposophists we are called upon to become Michaelites[128] in faithfulness and in a relationship that does not allow any compromise in regard to what was given to us through Rudolf Steiner by Michael himself as his example. In any case, we still find ourselves quite at the beginning of the path to this goal.

And yet we are directly addressed as students of Michael in the mantric verse through which Rudolf Steiner concluded his last lecture. We feel ourselves spoken to quite directly by Michael himself who in these words reveals himself as the great hierarchical co-worker of Christ. The entire cosmic-telluric connection of Michael to Christ becomes visible in this verse. Thus in this mantra, it is not Michael alone, it is not the Christ alone who speaks; there speaks a new being whom Rudolf Steiner denotes as *Michael-Christ*. Encompassing heaven and earth, this being now turns to Rudolf Steiner's disciples; to their will, their courage, and to their inner strength which is to make them capable to actually walk on this Michaelic path to the Christ so that the most significant tasks of our age can be fulfilled.

# IV

# The Michael-Imagination as a Revelation of the Michael-Mystery

The mighty presentation of karmic relationships – with their consequences in humanity as well as the cosmos – that Rudolf Steiner had discussed in detail in 81 lectures during the year 1924 was brought to a culmination by him with the festive Michaelmas-address on 28 September. In this address he referred once more to the spiritual origin of his karma revelations, namely the mantric verse with which he had ended this last lecture. With this verse's direct turn to Michael and all the Anthroposophists as his disciples, it thereby became like a last spiritual will by Rudolf Steiner and simultaneously a testament to the deepest connection that exists in the spiritual world between Michael and Christ. In this sense, the Michael-path of the new Mysteries described in this book leads to Christ in a way that is appropriate for contemporary humankind.

Now in this chapter we shall turn directly to the content of this unique Michael-meditation in order to further pursue the most important component-parts of the Michael-Mystery already described in the previous chapter, which in its mantric concentration receives a still more profound expression. We start with the first verse:

> "Springing from Powers of the Sun
> Radiant Spirit-powers, blessing all Worlds!
> For Michael's garment of rays
> You are predestined by Thought Divine."

These four lines lead us directly into the Sun-sphere of Michael, and simultaneously into his supersensible school in the region where the instruction was given. As we have already seen in his many descriptions of the Michael-School, Rudolf Steiner refers to the fact that not only human beings – who in their life between death and rebirth were predestined to shape the coming Michael-epoch on earth – but likewise many entities of the spiritual world also took part in this instruction by Michael.

Who are these beings? Rudolf Steiner mentions them over and over again in his lecture dealing with the Michael-School. First, there are a large number of elemental beings; then there are also spirits of the Third Hierarchy who also belong to the Michael-stream in the spiritual world, and due to the Cosmic-will of Michael they work in the evolution of humanity. These entities are those *spiritual* beings that were called upon at the behest of Michael to be present at the Christmas Conference for the founding of the new Mysteries on earth, and to help guide these Mysteries since then. Rudolf Steiner repeatedly makes reference to all these spiritual powers that are subordinate to Michael in the same way that Michael follows and serves the will of Christ.

Concerning the relationship of the Michael-will to the will of Christ who is effective as the "Will of Worlds", Rudolf Steiner states verbatim: "Only then when this work, the great mighty permeation of the Michael-power with the *Michael-will* – which is nothing else but what precedes the *Christ-will*, so that this Christ-power becomes implanted into the life on earth in the right way – only then will matters move in the right direction, namely when this Michael-power can really be victorious over the demonic dragon-like element which all of you know too well ..." (ibid.). Rudolf Steiner also speaks about what it signifies when this is fulfilled and that thereby the possibility arises for human beings to become "faithful servants" (ibid.) of Michael in this battle.

Rudolf Steiner then speaks about participation of the entities of the Third Hierarchy in this work by Michael for which they were prepared already in the supersensible Michael-School. In this regard he first said in Holland: "Michael gathered his hosts together; those who as supersensible beings belong to him from the realm of Angels and Archangels. He likewise gathered together those human souls who in one way or another had come into a connection with him" (GA 240, 20 July 1924).

Then, however, we come across a further passage in a lecture from the cycle that Rudolf Steiner gave in August of 1924 in England, where he enlarged this composition of the Michael-School. There he relates that not only Angels and Archangels belong to the Michael-stream, but even Archai who are connected with Michael and who minister to him as the *Countenance of Christ*. Although Michael today belongs to the Hierarchy of the Archai, by virtue of the fact that he became the countenance of Christ, he stands on a much higher level than the entire Third Hierarchy. From the Sun, it is Michael that has the task of representing the Logos itself; the highest creative principle of all worlds. Therefore, one need not be surprised to learn that there are even Archai who minister to Michael, and who have participated along with the Archangels, Angels, elemental beings and human souls in his instruction in the supersensible school.[1]

Rudolf Steiner states in this regard: "All the discarnate human souls that belonged with Michael participated in that great school which ran its course supersensibly in the 14th, 15th and 16th centuries. All those beings from the Third Hierarchy – the Angeloi, Archangeloi, Archai – and numerous elemental beings who belonged to the Michael-stream, participated" (GA 240, 27 August 1924).

What is stated here can explain a further riddle for us. It is linked with the coining of the expression "spiritual forces", which Rudolf Steiner uses several times in connection with the esoteric nature of the Christmas Conference. Thus in May of 1924 in Paris, he speaks about the "forces of the alliance that we were permitted to bring about with good *spiritual* forces" (GA 260a, 23 May 1924), so that in future times the anthroposophical movement could be protected from all attacks by the opposing powers. Then in Arnhem he says that, following the Christmas Conference, "those *spiritual forces* which guide the anthroposophical movement in the spiritual world now come to meet with a [still] greater generosity, with a higher benevolence... with that which flows through the anthroposophical movement" (GA 260a, 18 July 1924). Rudolf Steiner likewise mentions in this regard that at the Christmas Conference, these forces "were given a promise" by him personally and that "this promise ... will be fulfilled in an unbreakable way" (ibid.).[2]

In other reports concerning the Christmas Conference, Rudolf Steiner reinforces the significance of these spiritual forces for the further development of the anthroposophical movement on earth and speaks of "those *spiritual powers* from whom we have our revelations" (GA 260a, 12 August 1924), above all the karma revelations of the year 1924 and the revelations from the spiritual world that represent the foundation for the communications of the First Class of the School for Spiritual Science.[3]

A sort of culmination is attained in September 1924, namely in that lecture in Dornach, where – like a re-evaluation – Rudolf Steiner speaks for the last time to the members about the events of the Christmas Conference. He makes a direct reference that here one concerns oneself with the "spiritual *powers* that bestow Anthroposophy on us" (GA 260a, 5 September 1924). One need only compare these words with the other words – already quoted here – that "this spiritual insight is the gift of Michael" (GA 152, 2 May 1913), in order to come a step closer to the solution of the above-mentioned riddle.

From all that has been delineated here, one can reach the conclusion that with the expression "spiritual powers" in the above-described context, it is a matter of Michael himself and diverse spirits of the Third Hierarchy that are filled with Michael's creator-will, and which therefore form a kind of unity with him. In occult-imaginative language, however, it is understood that these "powers" belong to Michael's spiritual "garment" and therefore can be designated together with him as *one being*. That this is actually the case is vouchsafed by the following written remark by Rudolf Steiner found in the *Michael Letters*: "Beheld in the supersensible, the matter is as follows. *The spiritual powers that one can designate with the name "Michael"* administer the ideas in the spiritual cosmos."[4] And in this "administration of ideas", Michael and all the hierarchical beings belonging with him work together inseparably.

If on this basis we now consider the first verse of the Michael Mantra, we find – delicately indicated – that here the entire host of Michael in the spiritual world is addressed. "Powers of the Sun" – we find ourselves in the Sun sphere with these words. From the beginning, we deal with those paths that are linked to the Sun-kingdom of Michael. Next in turn, something else is linked that "has sprung up", and has to do with the plant-kingdom. Naturally, there are no plants on the Sun, but there exist elemental spirits that moreover reveal themselves in certain earth-processes. Out of the Sun-powers originate what "springs forth" – hence the various elemental spirits who now participate in the Michael-School.

On the next stage a radiant quality is fitted in. This is a quality of the Angels. All appearances of Angels bear a power of radiance in them. But here in the spiritual world, we deal only with Angels that belong to Michael's kingdom and that have gone through his supersensible school.[5]

Then there appear still higher spiritual entities who even work in a "world-blessing" manner. These are the Archangels who participate in the Michael-School. They have the task of intervening formatively even into the karma relationships of human beings. They are to bring the new grace of the Christ as Lord of Karma to all human beings, quite in accord with the lines from the second part of the Foundation Stone Meditation:

> "For the Christ-will holds sway in the circumference,
>   Blessing souls in the rhythms of worlds."
>                     (GA 260, 25 December 1923).

At this point, Christ Himself works in the spiritual world through the circle of twelve Archangels.[6]

After that, there appear the highest of the spirits that participate in the Michael-School, the "Spirit-powers" or Archai that belong to Michael's stream.

All these hierarchical beings are part of the "radiant garment" of Michael, his cosmic aura, in which he, "the Teaching One", appears in his supersensible school in the midst of the Archai, Archangels, Angels and elemental spirits or – in the verbiage of the Michael-meditation – in the accompaniment of the *spiritual powers*, the *beings blessing worlds*, the *radiant beings*, and the *elemental beings* who have sprung forth from the Sun.

In the first lines of the Michael-meditation, we also discover an indication to the secret of the threefold Sun in which the "radiant Spirit-powers", who are most strongly involved in shaping "Michael's garment of rays", initially reveal themselves. Then we have the beings that "have sprung from" the Sun and "bless worlds". And in conclusion, from out of the Sun centre, we have the "Powers of the Sun". With this, after the external revelation of the Sun as the light-source, there follows a deepening backward movement to above – see diagram below for the working of Grace and Life – and from there still further up to the Sun and Spirit-powers that belong to the very spirit centre of the Sun and jointly transform "Michael's garment of rays" into the "Light-ray garment of the Sun" (GA 238, 28 September 1924).

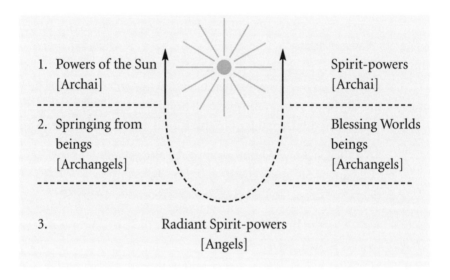

Thereby, through the entities that shape it, the "Sun-garment" of Michael is at the same time a reflection of the threefold Sun from which the great Zarathustra was the first to speak in the Mysteries he had established during the post-Atlantean age.[7]

From this comprehension of the first verse of the Michael-meditation, we find that the designation in the first line "Powers of the Sun", points to still loftier hierarchies than the Archai or "Spirit-powers". Initially, Rudolf Steiner mentions the "Light-Spirits";[8] these are the three kinds of entities of the Second Hierarchy, the Kyriotetes, Dynamis and Exusiai.[9] They are particularly linked with the Sun, and among them chiefly the Exusiai or Spirits of Form – in the Bible likewise called the "Elohim" – who are the actual Creators of present-day earth and humankind.[10] At around the midpoint of the Lemurian Age, they sacrificed their own substance for the individual "I" of the human being[11] and are moreover those, among all the beings of the Second Hierarchy, who are most strongly united with the Sun (see GA 110, 15 April 1909-II). This is why they, and among them particularly the six leading beings, stand in a direct relationship with the Christ after He had descended downwards at the beginning of earth evolution from still higher spiritual spheres of the Sun.

In the lecture of 20 May 1908 (GA 103), Rudolf Steiner describes Christ's work on the Sun through these six Sun-Elohim. They represent "the nature of the divine love of the Logos" in the cosmos, and send this divine love, along with shining rays of sunlight, to human beings on earth. For in the Sun's light as purely spiritual activity, live the Exusiai who are the inhabitants of the Sun.

As the actual creators of the earth and ego-endowed human beings, these Spirits of Form live at present within the process of passing on their guidance of earth and humankind to the most advanced beings of the Hierarchy of the Archai, or Spirits of Personality, who stand directly under them. The Spirits of Form in turn ascend to a higher stage of "cosmic creator-hood" and the Archai begin to be active with the "creator-qualities" of the Exusiai. This signifies that these Spirits of Personality are involved at the present time in the process of transition from the Archai-stage to that of the Spirits of Form. This implies that they already bear within themselves the qualities of both the Third and the Second hierarchies. Or to put it into the language of the Foundation Stone Meditation: From the "Soul-Spirits" of the Third Hierarchy the guidance passes over to the "Light-Spirits".[12]

Now, the "Soul Spirits" have the possibility of engaging in a direct relationship with individual human souls (this is why they are called Spirits of *Personality*), something the "Light-Spirits" of the Second Hierarchy are not allowed to do, for their spiritual power cannot be tolerated by the human soul. Thus, these spirits work above all from outside – as does the spiritual side of sunlight – and they shape sunlight with their spiritual forces into countless natural processes. By contrast, the new Spirits of Personality possess both qualities and are therefore especially qualified to guide a human being to a modern initiation; something that is offered today in Anthroposophy. "The Spirits of Personality assume a new character. The new initiation is essentially connected with this new nature of the Spirits of Personality" (GA 187, 27 December 1918).

All this likewise has a connection with Michael and his super-sensible school. For in that school, among other matters, Michael spoke the following to all those who were present: "Let us redesign the mighty initiate-teaching that once poured down in the ancient way to the earth through the Mysteries; let us design it for the souls of those who in an intelligence-filled manner were connected with Michael" (GA 240, 20 July 1924).

One sees in both cases – in the School of Michael as well as in the new activity of the Spirits of Personality – that it is a matter of achieving the same goal, namely the founding of the new modern initiation on earth. Thus, these two streams are connected and effective together in Anthroposophy as initiation-science.[13] Thereby on the one hand a new cooperation is commencing between gods themselves, Michael and the above referred-to Spirits of Personality, and on the other hand a new coop-eration between gods and human beings.

Rudolf Steiner considers the ascent of these Spirits of Personality to the point where they are new creators, and the subsequently changed relationship to human beings that follows from this – a relationship that fully includes their freedom – "to be the very most important and essential element as regards cognition of the contemporary age" (GA 187, 1 January 1919). Rudolf Steiner links this with the origin of spiritual science on earth which he characterizes in this context as follows: "We receive it in a living way, this spiritual science, and I have described it as a revelation of the Spirits of Personality, who as creators newly intercede" (GA 187, 31 December 1918). And it is indeed this fundamental secret of our age that is contained in the first verse of the Michael-medi-tation, namely in the transition from the "Powers of the Sun" (Exusiai) to the "Spirit-powers" (Archai), of whom some are destined for the forming of Michael's "garment of light-rays", and as hierarchical servants of

Michael will work together with him on the above-described process in the supersensible worlds.

For, it is the "Thought Divine" itself, meaning the cosmic thoughts of all nine hierarchies, who together form and represent cosmic intelligence. They have brought it about that a number of entities of the Third Hierarchy participated in the supersensible Michael-School, and in so doing became the celestial "garment" of Michael in which he works since the beginning of his contemporary regency on earth. Therefore, they can be designated in the plural as "Spirit-powers" who guide the anthroposophical movement in the higher worlds.

Having become acquainted in this part of the verse with all the beings that belong to the Michael-School, there follows the communication concerning the content of their instruction which, however, is limited in the meditation itself only to the most essential elements and summed up in the next two lines:

"He, the Christ-messenger, reveals in you – ..."

Now, Michael stands before us as the radiant heavenly teacher of his Sun-School, and in it his instruction begins that he offers to all of whom mention was made earlier, including human souls that belong to it. Principally, he refers to what must definitely be effective in his instruction pervading all of it, namely:

"Bearing mankind aloft – the sacred Will of Worlds."

And now Michael moves forward before his hierarchical-human disciples in his highest office as "Christ-messenger" who not only has authority to reveal the "sacred Will of Worlds", that is none other than the Cosmic-will of the Christ Himself, but to permeate the diverse entities who participate in his school with this will, so that through the mediation of Michael they can become servants of Christ[14] that inwardly bear and bless human beings in accordance with the already quoted lines from the Foundation Stone Meditation:

"For the Christ-will holds sway in the circumference,
    Blessing souls in the rhythms of worlds."[15]

That we are dealing here with the Christ-will is assured by the fact that it bears and supports human beings. For, since the Mystery of Golgotha, His Cosmic-will holds sway not only in the universe but likewise on earth, for He is inseparably connected with it. And on earth, this will of worlds by the Christ becomes "the hold" of human beings because in the Mystery of Golgotha the human ego and the physical body were both redeemed.[16] New spiritual forces work in human beings. And these Christ-forces in us are literally supportive of and bear us as human beings. Thus one can say that with the words "bearing and supporting", the mighty all-encompassing secret of the Mystery of Golgotha is being referred to.

As we have already seen, a panorama of all true Mysteries of the past were "opened up", as it were, in this Michael-School by Michael himself; and their metamorphosis through the Mystery of Golgotha into future ages was furthermore presented. And what does this entire Mystery-evolution signify, which from the very beginning was directed towards the Sun? It indeed signifies its absolute conformity with the Will of Worlds which, however, prior to the Mystery of Golgotha, did not as yet have its fount on earth but on the Sun, and therefore could not be as "supportive" of humanity. Now, all those who had participated in the Michael-School learned that this Will of Worlds had become supportive along with the Mystery of Golgotha. And from this emerged the most important task for them. For all beings that had participated in this Michael-School now had to become conscious and willing executors of this Will of Worlds in earth's ongoing development.

It can be said that in two lines of the second stanza, we have in abbreviated form – something which is only possible in mantric speech – a summation not only of the instruction by the supersensible Michael-School, but likewise what was to be brought about in those beings who participated in the instruction of this school. That in turn was an actual spiritual communion with the Cosmic-will of the Christ, transmitted as if from a heavenly high-priest. That would be His Sun-messenger.

A subsequent step on this newly begun path is contained in the next two lines of the second verse:

> "You, the radiant Beings of Ether-worlds
> Bear the Christ-word to man."

Now, we no longer find ourselves in the lofty Sun-sphere but in the "Ether-worlds" that directly adjoin the earth. What variety of beings is effective here? Here, they are designated as "radiant" beings, something that points to the Hierarchy of the Angels. In the first verse, they reveal themselves in the Sun-region as "radiant". Now, while Angels appear in the spiritual circumference of the earth in the same quality of radiance, they do, however, find themselves already in their own region, for their field of activity is chiefly the "ether-worlds" in which they come closest to the terrestrial, earthly, world in order to be in a position to fulfil their manifold tasks in regard to earthly human beings, and in obedience to the direction by higher hierarchies.

Today, the etheric Christ works in this sphere as well. And what is more, He Himself passed through this angelic kingdom in the middle of the 19th century inasmuch as He fulfilled the second supersensible Event of Golgotha, in consequence of which His appearance in etheric form was called forth beginning from the twentieth century onward. Rudolf Steiner describes it like this: "Thus, the Christ-consciousness can be united, beginning in the twentieth century, with the earthly consciousness of humanity, for the dying away of the Christ-consciousness in the angelic sphere during the nineteenth century signifies the resurrection of the direct Christ-consciousness in the earthly sphere, meaning the life of the Christ will be sensed more and more beginning from the twentieth century onwards in the souls of human beings as a direct personal experience" (GA 152, 2 May 1913).

And a little further in this lecture, Rudolf Steiner defines this process moreover in the following words: "Thus, we can behold that in those particular worlds which lie directly "behind" our own world, a sort of spiritual death, a cessation of consciousness did occur, and with that a repetition of the Mystery of Golgotha so that a re-enlivening of the earlier hidden Christ-consciousness can take place in the souls of human beings on earth" (ibid.). Thus, in this process, we have summarized three stages. The Mystery of Golgotha (including its supersensible repetition) consists always of two stages, death and resurrection. And then as a third stage comes what emerges from this process; what has led and shall lead further to a shining forth of the new Christ-consciousness in human beings beginning from the first third of the twentieth century[17] leading onward to a more pervasive perception of the etheric Christ.

At this point, one more question can be posed. In what sort of connection does Michael stand to this supersensible event? Or formulated differently: What else did Michael do after the conclusion of the supersensible cultus? Rudolf Steiner reports that beginning from the year 1841, as if in imitation of Christ, Michael had begun his passage from the Sun into the next sphere of the spiritual surroundings of the earth, so as to embark on his task, beginning from 1879, as the contemporary Time-spirit of humankind. And there can be no doubt that it was this very path which led through that spiritual sphere where the second supersensible Mystery of Golgotha occurred at that time. Thus, Michael became that second Mystery's direct witness, if not even a helping co-worker. This is why Rudolf Steiner states further on in the same lecture: "What I have only been able to indicate in a few words concerning the second Mystery of Golgotha, will gradually penetrate into human souls, and its herald – its mediator – will be Michael himself who is now the envoy of the Christ" (ibid.). As a witness who proclaims this truth based on his own cosmic experience – a truth which originates out of the world of the "bright beings of ether-worlds", or put differently, a truth which originates out of the sphere of the Angeloi that have the task "to bring the Christ-word to the human being" – Michael begins his vocation as Time-spirit.

There is moreover much that speaks for the fact that some participants of the cosmic cultus – not all of them but those who were leading human souls in that cultus – were also witnesses of the supersensible Mystery of Golgotha. As a result they could bring the message of this event later on to the earth based on their personal recollection. This was the case for these particular human souls based on what they "co-experienced" there. Their individual access to the new Christ-consciousness took place as yet quite differently from the way it will gradually spread in mankind over the next three millennia.[18]

One can now go one step farther and pose the question as to a direct connection that exists between the cosmic cultus and the supersensible Mystery of Golgotha. Were the Imaginations that harboured the nature of the "new Christendom" not at the same time like a spiritual chalice into which the new Christ-consciousness poured as a result of the second Mystery of Golgotha, so as to be preserved there until after the first third of the twentieth century?[19] And would this new Christ-consciousness not have been carried into humanity by the Angels so that human beings could begin to behold the Christ in the etheric realm? (See more on these Angels further below.)

From this cosmic cultus comes the unique relationship of Anthroposophy to the etheric Christ. For, the cosmic cultus *was* the second stage of Anthroposophy's supersensible preparation. And the just-described relationship makes the deeply profound connection with the etheric Christ that Anthroposophy is called upon to assume in the future more comprehensible. The subsequent words by Rudolf Steiner in the Christmas-lecture of 1914 in Dornach – following the outbreak of the First World War and as if called into this dark atmosphere – point to the following secret: "And let us build in our souls the confidence in the fulfilment of this proclamation: The confidence that what we feel today for that child whom we worship – the new Christ-comprehension[20] is this child – that this child may live (and in not too long a time) may grow up in such a way *that there can incarnate in it* the *etherically appearing Christ* just as He could incarnate in a body of flesh at the time of the Mystery of Golgotha" (GA 156, 26 December 1914).

And this incarnation of the etheric Christ into the then developing Anthroposophy (and likely also through the spiritual work of anthroposophists) only became possible because earlier it had received the new Christ-consciousness into itself in the above-depicted manner; something that had originated through the supersensible Mystery of Golgotha.

Thus in total, we have a threefold connection of Anthroposophy with Christ. First, there is the connection with His cosmic Sun-secret that was made relevant in the supersensible Michael-School by Michael as Sun-Archangel. Secondly, we have the union of Anthroposophy with the new

Christ-consciousness that it takes into itself following its preparation in the cosmic cultus. Thirdly, Anthroposophy can receive the etheric Christ Himself into its own being already on earth.

Let us now return to the consideration of the Michael-Mystery.

With the line, "You, the radiant Beings of Ether-worlds", the entire hierarchical surroundings of this cultus, but primarily the Angels, are being called. Now in the second line of the second verse, the most essential aspect of this cultus comes to the fore, namely that in it (though at first still in the spiritual world) the new Christianity was established. What this new Christendom is to become for human beings on the earth is then found in the fourth and last line:

"Bear the Christ-word to man."

The Christ-word, the etheric-word, the words of the etheric Christ, must be borne by the Angels into humanity – by the "radiant Beings" of light that belong to the Michael-stream. For, only this Christ-word can awaken the Christ-consciousness in human beings today, whereby the new Christ-experiencing can become a quite personal inner event in man.

In the booklet, *Spiritual Guidance of the Individual and Humanity*, Rudolf Steiner speaks of the Angels who were involved in the guidance of the ancient Egyptian civilization long ago and – in contrast to other Angels[21] – fully and completely accepted the Christ-impulse later on; and this is the reason why in our time they can bear spiritual science into humanity. This means that today these Angels bring Anthroposophy to human beings as a gift of Michael, and with that they avow that they are connected with Michael and his stream. Concerning this contemporary function of the Angels who today work in accord with Christ and Michael, Rudolf Steiner speaks as follows: "And if one is involved today with Anthroposophy, this signifies nothing less than an acknowledgement of the fact that supersensible entities [the Angels] who have guided humanity [during Egyptian times] continue their leadership in such a way that Angels find themselves today under the guidance of the Christ" (GA 15, Chap. III).

With the above, a condition is likewise depicted under which Angels could participate in Michael's supersensible school. So as to be present at the instruction of the Sun-countenance of the Christ, they had to have taken the Christ-impulse into themselves earlier. Only then, following the two-fold preparation in the Michael-School and the Michael-cultus, could they begin to guide human beings in the twentieth century to a conscious experiencing of the etheric Christ. For the Angels in particular, this twofold spiritual preparation was the foundation on which they could fulfil their task since the first third of the twentieth century in regard to the appearing of the etheric Christ. "And just as in our age, the same great teachers [the Angels] are the ones who already guided human beings in the Egyptian-Chaldean culture, so will they moreover be the ones who guide human beings upwards to a beholding of the Christ in the twentieth century, as Paul beheld Him. They will show human beings how the Christ not only is effective on the earth, but spiritualizes the entire Sun-system as well" (ibid.).

The last sentence of this quote in particular indicates the central teaching of the supersensible Michael-School as well as the cultus that followed, in which foundations of the new cosmic Christendom were worked out by Angels and human beings together. However, so that this could actually take place, the Angels in the supersensible cultus who were connected with Michael had to learn more than anything else "to bear the Christ-word to human beings so that we humans could learn a new Michael-Christ language from it; Christ-words in Michaelic form which are accessible to the free forces of cognition in every human being.

What this signifies is described by Rudolf Steiner in the lecture of 6 February 1917, where he first raises the question: "What is Anthroposophy?" And then he gives the reply himself, namely that Anthroposophy is nothing less than a new spiritual language that we learn so that we can converse with the *etheric* Christ. And today when we pose true heart-questions in this language of spiritual science to the Christ, He will reply to them. "Why do we occupy ourselves with spiritual science? It is as if we had to learn the vocabulary of that language in which we draw near the Christ. And one who tries to think about the world in the way that spiritual science tries to work; one who makes the effort to look into secrets of the cosmos in his or her head, in just the way spiritual science wills it; to such an individual there will appear today – out of dim and dark foundations of worlds – the form of the Christ, of Christ Jesus. And He will then be the powerful force for such a person in which he or she will live; standing by his or her side in a brotherly fashion so that this person might be strong and powerful in heart and soul. Such a one will be up to the tasks of the future evolution of humankind. We should therefore not merely seek spiritual science as a teaching, but learn to acquire it as a language and wait until we find the questions in this speech which we then may pose to the Christ. He will reply; yes, He *will* reply" (GA 175, 6 February 1917; italics by Rudolf Steiner).

It follows from Rudolf Steiner's further remarks below that Michael, who in our age guides one to Christ, is also in the deepest sense connected with this language of spiritual science: "But aside from *this* language [that of natural science], Anthroposophy indeed speaks yet another language, namely that of the nature of man, about the development of the human being, and about the evolution of the cosmos; Anthroposophia would like to speak the Michael-Christ language."[22] Thus, the above-mentioned Angels are the most important mediators of this new language of spiritual life today. And they have indeed learned the foundations for this task both in the Michael-School and in the cosmic cultus.

Let us proceed further through the Michael-meditation. The next verse contains the third stage in the evolution thus far depicted. Following its heavenly preparation, Anthroposophy can now appear on earth among human beings. "And thus we have a dual supersensible preparation for what is to become Anthroposophy on earth: First, we have that preparation in the great supersensible school of instruction beginning in the 15th century; and then ... we have that which replicated itself as an Imaginative-cultus in the supersensible realm at the end of the 18th and beginning of the 19th century. What Michael-students had learned in the supersensible school of instruction through mighty imaginative images was then formalized. Thus were these souls prepared who then descended into the physical world, and after all these preparations were to receive the urge to move to what Anthroposophy is supposed to accomplish on earth" (GA 237, 28 July 1924). With this, the threshold

of the year 1879 is attained at which time the new Michael-epoch begins.
Now, Michael descends from the Sun to the earth and stands before
human beings with his "Sun-countenance" which at the same time is the
cosmic "Christ-countenance."

>     "Thus shall the Herald of Christ appear ...".

To be a "herald" means to be able to bring someone a message composed
of words. Here, however, we deal with the most elevated interpretation of
the meaning of the word "herald" because there steps before us the Herald
of the Christ-word (Logos). In our age this is Michael. He appears to
humankind surrounded by the Angeloi who minister to him from out of
the circumference of the second supersensible Mystery of Golgotha;
Angels who likewise belong among the followers of the etheric Christ.
And He turns

>     "To the thirstily waiting souls,"

In reality there are many more contemporary souls who seek this
Michaelic wisdom, this Michaelic access to the spiritual world, and above
all access to the Michael-Christ sphere; a realm that with the help of
Anthroposophy we are allowed to enter into owing to full comprehension
of this wisdom. And overall this may perhaps be the only genuine
and quite modest task of the Anthroposophical Society: namely to
nurture this Michael-Christ-message – this Michael-Christ-wisdom – as
Anthroposophy so powerfully that it takes hold of the entire human being
and shines out of his or her soul even for other souls who seek this wisdom
the entire world over. Even if some of these people have not participated
in the Michael-School and supersensible cultus, they nevertheless have
come down during this Michaelic age to the earth and therefore belong –
if they only understand themselves rightly – among those individuals
concerning whom the above meditation speaks of as "abiding, thirsting
souls" in such an insistent manner.

Already during the foundation-stone laying of the First
Goetheanum that was to become a visible expression of the above
mentioned new spiritual language, Rudolf Steiner refers to such souls who

seek for the spirit, and indeed call for the true spirit. For the First
Goetheanum was in its esoteric nature nothing else but the visible revelation of the Christ-Michael language of Anthroposophy. "Look around
you, my dear sisters and brothers how this undefined longing and
undefined hope for the spirit holds sway in people today! Feel, in listening
for an answer here at the foundation stone of our landmark (this
structure), how in the undefined longing and hope of human beings
the cry for the spirit will be audible for an answer; for that answer which
can be given where spiritual science can hold sway with its gospel of
proclamation for the spirit" (GA 245, 20 September 1913).

So through this science of the spirit, Michael himself turns to
souls of contemporary human beings, and particularly to his disciples who
have journeyed together with him on this path that passes through his
supersensible school and the cosmic cultus. And these are those human
individuals in whom the "undefined longing" and "hope for the spirit" has
turned into a conscious striving for Michael and lives in their souls with
a strength that Rudolf Steiner characterizes in the following words:
"Only those can be Anthroposophists who experience certain questions
concerning the nature of the human being and the world as a necessity of
life, just as one experiences hunger and thirst" (GA 26).

At this point, every Anthroposophist should really earnestly ask
him or herself: Do these words apply to me as well? Or is Anthroposophy
something I merely occupy myself with on Sundays, and during the
remaining six days I do something else completely different that is not
very Michaelic at all? What is the situation actually like in my case? One
really does have to pose this question concerning how it feels, physically
speaking, when one hasn't eaten or drunk anything for a somewhat longer
period of time thereby arriving at a certain limit. Does one wish to tolerate
[this condition] and for how long can one do that? And then one has to
face the next question – now entirely on a soul-spiritual level – whether
one is willing to arrive at such a boundary in Anthroposophy. For to
endure this borderline situation is the decisive criterion of our true relationship to Michael. We only become his true disciples when his gift,
Anthroposophy, becomes something that is essential for our lives and

life-determining – like hunger and thirst – something that at the same time signifies that our entire being is gripped by this.

Let us follow the course of the meditation further. Michael as the leading Time-spirit now turns directly to all human beings of the present:

"To whom your Word of Light shines forth ...".

"Them" would indeed refer to those human souls who thirst for the true spirit; "your" points to what streams forth from the Angels, the "radiant Beings of Ether-worlds" who are enfilled by the Christ-impulse, and who today stand in Michael's service and together form his cosmic garment. Michael now gives those Angels belonging to his stream a new task in regard to what in the cosmic cultus as "Christ-word" is to be the basis for the "new Christendom". What is to be carried down to human beings as the further metamorphosed cosmic "Word of Light" takes hold of cognitive forces in human beings. The cognitive forces referred to here are no longer the regular intellectual head-forces that do not shine. The "Word of Light" represents the forces of transformed thinking that illuminate and bring about a new cognition, through which alone we can understand spiritual science today in such a way that it reaches our hearts and fills them with genuine enthusiasm for true spirit-knowledge.

When that can happen, Michael himself is effective in this process. "He liberates thoughts from the region of the head; he frees the path to our heart for them; he loosens enthusiasm out of our heart and mind so that we can live in soul-devotion to all that is possible for us to experience in the *light of thoughts*."[23] It is Anthroposophy that is filled and penetrated by this thought-light of transformed thinking, for Anthroposophy has emerged out of spiritual research which is rooted in heart-thinking, and can only be truly grasped by this heart-thinking.[24]

Then people in anthroposophical settings will cease from always repeating: We must finally refrain from relating everything to Rudolf Steiner by asserting that "Rudolf Steiner said...," or: "He has once again quoted Rudolf Steiner." For then our hearts burn for Anthroposophy and every word by him. In his own words it sounds like this: "Thoughts that nowadays strive for comprehending spiritual truths must stem from hearts that beat for Michael as the fiery Lord of Thoughts of the world-all" (ibid.). And why do human hearts burn; why do they then beat for Michael? Because, in Anthroposophy, the "Christ-word" as "Word of Light" takes hold of our cognitive forces in the Michaelic sense and thus enfires us in such a way that in every word by Rudolf Steiner we can experience this Michael-Christ substance as the spiritual background.

The third verse of the meditation finds its conclusion through the line:

> "In cosmic age of Spirit-Human."

One could almost be shocked by this mighty perspective. Not even once have we come close to the Spirit Self, yet here mention is already made of Spirit-Human [please refer to note 25 on page 266]. So as to understand this better, we should call to mind that as earthly human beings we only have our "I" available as the highest part of our entity. It forms the inner centre of our entire nature. The Angels have no human ego. Their "I" is "melted together" with their Spirit-Self; and the "I" of the Archangels is by now inseparably linked with their Life-Spirit; and the "I" of the Archai already now works out of the "very core connection" of being with Spirit-Human. Michael too as an Archai has his "I" in Spirit-Human. As the one who leads the Sun-region, this is why Michael finds himself in a special relationship to the cosmic Spirit-Human of the Christ, whom on His way to the earth Christ left behind on the Sun. "Christ died on the Sun; He died cosmically from the Sun down to the earth; He came down to the earth ... After this cosmic death, Christ left the Spirit-Human back on the Sun" (GA 240, 27 August 1924).

Out of the power of this Christianised Spirit-Human, Michael likewise works today on the earth. He thereby has a very special relationship to the Christ, something that places him in the hierarchical totality much higher than what corresponds to his actual stage of development as that of an Archai.

The next topic referred to in the meditation is "cosmic age". What is meant by that? We find the answer when we consider the future evolution of humanity. Today in the fifth post-Atlantean epoch [during the fifth cosmic age] of the consciousness-soul, we stand on the stage of the "I" or ego. In the sixth cultural epoch, the provisional and grace-filled outpouring of the Spirit-Self into humankind will come about. During the seventh epoch, despite all the catastrophes relating to the "war of all against all", a similar grace-filled outpouring of the Life-Spirit will take place. And only after the "catastrophe of worlds" following the conclusion of an entire cosmic age (including in this case all seven post-Atlantean cultural epochs), we arrive at the next "cosmic age", the "*great* sixth age", which in turn will consist of seven sub-stages. This sixth cosmic age then begins with the grace-filled outpouring of the Spirit-Human [element] into humankind. Moreover, this sixth cosmic age will be the one at the end of which the union of the earth with the Sun occurs. This event is the one that Michael as the leading Sun-Archai already now wishes to prepare for during his contemporary guidance of humanity today.

This preparation consists among others in the fact that Michael increasingly reveals the secret of the Christ as highest regent of the Sun to human beings out of his cosmic Mysteries. For through knowledge of the fact that Christ is the Sun-being, something one can understand through Anthroposophy, we recognize that as a result of the Mystery of Golgotha a stream flowed out from the Sun-evolution into earth-evolution that is at the same time the first step for preparing the union of the Sun with the earth.

Through turning to Michael and his Mysteries, the human being can even today work alongside the preparation of this future event. This takes place by means of the fact that the power of Michael is voluntarily absorbed into the human soul during the present epoch; and as a result such a soul learns to speak of its own inner Sun. For, what is initially attained in one's inner being will then happen cosmically later on as well. "The Sun-like element that the human being only absorbed into itself out of the cosmos through long ages will become inner nature of soul. Man will learn to speak of an 'inner Sun' ... We will recognize our own being moving about on earth as *Sun-guided*."[26] At the same time this will signify that Michael as Solar Time-spirit "will make the human soul his new domicile" (ibid.).

Thus, this line of the verse points above all to forces of the future Spirit-Human, forces out of which Michael works in the cosmos even now, as well as in the much later earth-age of Spirit-Human as the great "cosmic age of worlds" during which earth will once again unite with the Sun. Then Michael will receive the totality of humankind, guided as we shall be by Christ Himself in Michael's own kingdom. This remarkable perspective, so states Rudolf Steiner, is already presently predetermined in seed-like form in the anthroposophical movement. For the path into the sixth great age – the age of worlds – will lead through the sixth cultural epoch, which in 1,500 years will replace our fifth cultural epoch. There, the mighty cosmic transition of the future is even now being prepared in accord with our state of consciousness.

This entire future development is inseparably connected with the destiny of Anthroposophy on earth, and not merely in the sense of the lone study of its contents but mainly through its various social establishments on the foundation of Anthroposophy – the branches, the national societies, and the General Anthroposophical Society.[27] For already now they are supposed to be the associations that prepare the sixth cultural epoch.

Rudolf Steiner says about this: "By means of our coming together, our uniting in brotherly associations to work on our spiritual science, we prepare for what as a culture, a civilisation, is to pervade the sixth post-Atlantean cultural epoch" (GA 159, 15 June 1915). And in an earlier lecture he moreover states concerning this theme: "The sixth sub-race will be the basic seed-race for the sixth root-race" (GA 93a, 31 October 1905). Differing from the Theosophical terminology still used here, this sentence says in anthroposophical usage of words: The sixth cultural epoch will be the fundamental up-and-coming community for the sixth cosmic age.

Anthroposophy is therefore the bridge that connects the spiritual work of this present age beyond the sixth cultural epoch all the way to the great cosmic age in which the union of the earth with the Sun comes about. Rudolf Steiner speaks about this in the following words: "As anthroposophists[28] we are in a position today that can compare with the one in which humankind found itself during ancient Atlantean times.

And just as life has changed since then, so during a certain future time it will change again in a catastrophe (the war of all against all). *But this great perspective should arise before our minds and souls"* (GA 109, 6 April 1909).

This perspective consists of our beginning even now gradually to prepare for that future with Anthroposophy. For that, we are constantly encouraged and called upon by the great Masters of Wisdom and Harmony of Feelings. "Today there resounds to a similar small group of people [just as was the case at the end of the Atlantean age] a call out of the spiritual world that we identify as the call by the Masters of Wisdom and Harmony of Feelings" (ibid.). Who are these Masters, these leading individualities of humanity's evolution? They are those who even now are at a stage where they can already consciously work on the transformation of their physical body into Spirit-Human. For the entire earth-civilisation works today on the gradual transformation of the astral body into the Spirit-Self, albeit unconsciously in most cases.

When a human being decides to become a spirit-disciple and enters upon the path of modern initiation in accordance with Anthroposophy, he or she then decides to work on changing his or her etheric body into the Life-Spirit. A true Master distinguishes him or herself by the fact that he or she has begun already now to work on his/her Spirit-Human.[29] In this process, the Masters of Wisdom and Harmony of Feelings move at the head of all other human beings. They are the genuine representatives of those who stride into the cosmic time of Spirit-Human, as mentioned in the Michael-meditation. Their work within humankind thus forms even now the foundation for the great sixth age of worlds. And Michael as the "Sun-Time-spirit" has assumed the task of making possible for us this development out of Anthroposophy. In it, he turns with a mighty accepting gesture to all mankind.

At this point, an additional and special subject must be indicated which is connected with the great sixth age as the one of Spirit-Human. For, just as in the transition from Atlantis (fourth great age) to the post-Atlantean age (fifth great age) a certain initiate has to be present to facilitate this transition, for this time as well a certain initiate always becomes the leader of all humanity. So it will also be at the end of the "war of all against all." Only in this case, the initiate – who in the earthly usage of the word is called Manu – will no longer be a superhuman being as was the case earlier, but for the first time in human history the initiate will emerge out of humankind itself.[30] Then, as the great leader of humanity, he will guide mankind into the sixth age – or:

"Into the cosmic age of Spirit-Human."

It is obvious that this first human Manu will be linked with all that this Michael-meditation has to do with, chiefly with the above-described guidance of Michael into the "cosmic age of Spirit-Human".

A further secret of the contemporary Michael-Mysteries is linked with this. In the lecture of 22 November 1919 (GA 194), Rudolf Steiner speaks of two great Michael-revelations in humanity's history. The first revelation was recorded shortly after the Turning Point of Time by the Evangelist John in the prologue of his Gospel that culminates in the sentence, "And the Word became flesh" (John 1:14, trans. by E. Bock). And today – according to Rudolf Steiner – we live in the age of the second Michael-revelation which states: "And the human flesh must once again become spirit-enfilled so that it might become capable of dwelling in the kingdom of the Word and beholding the divine secrets. The Word becoming flesh is the first Michael-revelation; the flesh becoming Spirit must be the second Michael-revelation."

This process of the physical human body's spiritualisation that in its emerging state can be commenced even now during the present Michael-age is, however, not possible without the cooperation of Spirit-Human. Or expressed differently, the human being must at least begin on the path to Spirit-Human so that he or she can gradually move closer towards the ideal of humankind's development which is inherent in the second Michael-revelation.

Let us trace the meditation further. In its fourth verse it all turns very intimate and moving. Now, Michael turns directly to his earthly disciples, meaning to all true anthroposophists who stand by him and are devoted to him in faithfulness:

"You, the disciples of Spirit-knowledge,
Take Michael's Wisdom beckoning, ..."

In the lecture of 13 January 1924, which is the first detailed lecture about Michael following the Christmas Conference, we come across a completely new description of Michael. Today, he has become a silent spirit who hardly ever gives directions, references, or inspirations on his own, but always waits on what human beings *do* with his gift of Anthroposophy. Rudolf Steiner describes this in the following words: "Now, Michael is an entity that actually reveals nothing unless one brings something towards him from the earth based on hard-won spiritual effort.[31] Michael is a silent spirit. Michael is a spirit that is reticent. Whereas the other ruling Archangels are spirits who say a lot – naturally in a spiritual sense – Michael is definitely a taciturn spirit who says little, who at most gives sparse directives" (GA 233a). And that he has to do above all with what human beings accomplish out of modern spiritual cognition or Anthroposophy is confirmed by the ongoing words in the same lecture where it is stated "that Michael involves himself the most with what human beings *create out of the spiritual*. He lives in the consequences of what human beings create. The other spirits live more out of the sources, Michael more out of the consequences" (ibid.).

In other words: Michael *waits* in the spiritual world chiefly for what human beings do in their own souls, from out of their complete freedom, with what was previously his cosmic intelligence that has now become human. Do human beings want to pervade this intelligence today with the mindset of spiritual science and then carry that towards him – or do they not wish to do this? Do members of the Anthroposophical Society have the impulse to attain this goal for all mankind in an exemplary way? "This is what matters presently, namely that the Anthroposophical Society takes hold of this, its task, which consists in not opposing Michael in human thinking. One cannot be fatalistic here. One can only say: Human beings have to work together with the gods, with Michael himself" (GA 240, 19 July 1924). So that this will come to pass, humankind "must combine intelligence in their hearts with spirituality", so that "the Michael-battle will be fought out in favour of the Michael-impulse" (ibid.). Only thereby can a new relationship arise between humans and the world of gods, the hierarchies, as a beginning of the union between earth and Sun. This relationship takes place first on the level of cognition, on which in the Michaelic sense all spiritual elements must be attained that have to do with the human being and his or her origin. In far future times, all of this will likewise become a cosmic fact. Yet even in our time now, the first actual steps can be taken in this direction.

Once this process has progressed far enough and human beings have attained to the stage on which – out of this spiritualized intelligence that is available to them nowadays in Anthroposophy – they are willing to be active on earth as well; and if in addition they are ready to appear with the results of these efforts before Michael,[32] he will then evaluate these deeds of men and women not with words but only with his glance and a "*silent gesture of approval* with his hand"[33] that is filled with the deepest and most profound cosmic wisdom, and therefore can be only designated as a "wise gesturing by Michael" – something that human beings must learn today to behold fully consciously.

What this "gesturing" means and what it actually looks like, emerges from a passage in the *Michael Letters*, where Rudolf Steiner makes use only of the word "gesture": "But as a majestic exemplary action, Michael can unfold in the visible and initially adjoining supersensible world what he wishes to clarify. With a light-aura, with a 'spirit-being's gesture', Michael can show himself there."[34]

As described already by means of Rudolf Steiner's biography in the 2nd chapter of this book, Michael then takes the consequences of human deeds – if they appear justified to "the Guidance of the Cosmos" – into his spiritual kingdom, where they are transformed into cosmic deeds.[35] They become the "first building-blocks for humanity as the Tenth Hierarchy, or the Hierarchy of Freedom and Love, which then has the mission out of freedom to create the new Cosmos of Love. And the actual reason why Michael only responds with a wink or gesture to such deeds by human beings is that he fully and completely takes into account human freedom, for he is preparing to become the 'the spiritual herald of freedom'" (GA 233a, 13 January 1924).

And now comes the decisive point. In a single line, the entire path described here – from the Michael-School through the Michael-cultus to the appearance of Michael as Time-spirit before humankind – is summarized with all the tasks and perspectives for his disciples and expressed as the most important challenge for our time:

"Take the Word of Love of the Will of Worlds ..."

Where does this Cosmic-will come from that we have already encountered in the first verse? It comes from Christ Himself. This is why it is will that is "holy", and at the same time will that permeates the entire Michael-School, and because we have attended the Michael-School in the supersensible realm, we may now recall all this. More yet, we must voluntarily and consciously accept this Christ-will into ourselves. Then, mediated through the Michael-School, the Christ-will becomes the "Word of Love" in us, which resounds out of the "Will of Worlds", out of the Logos itself – a wondrous threefold metamorphosis!

Already in the supersensible cultus, the spiritual *Christ-word* resounded, for only out of it could the new Christendom be established. Now this Christ-word must reach all human beings on earth so that from now on in their souls it can become the *Word of Light*. For nowadays it is possible for every human being, independently of his or her education or stage of inner development, to experience and to understand the spiritual science of Rudolf Steiner as the Michael-Christ language of the present age. The Christ-word in Anthroposophy will become the "Shining-word" of man's cognitive forces when they fully unite with Anthroposophy.

On the other hand, in order to be able to serve Michael consciously today, this is not yet enough. For that to happen, this Word of Light that reveals itself in Anthroposophy must still be deepened and made more inward by human beings; meaning that this Word should not only be received with the most profound forces of the head but likewise with those of the heart. This Word of Light as "Word of Cognition" by Michael-Christ must here become the *Word of Love*, the pure Christ-substance.

For the Christ-word that reveals itself as Spirit-sun includes both the Word of Light that *illuminates* the heads of human beings and the Word of Love that *warms* the hearts of human beings. All of this is quite in accord with the fourth part of the Foundation Stone Meditation:

> "Light Divine
> Christ-Sun
> Warm thou our hearts,
> Enlighten thou our heads"
> (GA 260, 25 December 1923)

The inner relationship between the two meditations can therefore be depicted in the following way:

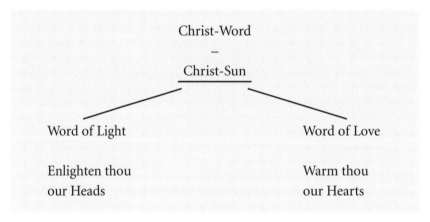

How the progression and intensification of the Christ-word to the Word of Love can take place through occupying oneself with Anthroposophy, is described by Rudolf Steiner in his first "membership lecture" in Stuttgart after the fire of the first Goetheanum, that Marie Steiner later published under the title, *Words of Sorrow, Research into Conscience, and Words of Becoming Aware of Responsibility*. There Rudolf Steiner says: "Ideas are for Anthroposophy the containers fashioned out of *love* in which the human being is brought down out of spiritual worlds in a spiritual way. Surrounded by lovingly nurtured thoughts, it is through Anthroposophy that the *light* of true manhood is meant to radiate. And cognition is merely the form through which human beings are given the possibility to gather the true spirit from widths of worlds into human hearts so that it can irradiate human beings. And because Anthroposophy can only be truly grasped by love, it is 'love-creating' when it is comprehended by human beings in its true form" (GA 257, 23 January 1923).

Thus, uniting oneself with Anthroposophy (when carried out in accordance with the above statement) leads first to the inner experience of spiritual light and then to that of spiritual love, which in the heart of the human being leads through the earlier entered-upon path by way of the Michael-meditation, ultimately forming itself into the Love-word of the Christ.

Here, we can remind ourselves of Rudolf Steiner's words concerning Michael's light of cognition and Christ's challenge for community-building love, though not in regard to all mankind and the life after death, but as regards our own participation in Anthroposophy (see also page 144).

Likewise in the statutes of the General Anthroposophical Society founded at the Christmas Conference, mention is made of this power of love that reveals itself through Anthroposophy and originates in the Christ's Word of Love. Thus, Rudolf Steiner writes in the introduction of the statutes' first publication: "She [Anthroposophia] opens her founts, and love-borne *human will* can then avail itself of these sources. Anthroposophia enlivens *human love* which then becomes creative in impulses of moral action and genuine social life-practices" (GA 260a, 13 January 1924). In these words we find this mysterious connection between the "human will" and "human love" that forms the foundation for every true anthroposophical action in practical as well as in social life. With that Anthroposophia weds love and will together in the human soul, something that leads to a new inner organ in the human being; first an organ only for perception, and later an organ also for experiencing what corresponds to this process in the macrocosm and what Michael poses as a task for all his disciples:

"Take the Word of Love of the Will of Worlds
Into your souls' aspiring, actively!"

Ultimately, this motif of love also appears in the statutes of the Anthroposophical Society. In Paragraph 3 it says: "They [the results of Anthroposophy which are nurtured at the Goetheanum] can lead to a real social life built on brotherly love" (GA 260a, 13 January 1924). But already in the year of preparation for the then forthcoming Christmas Conference, Rudolf Steiner – although in a more concealed form – had already referred to this secret of Anthroposophy's community-building activity: "If this true comprehension for Anthroposophy is present, then this comprehension is not only the path to the ideas of the Spirit but to community with the Spirit. Then, however, the awareness of this community in connection with the spiritual world is also community-building. And the communities that are determined by karma will form themselves" (GA 257, 27 February 1923).

This is how the Michael-community forms itself into a genuine karma community on earth – if with the help of Anthroposophy it becomes aware of its communal Sun-karma – and concerning which Rudolf Steiner expresses himself as follows in the *Michael Letters*: "Human beings, who in their previous earth life ... were servants of Michael, feel themselves ... urged towards such a voluntary Michael community." [36]

In this way, in the Society itself, the Word of Light – in anthroposophical spirit-cognition as Word of Love – can be strengthened into a powerful innermost element of the human soul from which a real Love-force streams that can be effective in all social relationships of this human community. A new brotherly foundation for living and working together can be created by this Love-force among the most diverse people and karmic streams represented by them. [37]

Now, however, after Anthroposophy as spirit-cognition has become Word of Light in human heads, and human hearts have received the Word of Love into themselves that speaks from one human soul to another, and with that allows a new fraternal community to be created on the earth, then Light and Love must be penetrated by "Will of Worlds" so that – out of the Light of cognition and Love for executing actions in the social life – human beings can become active and involved on the basis of Anthroposophy. [38]   Or, as Rudolf Steiner formulates it during the Foundation Stone laying at the Christmas Conference: "And the right ground into which we have to lay today's foundation stone [of love], the right ground would be our hearts in their harmonious working together in their good *love-pervaded will*, so as thereafter to bear the anthroposophical willing through the world together" (GA 260, 25 December 1923). These words too are connected with the secret of the line in the Michael-meditation, "Take the Word of Love of the Will of Worlds".

Here it is striking that among human beings we have to do with a love that furthermore enwarms and penetrates the will (*The Philosophy of Freedom*). By contrast in the spiritual world, the spirit-disciple receives the Cosmic-will into him or herself that reveals itself in the disciple as the Word of Love. So altogether we have the following sequence: The Cosmic-will in the human being becomes the Word of Love which kindles human love that can work socially, and which then pervades the human will. In this transformed way, human will is capable of carrying out socially constructive deeds in the world.

With what happens here, a stage is reached in which we think of the Christ-word not only as Word of Light and Word of Love, but we feel it in social relationships and in our relationships to each other. Now we are actually able to pass on to actual doings and actions in this world that are penetrated by the Cosmic-will from the Michael-School; doings and actions which then become deeds that Michael deems to be justified in the spiritual world and which can then be taken into his cosmic sphere.

This means that we must receive this threefold metamorphosis of the Christ-word out of the cosmic cultus: first as the Word of Light through our efforts of cognition in Anthroposophy, and then to experience it as the Word of Love in social endeavours of the Anthroposophical Society in order finally to penetrate it with Cosmic-will – which is at the same time Christ-will – on the third stage, based on our conscious recollection of the supersensible Michael-School, the way the Christ-will is active since the Mystery of Golgotha in earth-development. There it says:

"Take the Word of Love of the Will of Worlds ...".

We must freely create this synthesis in our soul as true Michael-disciples from what we bear in ourselves from the Michael-School, and what we have experienced together, but now permeated by the Cosmic-will of worlds of the Christ, a will we can experience on earth through our involvement with Anthroposophy.

Likewise in his introduction to the Michael-Imagination in *The Last Address*, Rudolf Steiner describes the path of the Michael-thoughts (the Word of Light) from their intensification in human hearts all the way to the pure quality of love (the Word of Love), and in conclusion the transition to concrete earthly deeds into which the "will of worlds" – as the will of Christ mediated by Michael – flows into the human will.

All of this is summed up by Rudolf Steiner in the introduction to the Michael-Imagination in *The Last Address* as follows: "And when all of you have received the Michael-thought into yourselves in the *light* of anthroposophical wisdom; when you have received this Michael-thought with faithful hearts and warm love; keep it and protect it there; and when you try to take this Michael-devoted mood of this year as the point of departure for what in all strength in all power can reveal this Michael-thought – not only in the soul but make it come alive in all your deeds – then will you become faithful servants of this Michael-thought; then will you be able to become noble co-workers for what wishes to make itself felt in accord with Michael through Anthroposophy in earthly evolution" (GA 238, 28 September 1924).

And that the above deals with the Will of Worlds, or Cosmic-will, is pointed out by Rudolf Steiner in the same passage of his address inasmuch as he speaks of the penetration of anthroposophical works on earth "with the Michael-power, with the Michael-will – which is nothing else but what precedes the *Christ-will* or *Michael-path* so that this Christ-force can then be implanted into earth life in the right way" (ibid.).

For "it is Michael's task to guide the human being *on the ways of the will* once again into the supersensible realm" (GA 26, Leading Thought 105). And this new Michaelic path "on the ways of the will" into the spiritual world is moreover the path of the "Michael-will" to the "Christ-will", or "the Michael-path that finds its continuation in the Christ-path" (GA 194, 23 November 1919).

How does this transition occur? Rudolf Steiner speaks further on this in the introduction to the Michael-Imagination as well: "Michael appears, who initially points to and indicates what is to take place so that this Michael-garment, this light-garment, can become waves of words that in actuality are Christ-words – Words of Worlds – that can transform the Logos of Worlds into the Logos of mankind" (GA 238, 28 September 1924). If in the Michael Mysteries the Logos of Worlds has become the Logos of humankind in this way, then the transition from the Michael-path to the Christ-path has been carried out at the same time. The Christ-will then works on earth in the hearts of human beings as the "Will of Worlds" that expresses the "Love-word" in our hearts.

At this point the first real step is accomplished in the direction of realizing the second Michael-revelation (the flesh becoming Word) the goal of which is only attainable through the working of Spirit-Human. This is the reason why the "spiritual time of *Spirit-Human*" is already being announced in the meditation today.

All this we must combine with the loftiest aims of our souls, meaning to make this into one of our most important tasks as Michael-disciples here on the earth. The last line of the Meditation speaks about this, challenging us to take up all that has just been stated:

"Into your souls' aspiring, actively!"

In doing so, the designation "aims of soul-work" relates particularly to the forces and karmic recollection of our higher "I", which has cooperated in all the here-described stages of the celestial evolution of Anthroposophy. In the just recently begun Michael Age however, the *earthly* "I" of the human being must receive all these contents at the same time as the highest aims for its life and work here on earth, and certainly not in a passive or dreamy way but in an "effective manner", meaning "to work actively in actual earth-deeds".

On another occasion, Rudolf Steiner furthermore communicates the following to anthroposophists concerning the above: "This is actually inscribed in the karma of every anthroposophist: Become a person of initiative" (GA 237, 4 August 1924). What is meant here with "the karma of every anthroposophist" pertains indeed to the content of the Michael-meditation that anthroposophists carry inwardly in their hearts as recollections of their higher "I". With this the entire path through the meditation is revealed as the path of modern men and women to their higher "I", out of which, in accordance with the Michael-Christ-will, all of us must learn to live and act nowadays.

If therefore we are willing to allow our being to be taken hold of by Michael, not just intellectually but so that our entire nature is thereby gripped by the Michael-Christ-will – meaning that our being is penetrated at the same time by the substance of the Christ-word – that substance which is present in the innermost core of the Illuminating Word of Love because Christ Himself is the Word, the Logos – then we are ready to receive what has been stated in this meditation in such a way that the Michael-Christ-will begins to shine in our heads, so that it becomes enwarmed with love in our hearts and unites with the Cosmic Will of Worlds. Then we know what we are called upon to do today as Michael-disciples regarding "Into your souls' aspiring, actively!".

Summing up the entire process, one can present it as follows:

Word of Light  – *individual* cognition through Anthroposophy

Word of Love  – social forming out of Anthroposophy

Will of Worlds – new working in the world out of which deeds emerge that receive cosmic dimension in Michael's kingdom, because the Christ-will joins actively in them.

The Will of Worlds, which can then be designated as Michaelic deeds in the world, bring out the truly *good* in us so that the entire process depicted above can correspond fully to the concluding lines of the fourth part of the Foundation Stone meditation:

|         | "That good may become            | – the deeds of men that have cosmic significance |
|---------|----------------------------------|--------------------------------------------------|
| Heart   | What we from our hearts would found | – penetrated by the Word of Love             |
| Head    | What we from our heads would direct | – penetrated by the Will of Worlds           |
| Limbs   | In conscious Willing"            | – Into your souls' aspiring, actively!           |

When all this has been done, and human beings are completely filled by Michael-Christ in their heads, hearts and limbs – in their thinking, feeling and willing – then we have an inkling of what stands before us as a lofty goal, and what it signifies in reality to be a *Michaelite* on the earth.

Everything that has been delineated in this chapter – which is only a very basic outline of what represents the Michael-Mystery in our time – can be summarized as follows (see outline on page 150):

| | | |
|---|---|---|
| Supersensible Michael School | Beings that work with us | (1) Springing from Powers of the Sun, |
| | | (2) Radiant Spirit-powers, blessing all Worlds! |
| | | (3) For Michael's garment of rays |
| | | (4) You are predestined by Thought Divine. |
| | Content | (5) He, the Christ-messenger, reveals in you – |
| | | (6) Bearing mankind aloft – the sacred Will of Worlds. |
| Michael-Cultus | | (7) You, the radiant Beings of Ether-worlds |
| | | (8) Bear the Christ-word to man. |
| New Michael-epoch (since 1879) | | (9) Thus shall the Herald of Christ appear |
| | | (10) To the thirstily waiting souls, |
| | | (11) To whom your Word of Light shines forth |
| | | (12) In cosmic age of Spirit-Human. |
| Anthroposophical Society Michael-School on the Earth | | (13) You, the disciples of Spirit-knowledge, |
| | | (14) Take Michael's Wisdom beckoning, |
| | | (15) Take the Word of Love of the Will of Worlds |
| | | (16) Into your souls' aspiring, actively! |

Here follows the facsimile of Rudolf Steiner's hand-written Michael-meditation. It was produced along with the eurythmy-forms belonging to it for the first eurythmy performance that took place on 12 April 1925 in the Schreinerei, the carpentry hall, following the death of Rudolf Steiner.

This final version of the meditation follows the wording of the same text that Rudolf Steiner wrote down for *The Last Address* in his notebook.

Sonnenmächten Entsprossene,
Leuchtende, Welten begnadende
Geistesmächte; zu Michaels Strahlenkleid
Seid ihr vorbestimmt vom Götterdenken.

Er, der Christusbote weist in euch
Menschentragenden, heil'gen Welten-Willen;
Ihr, die hellen Aetherwellen-Wesen
Trägt das Christuswort zum Menschen.

So erscheint der Christus Künder
Den erharrenden, durstenden Seelen;
Ihnen praßet euer Leuchte-Wort
In der Geistesmenschen Weltenzeit.

Ihr, der Geist-Erkenntnis Schüler
Nehmet Michaels weises Winken;
Nehmt der Welten-Willens Liebe-Wort
In der Seelen Höhenziele wirksam auf.

*Final version of hand-written meditation from "Contribution 67/68" page 1*

Sonnenmächten Entsprossene,
Leuchtende, Welten begnadende
Geistesmächte; zu Michaels Strahlenkleid
Seid ihr vorbestimmt vom Götterdenken.

Er, der Christusbote, weist in euch
Menschentragenden, heil'gen Welten-Willen;
Ihr, die hellen Aetherwelten-Wesen
Trägt das Christuswort zum Menschen.

So erscheint der Christuskünder
Den erharrenden, durstenden Seelen;
Ihnen strahlet euer Leuchte-Wort
In des Geistesmenschen Weltenzeit.

Ihr, der Geist-Erkenntnis Schüler
Nehmet Michaels weises Winken;
Nehmt des Welten-Willens Liebes-Wort
In der Seelen Höhenziele wirksam auf.

Springing from Powers of the Sun
Radiant Spirit-powers, blessing all Worlds!
For Michael's garment of rays
You are predestined by Thought Divine.

He, the Christ-messenger, reveals in you –
Bearing mankind aloft – the sacred Will of Worlds.
You, the radiant Beings of Ether-worlds
Bear the Christ-word to man.

Thus shall the Herald of Christ appear
To the thirstily waiting souls,
To whom your Word of Light shines forth
In cosmic age of Spirit-Human.

You, the disciples of Spirit-knowledge,
Take Michael's Wisdom beckoning,
Take the Word of Love of the Will of Worlds
Into your souls' aspiring, actively!

*Original outline of final version from notebook*
*Facsimile of hand-written meditation from "Contribution 67/68" page 2*

If one compares either the above final written version of the text [see pages 151-153] or the final version in the notebook [see page opposite], with the one that Rudolf Steiner spoke at the end of *The Last Address*, and for which short-hand notes were taken, one discovers in the latter two major variations in the third verse. Firstly, Michael is referred to a third time[39], so that in this version the names of Michael and Christ both occur three times. In the written versions the name "Michael" is only mentioned twice. And secondly [in the short-hand version from *The Last Address*], Michael appears as Herald of Christ not "To the thirstily waiting souls" of human beings but "In the thirstily waiting souls".

> "Thus Michael appears, the Herald of Christ,
> In the thirstily waiting souls,"

This corresponds to the process that Rudolf Steiner sums up as a further component of the contemporary Michael-Mystery in the following words: "Michael wishes in future times to take his seat in the hearts, in the souls of earthly human beings, and this is to begin in the present age. It is about a guidance of Christendom into more profound truths inasmuch as Christ is meant to find more understanding among human beings; to live His way into humanity as a Sun-being through that Sun-spirit – Michael" (GA 240, 21 August 1924). It is just this very deepening of Christendom through the revelation of the Sun-mystery of the Christ in our time, that Michael – as Sun-Archai and "Herald of Christ" – is charged with the promulgating of Anthroposophy for humanity as testified-to by all of Anthroposophy itself. In the somewhat rough way the verse was written down from *The Last Address*, and since the text of the shorthand notes does show the rhythm in which Rudolf Steiner gave this meditation, the text is recounted below:

Sonnenmächten entsprossene,
Leuchtende, weltenbegnadende
Geistesmächte:
Zu Michaels Strahlenkleid
Seid ihr vorbestimmt
Vom Götterdenken.
Er, der Christusbote,
Weist in euch
Menschentragenden,
Heiligen Welten-Willen.
Ihr, die hellen
Ätherwelten-Wesen,
Trägt das Christuswort
Zum Menschen.

So erscheint Michael,
Der Christus-Künder,
In harrenden, durstenden Seelen.
Ihnen scheinet euer Leuchtewort
In des Geistes-Menschen
Welten-Zeit.
Ihr, der Geist-Erkenntnis Schüler
Nehmt des Michaels
Weises Winken,
Nehmt des Welten-Willens
Liebes-Wort
In der Seelen
Höhenziele
Wirksam auf.

Springing from Powers of the Sun
Radiant Spirit-powers,
blessing all Worlds;
For Michael's garment of rays
You are predestined
by Thought Divine.
He, the Christ-messenger,
reveals in you –
Bearing mankind aloft –
the sacred Will of Worlds.
You, the radiant
Beings of Ether-worlds
Bear the Christ-word
to man.

Thus Michael appears,
the Herald of Christ,
In the thirstily waiting souls,
To whom your Word of Light shines forth
In cosmic age
of Spirit-Human.
You, the disciples of Spirit-knowledge,
Take Michael's
Wisdom beckoning,
Take the Word of Love
of the Will of Worlds
Into your souls'
aspiring,
actively!

*Facsimile of hand-written meditation from "Contribution 67/68" page 3*

Sonnenmächtige, ihr die leuchtenden
Kräfte, die ihr Welten begnadet.
Wallende, wellende Hülle wird euer Licht,
Hülle Michaels, des Menschentragenden.

So erscheint er, der Christusbote.
Künden mit ernstem Willen
Wird er die neue, die helle Zeit
Als die Zeit des Geistesmenschen-Waltens.

Ihr, der Geist-Erkenntnis Schüler,
Nehmt in eure Herzen seinen Willen –
Seht sein Weisen zu Christus,
Der da strebet in eurer Seelen Wohnung.

Then there is another notebook by Rudolf Steiner with an entry that represents a kind of pre-stage to the later-perfected text of the Michael-meditation. There it states:

> Sun-mighty ones, you the radiant
> Powers who bless worlds,
> Your light becomes a flowing weaving sheath for
> Michael who bears the human being.
>
> Thus he appears, the Christ-messenger;
> He shall announce with earnest will
> The new, the bright age
> As the time of Spirit-Human's reigning.
>
> You the spirit-knowledge disciples
> Take his will into your hearts –
> Behold his pointing to the Christ
> Who strives in your soul's dwelling.

In this likely earliest version of the Michael-meditation, the missing of what later became the entire second verse strikes us, which as we have already seen communicates to us the spiritual content and the main task of the supersensible Michael-School as well as the cosmic cultus. Rudolf Steiner only later inserted these two ideas into the text of the verse. This could be connected with the fact that initially he wanted to form the verse more exoterically, as was done during the first publication of the Foundation Stone meditation[40]. Then, however, he decided to include these essential contents as well, perhaps because of an inkling or awareness that this oral address to the members the evening before Michaelmas 1924 would be his last publicly spoken words.

Likewise in the early version, the words "who bears the human being" follows a different order. Here, this "character quality" concerns Michael himself. In the final version on the other hand, this character quality is already a part of the "Will of Worlds." This however does not represent a contradiction. This difference only proves the fact that in his cosmic deeds Michael only works out of the World-will itself; meaning that as the countenance of Christ, only out of *that being's* holy sacred will. Therefore in the second verse, reference is made to Michael's "earnest will" [that is enfilled by the Christ-will], because he appears before humanity as the "Christ-herald".

On the other hand, because the words "Herald of Christ" do not appear, since the second verse of the last text is not included in this version, Michael's own will is indicated directly. When he rises to the Christ-herald stage, it is no longer a matter of Michael's own will but the holy Cosmic-will of the Christ that now pervades Michael completely so that this willing can then be carried out into the world.

In this earliest pre-study of the Michael-meditation, the addition of the activity-emphasising word "reigning" is made to the word Spirit-Human. This means that already in our age the forces of Spirit-Human in humanity are beginning to become effective, and in certain situations assume a guiding or reigning nature – if only human beings create the conditions necessary for that to happen as described in the Michael-meditation.[41]

Michael's will is referred to twice in this pre-study. By this means, his will is decidedly linked first of all with the reigning of Spirit-Human,[42] something that Michael, as regent for "The new, the bright age", wishes to impart to human beings. At the same time, he would also like to bestow his will on human hearts, a fact which shows that Michael's will is inseparably connected with the Cosmic-will of Christ,[43] indeed irradiated and penetrated by Him. By this means, Michael becomes the main leader of humanity to Christ in our time:

> "Behold his pointing (us) to the Christ
> Who strives in your soul's dwelling."

Here, as is the case in many passages of the karma lectures, mention is not only made of Michael's entry into the hearts and souls of human beings, but also of the advent of the Christ Himself in our age. For, it is He who wishes to dwell in the hearts and minds of human beings today. This is what Christ wishes to achieve inasmuch as Michael precedes Him on this path and prepares His new home in human hearts. This can only occur

on the Michaelic path described in the third chapter of this book, a path
that leads to a thinking together and a being-free together with Christ.
And this preparation begins with the study of Anthroposophy.

Although this significant line, "Who strives in your soul's
dwelling", is missing in the final version of the meditation, through the
following words of the last version it stands in a direct connection to the
fully described process:

"Take the Word of Love of the Will of Worlds ...".

Although in differentiated form, these two lines point to the higher reality
that holds sway behind them. Even though Christ strives into human souls
today and wishes to establish His new home in them, He depends entirely
on man's free will to accept Him into his or her soul. We can do this only
when we voluntarily take into our inner being "the Word of Love of the
Will of Worlds" at the same time through our spirit-discipleship, to which
as "disciples of Spirit-knowledge" we ourselves must first find conscious
access. To accomplish that, Michael's will is blazing the trail, so-to-speak,
for us, just as he directs us to Christ, something that we have to accept into
ourselves, "into our hearts" – which then becomes a bridge for us during
this present age linking us in a Michaelic way with the Christ.

In Rudolf Steiner's mantric wealth of wisdom, the Michael-
meditation, rightly designated also as the Michael-Imagination, based on
its esoteric significance is only comparable with the Foundation Stone
meditation. Like two mighty pillars, they stand at the entrance to the invis-
ible temple of the new Mysteries, the founding of which is connected with
the Christmas Conference and the creation of the Fist Class of the School
of Spiritual Science. At the same time they point to the primal fount of
Anthroposophy that lies in the impulse of Michael-Christ. But how
Michael and Christ relate to each other in today's age and to humankind –
from their working together in the cosmos to permeating each other's
nature all the way into their wills – for Michael is the precursor of the
Christ's will) – this is something that the Michael-meditation above all
verifies for us. Like a final legacy to all anthroposophists, Rudolf Steiner
thus concluded his public activity on the eve of Michaelmas in 1924.

# V

# The Michael-Imagination in Eurythmy
# and its Esoteric Backgrounds

In the following consideration for the eurythmic representation of the Michael-Imagination, an attempt is being made to find a replica of the earlier depicted Michael-Mystery once again, but now in a completely different form. For, just as the basic truths of this Michael-Mystery had to be discovered in the text of the meditation itself, so this inner path can now be traced further in its eurythmic representation. It must however be emphasized particularly at this point, as is the case with all true works of art, that in regard to its content all explanations can merely be beginning indications of the spiritual reality that is concealed there, for this truth reveals itself directly only through the art itself.

During his lecture cycle on the Gospel of St. John in May 1908 given in Hamburg, and following the first lecture in which he spoke in detail about the prologue to this Gospel – still prior to the actual founding of eurythmy in the year 1912 – Rudolf Steiner posed the question below to the Russian painter, Margarita Woloschin: "Could you dance that?"[1] If she could have replied to this question in the affirmative, it would have been possible for Rudolf Steiner to present eurythmy from the very beginning in *cultic form* on earth. To perform the prologue in eurythmy, which moreover consists of the appearance of the Logos on earth, would likewise have signified the artistic representation of the first Michael-revelation on stage (see more regarding this on page 166).

Since, however, Margarita Woloschin could only give an insufficient reply to this question,[2] the earthly development of eurythmic art did not originate as early as 1908 with the prologue of the Gospel of John but instead ventured forth in other directions and became "a secular art". What Rudolf Steiner had originally intended with a cultic eurythmy, he tried to elaborate step by step until, following the Christmas Conference, it reached its full advancement, above all in the eurythmic representation of the Foundation Stone Meditation and the Michael-Imagination.

At the beginning of 1925, already on his sickbed, Rudolf Steiner created the eurythmic forms for the Michael-Imagination, and with his own hand wrote down their text in its final, ultimate formulation. (See facsimile on page 151.) Unfortunately, he could no longer experience the first performance on earth, but certainly he did so in the spiritual world in Michael's kingdom with whom he was connected in the deepest sense like no other Christian initiate during his entire earthly life.

Thus on Easter Sunday of 1925, which happened to fall on April 12th that year, the Michael-Imagination was eurythmically presented for the first time at the annual conference of the Anthroposophical Society at the Goetheanum. The most impressive thing was that here a lofty spiritual being – the Time-spirit Michael himself – was depicted in eurythmic form on stage. With that, this verse belonged to what Rudolf Steiner himself had described earlier as "cultic eurythmy", which was the same as had been described of the Foundation Stone meditation verse which had been performed in eurythmy at the Easter Conference of 1924.[3]

If one tries to substantiate this thought still further, one can discover the following. As early as in preparation for the Children's Acts of Consecration, Rudolf Steiner had slowly replied to the question by a teacher about the possible form of eurythmy for these acts: "Eurythmy? But isn't that a secular art? For these, I would have to offer forms of a special cultic eurythmy."[4]

Here, the word "cultic" does not refer to something cultic in a traditional or religious sense but simply to the fact that in cultic eurythmy performances, entities of the spiritual world appear on stage in a eurythmic form. For, just as had occurred earlier during a eurythmy presentation of the Foundation Stone Meditation Christ appears in such a way that He not only represents an intimate individual experience for *one* person but for an entire human community, as Rudolf Steiner has predicted for the future, so in this respect the Time-spirit is artistically portrayed in the eurythmy presentation of the Michael-meditation before the eyes of the audience.[5]

In the eurythmic presentation, Christ is shown in the Foundation Stone Verse with an uncovered face, for He once incarnated on earth and lived there as a human being among human beings. So on stage he shows His human countenance. Michael on the other hand was never a human being on earth. He remains a hierarchical being and therefore does not possess a human face. So His head is thus covered by a red cloth, and he appears to us as a mighty figure as if with a countenance of fire, sheathed in a veil seemingly out of golden light in a bluish-green garment (the life-forces directed towards the spiritual).

And how do the remaining eurythmists appear on stage? To begin with they appear in a way similar to what was the case during the perform-ance of the Foundation Stone Meditation.[6]  In both cases there are six representatives in a similar distribution of their roles. First, a spiritual being and then a human initiate who at the same time functions as the mediator between the spiritual world and human beings. Furthermore, there are four figures who are the disciples of this spiritual teacher on earth. These four fig-ures appear at the same time as representatives of the remaining humankind.

As we shall still see later, this division results in an accurate study of the eurythmy form for the prelude.  Here to begin with we observe a clear contrast between a central figure and a group: first the central figure who, with a large wave-like circular form, surrounds the entire perform-ance on stage thereby encompassing it; then the other five eurythmists who carry out their movements in straight lines. Yet one can likewise still find differences in their movements.  In contrast to the four others, one executes a slightly different form (see more on this further below) that subsequently allows the central figure to reach the centre of the perform-ance out of the periphery. With that it is made visible that this "fifth one" (in all the illustrated eurythmy-forms the fifth eurythmist is marked with the number "1") stands in a special relationship to the main figure that makes possible, as it were, their actions on earth among human beings.[7]

Let us now look more closely at the formation of the prelude. First, to arrive at their starting positions for the prelude, one of the five eurythmists dressed in a violet garment steps onto the stage from the right-rear forward to the forefront[8] with the sound-gesture "H", as if leading-in[9] the cosmic forces, and then ends in the position of the [zodiacal] Twins, something that signifies "the ability for doing the deed" (see GA 279, 7 July 1924). With that, this figure calls in the four other figures that enter the stage from both sides. Together, in one respect, the five eurthmists represent the spiritual entities who form the "Michael-garment" in the Sun-kingdom and, in another respect, they will become the mediators who carry the Michael-wisdom to the waiting thirsty human souls.

Next, Michael himself arrives inasmuch as he forms the gesture of the crab (Cancer) and places himself behind the four others completely in the background of the stage. On a sketch with the eurythmy-forms, Rudolf Steiner bestows the letter "A" on the outer eurythmy-form, in contrast to the five other eurythmists who are merely designated with numbers. Viewed in a eurythmic sense, we have here the transition from the "the ability for doing the deed" (**II**) to the "motivation for doing the deed" (♋) (ibid.), whereby alone human action, now also penetrated by the will, can be carried out. The culmination occurs a bit later in the gesture of Leo (♌) or "enthusiasm", the emotion that always accompanies every deed or action that originates out of the truly spiritual.[10]

In order properly to comprehend the main figure in the background of the stage, one has to know that in eurythmy the space of the stage is experienced in such a way that the foreground – the area nearest the audience – is experienced as the physical sense world, whereas the background of the stage corresponds to the spiritual world. Now the eurythmic prelude of the meditation begins. The form that Rudolf Steiner gave to the eurythmic prelude is such that it emerges from four different directions of movement by four eurythmists. This form certainly appears also to be connected with the Michael-sign that Rudolf Steiner set in place already in September of 1924 in the Recapitulation Lessons of the First Class of the School of Spiritual Science. In contrast to the other four, the fifth figure – as the Michaelic initiate wearing a red garment (like Michael's countenance) – makes five movements in five different directions, by means of which this fifth eurythmist moves through a complete pentagram when one views the sketch as an entirety.

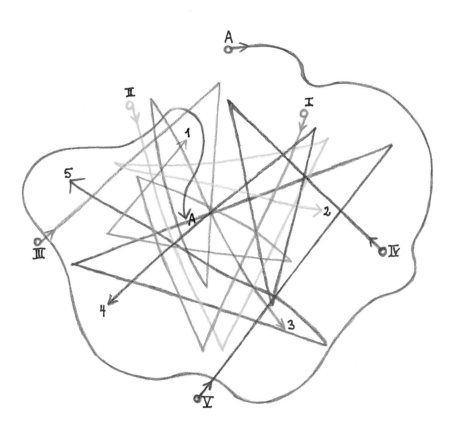

*Prelude*

This pentagram opens at one certain point so that the central figure – that earlier moved about from all sides of the periphery in a large wave-like circular form and thereby influencing the figures in the centre – can now enter into the inner formation which is about to shape itself so as to arrive into the centre of what is taking place. Thus a living image arises in this eurythmic form that depicts how Michael enters into the heart and soul of the human being, something that becomes possible through the involvement of the human initiate that serves Him (Michael).[11]

The purely straight lines of movement by the five eurythmists are expressions of the inner path that has its point of departure in human thinking. (In eurythmy, a straight line is always linked with thinking.) Michael on the other hand moves about on a wave-like circular line that corresponds to the will-forces in the cosmos as well as in the human being. (In eurythmy, round forms indicate the will.) And the will indicated here is the representative and bearer of "Cosmic-will".

If we compare the initial positions of the five eurythmists in the prelude with their final positions, we discover a pentagon and a pentagram. One of these formations points with its peak towards the audience the front. The other formtion points to the back of the stage. This signifies that in the course of the prelude the position changes, so that at the beginning of the prelude the pentagon points to the audience in the front, and at the end the pentagram points to the rear. If one also considers here that the pentagon and pentagram reflect the image of man, this then becomes a matter of man's soul turning from the physical-sensory to the spiritual world, something that in esoteric language signifies an inner "turning around" for the human being.[12]

Thus, we here confront three stages of a unified process. The human being, represented by the pentagon, first looks into the physical-sensory world, then turns to the spiritual world and fulfils with that the most important task of the contemporary Michael-epoch. Then he or she brings his/her transformed and spiritualized intelligence (the straight lines on which the five eurythmists move during the entire prelude) back to Michael, represented by the pentagram. And on the third stage, the

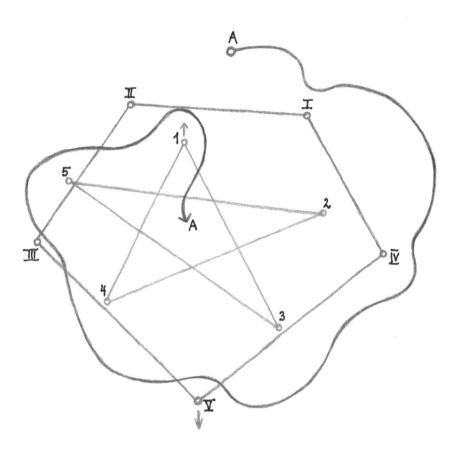

*Figure A with Complements*

human being opens to Him – Michael – his/her heart so that Michael can then occupy his new domicile there. In a meticulous consideration of the positions of the eurythmists, it is striking that during his/her appearance on stage the first figure moves all the way to the very front of the stage, and thus finds him or herself in the position of greatest polarity with Michael, who then appears completely in the rear of the stage. When first entering the stage on the other hand, the Michaelic initiate stands closest to Michael.

As far as eurythmy gestures are concerned, Michael (eurythmist "A") appears as representative of all the hierarchies who performs the word "FIAT" meaning "May it become". The five others respond to this with the eurythmy-gesture of the word "hallelujah" which means, "May the becoming be praised". For, everything that is to originate and thrive in the world must culminate in a "creation-process of becoming". Even in the "Prologue in Heaven" of Goethe's *Faust*, we discover a similar situation. What God creates in the "becoming of worlds", the hierarchies praise in their songs. But what takes place in the "Prologue" of Goethe's poetic work is something that happens between God and the hierarchies, and in our age becomes a course of action between Michael as leading spirit of our time and human beings.

Rudolf Steiner moreover explains the inner meaning of the word "hallelujah" as follows: "I purify myself of all that hinders me in beholding the most high" (GA 277a, 22 September 1912). If one considers that today Michael works as the countenance of Christ, one can experience him as a representative of the "most high". One must therefore liberate oneself from all that defiles the soul so that it can become possible to encounter Michael in the spiritual world. The ancient Rosicrucians who sought such a spiritual encounter (see GA 233a, 13 January 1924) were first supposed to cleanse and transform their souls to such an extent that for a certain time nothing connected with earthly matters or sense impressions could find access into their hearts and minds. And Rudolf Steiner describes the fundamental attitude of Michael like this, namely, "that he (Michael himself) does not wish to come into any contact with the physical presence of earthly life with his own nature". For any such contact with something earthly in the human soul "would be viewed by Michael as a contamination of his entity".[13]

While in former times it was above all a matter of the moral cleansing of the soul, nowadays it is more a matter of the corresponding cleansing of the human powers of cognition, something that begins with the transformation of the ordinary thinking into *pure thinking*. In other words, for the *cognizing* soul itself an inner "hallelujah" has to resound as fundamental mood of cognition.[14]

If we want to respond to this stream of world-becoming that proceeds from Michael as the Day-Spirit, as Spirit of Will,[15] as his disciples we may inwardly speak the word "hallelujah" only if we at the same time voluntarily and consciously enter into a practice of becoming; a process of inner development. For, to experience along the lines of the cosmic "means of development" or the cosmic "FIAT", we may only respond with our own evolution, with our own actions[16] and efforts of will, whereby we can gradually become actual Michaelites. This corresponds precisely to the last lines of the Foundation Stone Meditation that state:

> That good may become
> What we from our hearts would found
> What we from our heads would direct
> In conscious
> Willing.
> (GA 260, 25 December 1923)

In these few words, the inner mood of the "hallelujah" in the purely Michaelic sense is already present. Here we have to do with the birth of the true human being!

If we now make a large curve from the prelude to the postlude, we find a completely different situation there. Just as in the fourth part of the Foundation Stone Meditation,[17] we can immediately recognize two contrasting groups among the six participants, wherein the main difference is found in their convex and concave forms which, despite their polarity, work together here in the service of Michael. These two

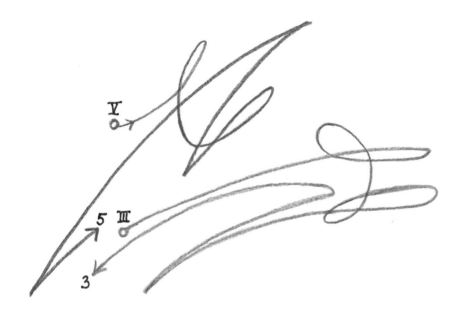

*Postlude* (*Extract*)

groups have the primal image in the shepherds and kings of the Turning Point of Time,[18] and correspond to the old and young souls in the Anthroposophical Society and movement (see GA 240, 18 July 1924). Now, however, they all begin to work together – and Michael is present in their mutual activity.

In the prelude the Michael disciples have received him into their hearts; in the postlude they work out of the common Michaelic karma in the world. In this way Michael remains connected with his human disciples even on the earth, and the Michaelic initiate who serves him is the mediator between Michael and his host.

In the eurythmy-forms, one discovers a harmonious cooperation between the slightly bent straight lines (that slash in like lightning flashes or sword-strikes) and the generous rounds that pass over into curves. Their working together speaks of the inner harmony of thinking and willing, and of cognizing and doing. In other words, we deal here with the activity of the will in thinking (meditation), and thinking in willing (karma awareness), which as the two central elements of Michaelic esotericism are in full accord with each other.

Likewise in the postlude, the original sounds "FIAT" and "hallelujah" resound again. And in the sweeping movement that is carried out from the right side at the back of the stage to the left-front of the stage, Michael works together with his disciples. One can experience in particular this movement by all six eurythmists like mighty strikes with swords. In so doing, the basic difference between them viewed eurythmically remains intact, inasmuch as the central figure sounds out the "FIAT" and the other five respond with the "hallelujah".

After the entire form has been completed, the eurythmists take three steps back as if in the direction of the spiritual world and reconnect the last "a" of the "hallelujah" again with the earth inasmuch as they turn the movement of "hallelujah" downwards. With this backward-movement, a turn is likewise connected that points, in the last part of the postlude, from a diagonal direction on the part of all eurythmists to a front-facing one, whereby they all stand facing the audience at the end of the performance, something that in eurythmy corresponds to the

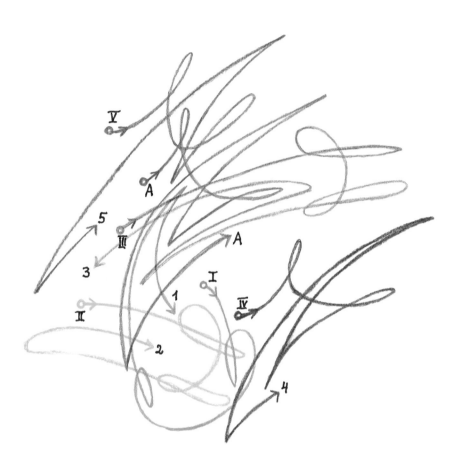

*Postlude*

ego-direction, or "I"-force. On the whole, the entire orientation of the eurythmists on stage moves alternately from a front-facing "I"-direction to the Michaelic diagonal direction towards the front-left. Here it is particularly striking that when the name "Christ" occurs in the text all participants assume a front-facing position.

Here, a brief reference follows concerning the colours on the garments and veils of the eurythmists. The ones on the main figure were already described. All the others wear the five colours of the shortened rainbow, where at the sides the polar colours orange and indigo are left out. Hence we deal here with the following colour-sequences: Red, yellow, green, blue and violet. The veils have the same five colours; however, they alternate from eurythmist to eurythmist, and in three of them colours appear as specific complementary colours to the colours of their [outer] garment.

As indicated already in the Old Testament, the colours of the rainbow always represent a new union between heaven and earth; between the hierarchies and humanity. This is why the rainbow in the Bible at the end of the flood, shows human beings that in the first post-Atlantean epoch the relationship to the spiritual world will become possible for human beings again, though in a different form than it was the case during previous ages. The colours that appear in the garments of the eurythmists point out anew that in our time also, a new union of human beings with Michael begins, and through him – in the way the Michael-meditation speaks of it – a new union with Christ can also form.

Concerning this new union with the leading higher powers that guide Anthroposophy in the spiritual world, Rudolf Steiner already speaks in his reflection on the Christmas Conference, saying: "But we can certainly hope that the forces of the union that we could form with good spiritual Powers will help us in the future to be in a good position to vanquish those opposing powers in the spiritual realm that serve themselves nevertheless through human beings on earth in order to attain their effects" (GA 260a, 23 May 1924).

In the eurythmic forming of the Michael-Imagination, another important element turns up: This is the turning of the eurythmists toward different directions of space. This occurs in a fourfold way:

- All stand on stage and look straight at the audience, whenever the word "Christ" comes up (for example in "Christ-messenger").[19] Likewise the appearance on stage in the prelude and the first two lines of the first verse of the meditation are carried out in this forward facing position.
- When mention is made of Michael, the entire group always turns diagonally facing left-forward.[20] The active vigour of Michael with the sword in the right hand is thereby recognized.[21]
- The group presents a third direction when it is addressed as the "radiant Beings of Ether-worlds", to the right-front. Here, the "Christ-word" is borne into the heart-forces.[22]
- At the challenging call, "You, the disciples of Spirit-knowledge", four of the eurythmists turn in a radial form outwards to all human beings in the world. Eurythmist No. 1 – as representative of the main figure – stands at the back of the stage in a frontward facing position, as does the main figure A.

These alternating space-directions transmit the will-emphasized element, and at the same time exert a consciousness-awakening effect on the audience.

Before we move on to the four verses of the meditation in our consideration, we shall briefly refer to the further destiny of the Michaelic initiate in this connection (the eurythmist with the red garment is pictured on the sketch by a red line). So as to form the sheaths for Michael at the end of the first verse, the eurythmist is positioned closest to the Time-spirit and thus represents the innermost nature or esoteric focal point of the human chalice, so to speak, that must originate on earth in order to receive the Michael-substance into itself.

At the conclusion of the second verse, Michael and his earthly initiate (represented by eurythmist "A" and "1" respectively) stand diagonally at the two opposite sides of the stage. Michael is represented standing on the left rear of the stage and the human initiate on the right-front. In so doing, together they form the outer limit or a spiritual sheath effective from up above to down below for the cosmic-cultic happening that the second verse of the Michael-meditation proclaims.

Here too, one can fathom the special role of the Michaelic initiate. He is called upon by the human side to carry and form the entire event of the cultus at the behest of Michael in the field of tension between the earth and Sun where Michael is to be found in our time.[23] The human initiate governs in the name of Michael, as it were, in the entire cultic process; the human initiate alone grasps and oversees this event, but in such a way that his inner glance is constantly directed on Michael as the "Christ-messenger". The human initiate is also the one, among all the participants of the cultus, who has received the "Christ-word" most powerfully into himself and goes on working only out of it.

In the form of the third verse, there now takes place a decisive change in the entire demeanour of this leading figure in regard to the four others, for at this point he executes the same form as they do. In doing this, the initiate has descended into the midst of his students. We can decipher what that signifies from the attitude of Benedictus in the Mystery Dramas. This is particularly true of the first two dramas, where it states on the title-page that both of them were written *through* Rudolf Steiner. As the leading hierophant of the Sun-temple, Benedictus ranks far above all his disciples. He is even characterized as the advisor of the higher hierarchies in the spiritual world.[24]

In the two subsequent *Mystery Dramas* – which, as stated in them, were written *by* Rudolf Steiner – at the beginning of the final drama during the listing of "persons, spiritual figures, and happenings", the following is recounted concerning Benedictus: "In *The Soul's Awakening*, Benedictus should not be considered as merely standing above his students, but as interwoven with his own soul destinies in the inner experiences of his students" (GA 14). Now in the modern Michael-Mystery, the teacher works *with* his students; he is linked with them even into his own karma. This is the situation that actually took place after the Christmas Conference in Rudolf Steiner's biography, when he linked his karma with that of the Anthroposophical Society out of his own free will.[25]

This occurred quite in accord with the words by Benedictus as related in the *Third Mystery Drama, The Guardian of the Threshold*:

"I must bear company with everyone who has received
  The spirit light from me on earth.
  Whether with knowledge, or unconsciously,
  He has come to me as student of the spirit,
  And I must guide him further on the paths
  On which he has set out through me."
                                        (GA 14, Scene Six)

In the fourth verse of the Michael-meditation, the particularly close connection between the Michaelic initiate (red) and the central figure is emphasized once more. This relationship becomes evident in the eurythmic form of the fourth verse by means of the fact that only "Figure 1" crosses over the path of the main figure *five* times. None of the other four figures is capable of achieving this feat. One figure does not cross the path of the Time-spirit at all; the other three in each case once, twice, and four times. This naturally reveals their inner relationship to Michael as well as their faculty of working together with him.

If one now compares this with Rudolf Steiner's biography, one can experience this as the new situation described by him which came to pass in the anthroposophical movement after the Christmas Conference. After that when revelations flowed even more abundantly out of the Michael-sphere in the spiritual world, the Anthroposophical Society thereby received a new "esoteric direction" out of which the Michael-School on earth originated. This was only possible due to the new way of cooperation that had come about between Rudolf Steiner and Michael as a result of the Christmas Conference.

Let us now look at the four-fold sequence of the eurythmy-forms in connection with the four verses of the Michael-meditation.

The first form mirrors the events of the supersensible Michael-School depicting for us the appearance of Michael in connection with the manifold processes that were taking place. These processes are portrayed by the five other eurythmists that in the Sun-sphere call forth the formation of his "garment of rays".

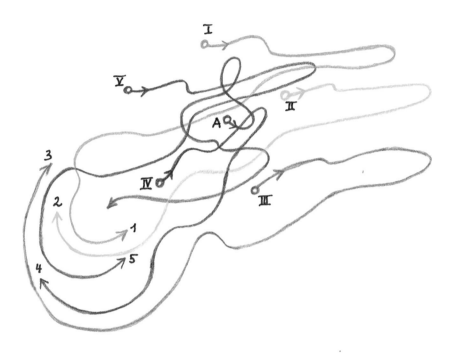

*1ˢᵗ Verse*

The central figure first performs a kind of open lemniscate on stage that is turned to the spiritual world (the rear of the stage) in order, from the kingdoms of the higher hierarchies, to obtain the necessary forces for instruction in the supersensible school. The form with the [middle] cross-over of the two directions of the lemniscate is the eurythmic expression for the word "you" [singular] or "you" [plural]. Now in the meditation itself, the "[plural form] of the pronoun "*you*" only occurs in the fourth verse, but the entire presentation of the text – viewed purely in a eurythmic sense – begins this way. In more clearly viewing the movements of figure "A" in the directions from front to rear, right and left, one can moreover recognize the form of a cross, something that indicates the relationship of the Michael-School to the events on Golgotha.

At the same time, the other five eurythmists make an extended movement from right to left so as to receive from this the forces they require to form a chalice-like sheath or garment for Michael. Thus his Sun-garment comes into being consisting of five layers (or curves) that are shaped out of the five kinds of natures that were depicted in the previous chapter: Archai, Archangeloi, Angeloi, human souls and elemental beings.

The orientation of the eurythmists in the space plays a special part in this verse. Up to the appearance of the name "Michael" in the text, all six eurythmists stand positioned with their face turned to the audience; but then they turn diagonally in the "Michaelic direction", which comes about again and again in performing the verse in eurythmy, and directed from the right-rear to the left-front.

Beginning from this moment, the eurythmic form carried out by the main figure visibly becomes more similar to the forms of the five others, something that affirms that the process of the sheaths, meaning the "forming of the garments," has begun. The concluding words of the verse, "Thoughts Divine", correspond to a weaving together of all figures in a curve from left to right and from right to left, which at the same time represents the form of a "receiving" chalice out of the waft of the celestial intelligence. It is significant here that the opening of the chalice points backwards, something signifying that it is open to the spiritual world; open in regard to the receiving of a higher being.

*Figure A in the 1st Verse*

The second verse begins with the pronoun "He", in which all six eurythmists turn again to the front. In this first line, the Christ-messenger speaks. The front facing position is maintained until the words, "Will of Worlds", with which the representation of the supersensible school's activity comes to a conclusion. In the third line, the eurythmists once again place themselves in a diagonal line, but now in the opposite direction, from the left-rear at the back of the stage to the front-right with a "sounding" upwards to the bright light-region, where the cosmic cultus is carried out in Ether-heights.

It is as if the main figure were to send out the five others. In the last line once again there resounds the name of the Christ, and again the front-facing position is assumed.

Thus, in the first line of the second verse where it is still a matter of the supersensible school, the central message is purely linked with Michael. Here, however, he appears as the Sun-messenger of the Christ before all of those who participate in the school. In the last line on the other hand, where we already find ourselves within the cosmic cultus, it is in particular the Angels who serve Michael who bear the Christ-word to human beings and allow them to participate in the creative activity of the Word of Worlds, whose spiritual forces are included through the cultic ceremonies in bringing about the origination of the mighty Imaginations.

The eurythmic form of the second verse demonstrates the greatest polarity between the main figure and the five other eurythmists. The movements of the latter are a kind of continuation or metamorphosis of their paths in the previous lines. The figure "A" on the other hand, demonstrates a quite different and unexpectedly clear and mighty thought-form, which consists of four corners and a closing off of itself.

Here we deal with the thought-contents of the Michael-School, the revelation of which Rudolf Steiner designates as "cosmic intelligence" that has been administered in the spiritual world at the behest of the higher hierarchies since the primal beginning. These contents must now be brought to awareness in the consciousness-soul, which is especially connected with thinking, by those participating in Michael's instruction.[26]

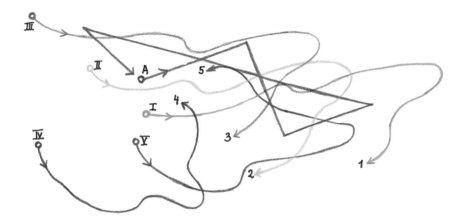

*2nd Verse*

In this unusual form it is striking that its first two triangles corre-spond to the first half of the verse. Then there follows a long diagonal path of the main figure from the right-front to the left-rear of the entire stage, bringing to expression the lines:

"You, the radiant Beings of Ether-worlds
Bear the Christ-word to man."

With this, the fact is connected that here at the beginning of the cosmic cultus, Michael leaves the region of what is happening here and slowly withdraws back into the region of the Sun. For in the cultus, the will-forces of all participants come to expression individually; this is why their eurythmic forms are so "wavy". This is connected with the fact that in the cultus not only are teachings conveyed but the participants themselves become active. In conclusion, the main figure turns around and moves forward towards the other five eurythmists so that they can receive their further task from the hands of the main figure, namely to bring to the earth – together with the Angels – the contents of the Sun-School and cosmic cultus so that Anthroposophy can come into being there.

Due to the fact that this verse relates directly to two stages of the celestial preparation of Anthroposophy, all forms have a twofold character. In five of them, there is a clear change of direction from the front-facing position to facing towards the right in the transition from the first two lines of the verse to the two further ones. In the case of the main figure, this transition becomes even more obvious. The two large triangles corre-spond to the first two lines with their corners to the rear and front. Then at the end there is a correspondence toward the middle (in comparison to the previous high and low points). Here we find a reference to the basic teaching of the supersensible Michael-School, where the view of the participants is first directed upward to the divine-spiritual origins of all true mysteries of the past and then below to the nature of the Mystery of Golgotha on earth.

In connection with the two further lines of the second verse, there corresponds in the eurythmy-form of the main figure a long upward-rising straight movement from the right-front to the left-rear of the stage.

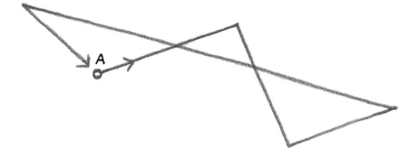

*Figure A in the 2nd Verse*

This path is connected with the cosmic withdrawal by Michael. During the heavenly cultus, he remains above in the Sun realm. For, now it is the souls of humankind who in working with the hierarchies must create the new cosmic Christendom.

Then there follows a powerful movement to the front-right side. Here, the content of the Imaginative-cultus is borne downwards to human beings. At the same time in this concluding eurythmic form, we discover a reference to the path from the Sun to the earth which Michael entered upon in 1814.

With all this, Michael proves himself to be Lord of the celestial intelligence which, however, must be permeated ever more clearly by the "Christ-word" since the Mystery of Golgotha. This is why the "Christ-word", in which all the eurythmists stand in a front-facing position, must be taken up by the five other figures and brought to human beings. At the conclusion of the verse, all the eurythmists stand on stage in such a way that the main figure is back to the left and the others to the right, further in front, as his spiritual servants and co-workers, aside from the first one who closes off his form at the right-front, thereby standing at the diagonally opposite end of the stage to the main figure. By means of this they together form the borderline of what can happen, embracing and carrying the Christ-word from two sides, as it were, from the Sun and from the earth.

The eurythmic form of the third verse has a special beauty and harmony. At the beginning of this verse, the five eurythmists still stand in front of the main figure. Then with a determined will-movement everyone of the five begins to build his/her individual house that consists of a developing spiral. Eurythmically, this signifies a finding of oneself in one's own self, or seeking one's soul in oneself. At the same time these five figures represent the "thirstily waiting souls" who are called upon to find Michael and receive him into themselves. In order to attain that, however, they must thoroughly prepare themselves for this, and to that belongs what Rudolf Steiner in his book, *Knowledge of the Higher Worlds and Its Attainment* calls "building a hut in higher worlds."[27] Only at a spiritual location, where the human being firmly secures his or her individuality

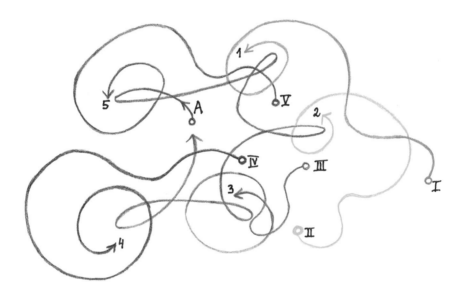

*3rd Verse*

in the supersensible world – because something like a sheath is received through the building of this hut – can a meeting occur between the human being and Michael. For, now it is no longer a half-conscious encounter but one from "I" to an "I", that is from Spirit-being to Spirit-being.

In a wondrously dynamic form that represents a pentagon with the tip pointing towards the back of the stage – representing the spiritual world – Michael now "visits" the soul of every human being who has prepared for this encounter in his or her spiritual hut. Into it, Michael brings the "Word of Light", carried by Angels who accompany him, so as to fill the human soul with it and make the human soul capable of beholding the spiritual world out of the lofty Michael-perspective. For only in this sphere can the forces of "Spirit-Human" be found and experienced.[28] In doing so, the connection between human beings and Michael comes about on the level of will, for the forces of Spirit-Human meet in the interplay of curvatures and spirals. Here we discover the affirmation of the earlier-quoted words by Rudolf Steiner that Michael today would like to guide human beings in the directions of the will into the spiritual world. (See page 146.)

When these forms are "eurythmy-sized", one can observe that with each curve, Michael comes a bit closer to the eurythmist in question. If, for instance, he visits the first eurythmist in his "house" – the eurythmist's position on stage – that person has not yet arrived in his or her house but is merely at the start of his/her form. In the case of the second eurythmist, they draw a little closer. And in the case of the fourth and the fifth eurythmists, they almost meet together in their movements. (This signifies that we are dealing here with spirit disciples who stand at differing stages as regards the "building of their house" in the spiritual world, out of which they are then capable of working as sovereign egos.)

Now, Michael has visibly arrived at the goal of his annunciation, and the "cosmic age of Spirit-Human." can begin. The totality therefore points to the process in which Michael transmits the forces of Spirit-Human to human souls, something that corresponds to the nature and content of his second revelation to humankind. Thus, it is part of the

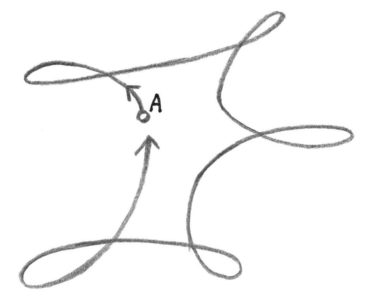

*Figure A in 3ʳᵈ Verse*

properties of the eurythmic presentation of the third verse that in it, all six participants uninterruptedly perform their eurythmy in a forward-facing position on the stage with their faces turned in the direction of the audience. With that the annunciation from the final verse is prepared, and at the same time so is the Michael-epoch that has begun on earth.

In the fourth verse, all the "disciples of Spirit-knowledge" are called upon to follow Michael's gesture, in which lives cosmic wisdom and at the same time his power of "ruling over worlds", and to receive this into their souls in order to be able to follow him. Now, at the beginning of the verse, the five eurythmists begin forming a circle around Michael, or put more accurately to form a five-cornered figure into the circle, in the midst of which stands the central figure.

Out of this Michael-sphere, they now call out in all directions of the world:

"You, the disciples of Spirit-knowledge ..."

With this we have the challenge, which at the same time contains a posing of tasks to all Michaelites in the world.[29]

In the eurythmic movement, all five figures first form the shape of an open triangle which here is a thought-form. One deals with the acceptance of the "Michael-thought" – a terminology that Rudolf Steiner often makes use of in numerous later lectures, and above all in *The Last Address* in the introduction to his Michael-Imagination. Then, the thought-form continues on into a wave-like movement of will. In a large "curvature-like" movement that almost embraces the entire space of the stage, the revelation of the "Word of Love" proceeds which is imbued with the "Will of Worlds", and after that an acute-angled turn is performed which calls forth a resolute striding of all eurythmists towards the proscenium. This forward-move corresponds to the last line of the verse. The entire form of the main figure embraces all four directions of the stage's space: Towards the rear, to the left, then to the right and finally to the front.

The above descriptions summed up together represent the inner development of a human being. It leads from grasping the Michael-thought to its intensification in one's own heart, and then on to its transformation

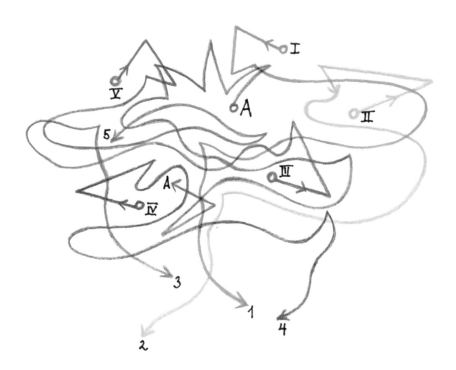

*4th Verse*

*Figure A in 4ᵗʰ Verse*

into an inner force that can bestow impulses on human deeds in accordance with Michael's goals. This is what Rudolf Steiner describes in the introductory words for the Michael-Imagination in his *Last Address*.

As far as the orientation of the eurythmists on the stage is concerned, the fourth verse offers the following picture: At the beginning, the five eurythmists are gathered in a radial pattern, facing the figure the centre. Only the main figure in their midst stands in a front-facing position and looks straight ahead. With the second line, when the name "Michael" resounds, all six turn diagonally to the left-front, something whereby the word "Take" is given a special dynamism. Then in the third line that deals with the central task of the entire meditation – the "Word of Love" by the Christ which is penetrated by His "Will of Worlds" and which is to be taken into oneself – the eurythmists once again rise up and assume their front-facing position. Thereby, the verb "take in" [German: "aufnehmen" which is separated into "nehmet" ... "auf"] – which is spoken a second time and, in German, shortened – receives a further intensification. Thus, this last verse is like a direct speech to the Michael-disciples who, with a decisive final step at the end of the last line, prove their readiness to receive the sacred content of the third line into their "souls' aspiring", and then to follow this aspiring in a sternly Michaelic sense of devotion. In German, the decisive final step is taken on the syllable "auf".

While the forms of the five eurythmists clearly resemble each other, the form of the main figure is completely different. It starts with fiery zigzags that appear to consist of three tongues of fire, all of which are directed backwards toward the spiritual world. This brings to expression the reality that in the cosmos Michael is always connected with threefoldness (all the way to the Holy Trinity where the primal image of all threefoldness has its roots), and he rejects any duality. In a lecture given on 21 November 1919 (the opening lecture of the cycle *The Mission of the Archangel Michael*), Rudolf Steiner speaks again and again about the erratic wrong ways of twofoldness, in order to hold up against that the true threefoldness which in our time is necessary most of all for finding the Christ. It is a matter of the threefoldness of Christ between Lucifer and Ahriman which finds its artistic expression in the sculpture-group of the Representative of Man. Rudolf Steiner concludes the lecture on this theme with the words: "All of that is linked with Michael's mission regarding those beings of the higher hierarchies with whom he in turn stands in a relationship." (GA 194). It is just this mission of Michael – regarding the higher beings in reference to the nature of threefoldness – that is placed at the beginning of the eurythmic form.

Viewed from another side, this very special form, which is also reminiscent of a crown and consists of slightly bent straight lines, is an indication of how the working of the will takes place in thinking. In this consists the nature of every genuine meditation which on the modern path of inner schooling is the most certain means of guiding the human being into the spiritual world. Initially, this path leads into the adjoining Moonsphere, then still further and further into the spiritual spheres of the planets all the way into the Sun-realm where the kingdom of Michael originates.

Rudolf Steiner describes the path referred to here above all in his book, *Knowledge of the Higher Worlds and Its Attainment* but likewise in the corresponding chapter in *Occult Science, an Outline*. He designates this inner path in one of his later lectures as the "Moon-path, probably in accordance with its spiritual point of departure" (see GA 243, 21 August 1924).

The main figure then moves on a long wavy line to the right. Thereby, the element of feeling comes to expression until, following an angle-movement in a large wave to the left, the eurythmist moves to the left-front so as to conclude the path with an angle-arc in a triangular form that is performed forcefully and quickly.

Concerning the path in the first verse, we have already seen that the loop-movement of the eurythmist is a decided "will-form", but here it turns into a triangle with its tip moved to the front, and thus moved towards the physical-sensory world. With that, we have to do with the activity of thinking in the will, something that on the path of schooling leads to karma knowledge. In the later lecture mentioned above, Rudolf Steiner designates this path as the path of Saturn, a direction that in our age is suited especially for will-imbued or natural-scientifically oriented human beings who work chiefly based on observations dealing with nature.

With this, Michael demonstrates to his disciples in these eurythmic forms the two main paths leading into the spiritual world that were represented during Rudolf Steiner's lifetime above all by Marie Steiner and Ita Wegman.[30] The time-frame of this form likewise corresponds to the development of the anthroposophical movement. In earlier years, Rudolf Steiner had depicted the first path as that of the Moon. Then only in later years did he describe the Saturn-path and others. First he proceeded along the path of the book, *Knowledge of the Higher Worlds and Its Attainment.* Later, he would proceed more directly from observations of nature and practical initiatives in various regions of life that originated out of Anthroposophy.

This was moreover connected with the fact that Rudolf Steiner in earlier years was surrounded more by individuals of the first kind of schooling, but later on, and especially after the first world war, by the second kind. Through the Christmas Conference, he has however united these two paths, that of the Moon and that of Saturn, into a higher unity. In the further classes of the Michael-school, this was intended to become revealed more and more just as this unity of the two paths is already preconceived in the eurythmic form of the main figure.

In this special form of the central figure, the beginning and end of humanity's evolution (Alpha and Omega) likewise unite. At the beginning, human beings were still completely open to the revelations out of the spiritual world. They were to a large extent even guided because their individual "I" was still involved in a germinal state of development. This is demonstrated through the upper part of the form that is still open to what is up above and down below – in a sense the upper and lower gods.[31] In the lower part on the other hand, we behold a closed triangle that indicates the forming of the individual and independent "I", which in future times will become creative out of its own inner nature.

It is therefore important that in all eurythmic forms for the fourth verse – following the movements of the main figure – approximately at the middle of each wave-like movement a more or less sharp angle occurs as a change of direction: most clearly observable with eurythmist 5 and least visible with eurythmist 2. Here in the case of the Michael-disciples we deal with the essential turn of mind and soul from the first to the second path; from the Rosicrucian basis of Anthroposophy to its further Michaelic orientation that later led to the Christmas Conference.

Although in the case of Michael himself – his turn towards the new Mysteries and his participation in their founding has already been carried out – this step has not yet been made to a large extent by his disciples. Only based on their freedom and a deepened comprehension of the Christmas Conference, can they find the connection to Michael and his activity in the spiritual world. What follows from this is depicted in the postlude of the meditation in eurythmic form. (See beginning of this chapter.) To that also belongs, among other matters, the union of the two karmic streams that in particular stand behind the two paths, or put another way his disciples have the tendency to follow one or the other path.

As we have already seen, the first path has its point of departure in the Moon-sphere, out of which the spirit-disciples rise further to the Mercury and Venus-spheres all the way to the Sun-sphere. The second path proceeds from the forces of Saturn and descends downward through the spheres of Jupiter and Mars in order, likewise, to reach the sphere of the Sun, however from the opposite direction where the two streams must unite with each other in Michael's realm.[32]

Both paths that seek a connection with the spiritual world – in direct beholding of the hierarchies present in that world and in cognition of their own karma – have their model at the Turning Point of Time in the Kings and Shepherds. With that, they correspond to the two main karmic groups of the anthroposophical movement, which from the beginning were connected to Michael, his supersensible school and the cosmic cultus, and still are linked in the present day.[33]

Now, since both paths meet in the Sun-sphere and unite there, they have the potential from the very beginning to work harmoniously together and promote and fructify each other – if only they are pursued far enough. Here it is a matter of *both* groups having an inner relationship to the Sun, which means to Michael and with that the cosmic region where the future Sun-karma can be found. And out of the power of the future Sun-karma the dividing Moon-karma of the past is overcome.[34]

In conclusion, we should note that although all five eurythmists have rather similar forms in this last verse, the path of the first verse (the Michaelic initiate – red figure) is distinguished from the others by the fact that he or she is the only one who crosses through the form of the main figure five times (as previously mentioned), and of those five times at two quite significant points, namely at the back of the stage in the fiery crown and in the front in the triangular loop. Obviously we deal here with an initiate who on earth is fully acquainted with both Michaelic paths, and capable of bringing to human beings the cosmic revelation of the Michael-wisdom from out of the all-inclusive Sun-fountainhead.

The eurythmic presentation of the Michael-Imagination that harbours the entire Michael-Mystery in rudimentary form [in German: "ansatzweise"], is framed, as it were, in a prelude and postlude. As we saw, both respond to an important question for our age. How does Michael come into the souls of contemporary individuals nowadays so as to be able to work with them so that the mighty aims of the present-day Michael-epoch can be attained in accord with Michael-Christ?

The following three facsimiles of the eurythmy-forms for the Michael-Imagination that Rudolf Steiner sketched without any correction within a few minutes not only demonstrate his exceptional spiritual presence of mind but likewise his unique artistic sense and remarkable creative ability.

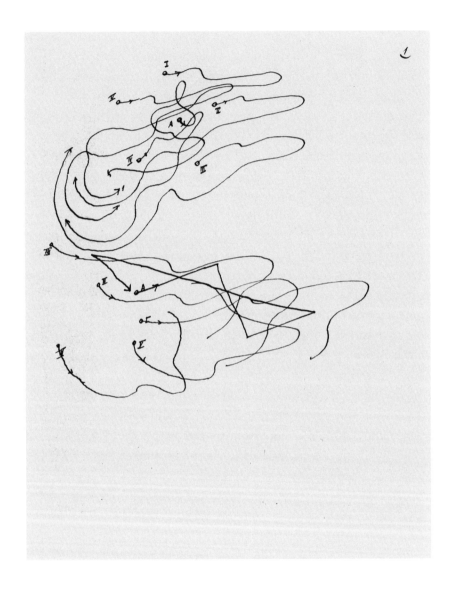

*Facsimile No. 1 with all six eurythmy forms by Rudolf Steiner*
*From GA K 23, pages 101-103*

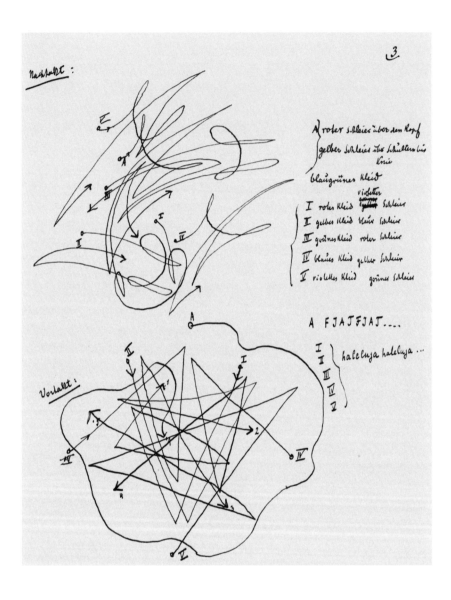

A $\left\{ \begin{array}{l} \text{Red veil over the head} \\ \text{Yellow veil over shoulders to knees} \\ \text{Blue-green dress} \end{array} \right.$

I      red dress, violet veil
II     yellow dress, blue veil
III    green dress, red veil
IV     blue dress, yellow veil
V      violet dress, green veil

A      FJAJFJAJ ....

I
II
III   $\left. \right\}$ Haleluya
IV
V

*Below and opposite is an alternative translation for the Michael-meditation, as printed above on pages 153 and 157 respectively.*

Springing from Powers of the Sun
Radiant powers of Spirit, blessing worlds
Preordained by thoughts divine
To become Michael's radiant garment.

Envoy of Christ, he shows in you
The holy will that holds us human;
You, bright beings of ether worlds
Bear the word of Christ to humans.

Thus the Christ-herald appears
To thirsting souls, long abiding;
To them your Shining-word streams forth
Into the cosmic time of Spirit-Human.

Disciples who would know the Spirit
Follow Michael's beckoning wisdom;
Take up the Love-word willed by worlds
Into the highest aims of soul-work.

Springing from Powers of the Sun
Radiant powers of Spirit,
blessing worlds;
Preordained by thoughts divine
To become Michael's
radiant garment.
Envoy of Christ,
He shows in you
The sacred will of worlds that
holds us human;
You, bright beings of
ether worlds,
Bear the word of Christ
to the human being.

Thus Michael appears,
The Christ-herald,
In thirsting souls,
long abiding;
To them your
Shining-word streams forth
Into the cosmic time of Spirit-Human.
You, disciples who would
know the Spirit,
Follow Michael's
beckoning wisdom;
Take up the Love-Word willed by worlds
Into the highest aims of
soul-work.

# Epilogue
## Michael and the Michaelites

In one of the last lectures that Rudolf Steiner gave in the Great Hall of the First Goetheanum only two weeks before its destruction on New Year's Eve of 1922, he presented an impressive image for Michael's relationship to his earthly pupils, meaning those human beings who today attempt – with the aid of Anthroposophy – to enter on the inner path of thinking's transformation as described throughout this book. This inner path begins with the transformation of earthly thinking, which initially moves only in spatial categories, and then changes into a thinking that is related to the stream of living time, and therefore can enter the spiritual world. With that, the first step is taken for returning the intelligence that has become human to Michael who formerly had administered this intelligence.

The just described image, or better put Imagination, is clothed by Rudolf Steiner in the following words: "The science that as anthroposophical spiritual science once again spiritualizes the judgements we make in space [physical earthly life] and makes these judgements once more supersensible; they work from below to above, stretch out their hands, as it were, from below to above, so as to grasp Michael's hands that are outstretched from above to below. This can then create the bridge between human beings and the gods" (GA 219, 17 December 1922).[1]

After the Christmas Conference, when Rudolf Steiner was allowed to speak about the Michael-Mystery quite openly and directly, he represented the goal of this path moreover as follows: "Michael – who aspired to descend from the Sun to those [human beings] who behold the spiritual in the cosmos – will in future times take his place in the hearts, in the souls, of earthly human beings" (GA 240, 21 August 1922).

So that this ideal might be fulfilled, and from grasping the hands of Michael to reach the possibility of his new domicile in human hearts, the next in-between steps must still be taken into account and realized. First, that condition in the human soul must be reached "where hearts begin to have thoughts".[2] This signifies finding a transition from the "thoughts in space" to those thoughts that take their course in the element of time and thereby are solely in a position to take hold of spiritual contents; and "thoughts that today seek for grasping spiritual elements must come from hearts that beat for Michael as the fiery Lord of Thoughts in the cosmos" (ibid.).

So that this may happen – and the following is only the other side of the same process – one must learn, with the help of Anthroposophy and its communications concerning the spiritual world, to develop the faculty in oneself of finding one's way from everywhere in the material dimension to the activity of the spiritual element. For only in so doing can one escape from the temptations of our present earth-civilization in which – in our time and from so many directions – the Ahrimanic powers hold sway. For this the human being requires a special inner strength of his/her soul; the strength of true spiritual thinking that seeks the possibility of understanding the world in accord with Michael everywhere, and to behold it with his eyes, from his perspective. "Michael is the Spirit of Strength ... Michael must pervade us as a mighty power that can see through the material element, and can behold the spiritual dimensions in the material at the same time, inasmuch as the spiritual is beheld in the material everywhere" (GA 194, 22 November 1919).

Only on this basis can the activity of the Ahrimanic dragon be overcome. And thus, Michael himself looks from the spiritual world adjacent to the earth down upon the deeds of human beings and the entire terrestrial civilization. Yet, only as long as these deeds are not occupied by the forces of the dragon can Michael accept the ordinary physical world. "He reigns as *an entity in a world* that can only affirm itself inasmuch as he affirms the world as if guiding down forces to the earth from all cosmic sites."[3] For he, Michael, only accepts a world that contains no Ahrimanic element at all.

This cosmic affirmation by Michael therefore rests upon the fact that nowhere does he compromise in anyway whatsoever with the

Ahrimanic opposing power and, or spoken more pictorially, constantly crushes the Ahrimanic dragon under his feet. In this regard he lives at the same time with the weighty question as to whether or not human beings can be found on earth who can and will assume his concerns. Here lies his mighty concern for humankind's evolution, but likewise also for the mental state of his disciples on earth. "He knows that *for himself* he will always have Ahriman under his feet, but will that also hold true for human beings?"[4]

In our age of freedom, Michael appears to human beings as the great example for everything they are supposed to attain in today's Michael-age. "But as a majestic exemplary action, in the closest directly adjoining supersensible world next to the visible one Michael can unfold what he wishes to unfold" (ibid.). To follow him in his mission signifies above all an utter lack of compromise regarding the Ahrimanic powers that in our age, as forces of the dragon, are at work under human beings.

Are human beings today capable of holding down these opposing powers under their feet following the example of Michael? Michael gives us the strength to do this. But whether we actually take hold of this force remains an open question, even for those who are actually his pupils on earth. Will the door remain locked for Ahriman in the Anthroposophical Society as the Michaelic community actually existing on the earth, or can Ahriman unfold his anti-Michaelic activity even there, where actually only the Michael-might may reign?

This is the decisive question for the Anthroposophical Society today and particularly for the visible centre in Dornach. Will it be possible for this society to be successful, proceeding as it does from the spiritual forces at this location where ninety years ago (1923-1924) the new Michaelic mysteries were established, to become a centre and source from which the Michaelic impulses can and indeed must flow into today's world? Or is it torn away into the whirlpool of the Ahrimanic forces that try to draw the entire earth-civilization into the abyss?

Stated from the level of the Michael-School on earth, this means: Will this school be in a position to be an opposing image – a counter force – against the temptations and influences of the subterranean Ahrimanic-school that are already now so mightily effective all around us? Are the

Michael-students in a position through their earnest and aimful work with the substance of the school entrusted to them to paralyse its manifold effects? So immeasurably much depends on this today!

In order to fulfil this task, we do require one certain characteristic that likewise belongs among Michael's fundamental virtues – great courage. For Michael is the Spirit of Courage, and for fulfilling his aims on earth he truly needs the most courageous of human beings. "Michael is a powerful spirit. He can only use brave individuals who are inwardly bold" (GA 237, 3 August 1924).

Therefore, the future festival of Michael is likewise connected with the nature of courage, courage that is particularly necessary if one wishes to be a genuine follower of Michael. For in a sense this does not suit today's human being. "He does not wish to be Michael's follower. For that requires inner courage. This inner courage must be attained through its own festival, through the Michael-festival" (GA 223, 8 April 1923).[5]

Now, one can ask oneself: What about this soul-quality among Anthroposophists today? Do they have true Michaelic bravery and have they made it into their most important virtue? Or do they act increasingly and only correspondingly to what the outer world pushes on them as Ahrimanic deception? In this sense regarding the anthroposophical movement and the Anthroposophical Society, we do in fact stand at cross-roads. The trials are there. For without them, no initiation-path can be pursued: The fire-trial, the water-trial and the air-trial. In the first trial, one learns to grasp the spiritual behind the physical; in the second, one is roused in one's activity through reading in the astral light – and today that signifies one's being roused through the communications of spiritual science – and in the third trial, one brings one's own deeds towards Michael, and in so doing must evoke the courage to bide one's time in empty space as if in a room without air, until Michael will proclaim his judgment concerning our activity at the behest of the higher powers.

This alone is how the path into the temple of the new Mysteries is formed today, where Michael's entry into human hearts becomes possible. Only thereby does the Michael-disciple become a true Michaelite.

# Appendix

## Excerpts from a few lectures by Rudolf Steiner for the theme of this book

i
### Rudolf Steiner's Encounter with Michael
(GA 240, 12 August 1924)

In order to familiarize ourselves with all the lesser known substrata that comes into consideration with the kind of questions that arise along with the first of these reflections today [...] I would like to make a kind of personal remark that nevertheless is meant in a completely objective sense.

As you know, the course of my life is being described by me in the ongoing issues of the *Goetheanum Weekly Newsletter*. But in a publication such as this which is likewise available to readers in the outer world, one cannot present everything that comes into consideration. It is therefore necessary to add a supplement here and there for those within our movement who in all earnestness wish to find their way into the spiritual world. Therefore, before I respond in the next lecture to questions such as those that come up now, I would indeed like to make this personal remark today.

You see when a person lived as I did from the 1860s to the present time [1924], one lived during that age which I have often characterized to you as the age when the Michael-rule came about in human civilization following the earlier Gabriel-reign of three-hundred and fifty years. The Michael-reign – meaning the inflow of the Sun-like Michael-impulse into the entire civilization in mankind's evolution – began at the end of the seventies of the previous century. During this particular time which followed, directly after the dawn of the Michael-influence in the eighties and early nineties of the nineteenth century – and one lived among other contemporaries of one's youth when the Michael-rule had begun to make itself felt behind the scenes of outer events – one had to work on one's mind-soul or intellectual-soul. You know that one develops that aspect of the soul between the 28th and 35th year of life. Now if one really lives in the way just described in one's mind or intellectual-soul, then one actually lives outside the physical world. When human beings experience themselves in their mind or intellectual-soul, when they consciously experience themselves in this way, then they are mostly outside the physical world.

We can observe that the human being consists of physical body, etheric body and astral or sentient body. With the physical body, we clearly stand within the physical outer world. With the etheric body, we likewise live in the outer world; with the astral body we also still live strongly in the outer world. Even in the mind soul, we still live in that outer world, but human individuals can also live quite outside the physical world when – prior to an awakening in the consciousness-soul at about age thirty-five – they awaken and live fully consciously in the rational or mind-soul. Then one enters completely into the soul-element. Thus in the previous eighties and nineties of the past century, the opportunity was there for someone who had the disposition for it to live more or less outside the physical world with his or her rational or mind-soul.

What does that mean? It means that by living outside the physical world with one's rational or mind soul, one can thus live in that region, in that sphere, into which Michael in particular entered into terrestrial life.

For you see, in the eighties and nineties of the 1800s, many things took place that people admired, matters in which they were educated, and matters through which they educated themselves. Well, through the use of many choice words on the part of more erudite literary individuals, this age has been astutely described. Take everything that newspapers have printed, what art has produced, and much that surfaced in the eighties and nineties of the past century. It takes its course like this: 1879, 1880, 1890, and so on. Yet, during these years, something else took place. There was a thin veil, and behind this veil there was another world strongly adjacent to our physical world. This was the peculiar characteristic during the later years of the nineteenth century, the time prior to the end of Kali Yuga – as we know the Kali Yuga ended in 1899 – when as if through a spider-web-like thin veil, which the ordinary state of consciousness cannot penetrate, there was an adjacent world beginning to show itself. What took place then must emerge more and more into the physical world showing itself through its effects from now on.

There was in fact something mysterious about this age at the end of the nineteenth century. Behind the veil, remarkable phenomena were taking place, and these phenomena grouped themselves around that Spirit-being we designate by the name Michael. There were powerful adherents of Michael, human souls who then were not in physical incarnation but between death and a new birth. Likewise, there were also powerful demonic forces under Ahrimanic influences that rebelled against what Michael was supposed to bring into this world.

Now allow me to utter a personal remark here, and it is this: I myself grew up in such a way that actually I never had any difficulties grasping the spiritual world. What the spiritual world brought me entered into my soul, shaped itself into ideas, and could form themselves into thoughts; but what seemed to be so easy for other people was difficult for me. I could quickly grasp natural scientific inter-connections, yet on the other hand individual sets of facts would not stay in my memory, and did not fit in. I could grasp the theory of undulations with ease, and the views of mathematicians, physicists and chemists. A mineral on the other hand I could not simply study once or twice and then recognize it again, as most other people could, whenever the same kind of mineral confronted me later. In order to remember it again, I would have to study it thirty or forty times. A set of facts for the outer physical world typically would evoke resistance whenever I tried to hold on to them and then understand them. It was difficult for me to go out into this physical sensory world.

For this reason, I had to remain standing within this world behind the veil with my entire intellectual or mind-soul. In this world of Michael I had to live and go along with what was taking place there. And it was there that the great challenges arose once and for all to deal earnestly with the reality of the spiritual world, and to bring these momentous questions to the forefront. Outer life offered no opportunity for this. Outer life continued to write down and continue with the old and well-worn philistine biographies of men like Darwin and Bacon. But there, behind the scenes, behind this thin veil in the region of Michael, there the great questions of life were raised. And above everything else one learned to know one thing: What a vast difference there is between raising these questions inwardly in one's heart, and speaking about them in actual words.

Today's human being is generally of the opinion that what one knows one can speak about in words, and indeed nowadays announce it as quickly as possible. However, when the questions at issue in Michael's sphere during the eighties and nineties took hold of a person, these questions worked on the person into the 20th century. And even after having lived with these questions for decades, every time someone wanted to utter them, it was as if opponents of Michael would approach and seal one's lips – for about certain matters one was not supposed to speak.

And you see, even in the lap of the anthroposophical movement, there was much that remained as Michael secrets for some time – above all the truths relating to historical connections of the kind about which reference has already been made. But for some time now – actually for months – these truths can be spoken of without restraint. That is why for me it has now become possible to speak frankly and openly about these matters, including the connections between earthly lives. Therefore, it happens, has happened, and should continue to happen here that one can speak unrestrainedly about the connections in earthly lives now. For this is part of the unveiling of those Michael-mysteries which took place in the manner I have described to you.

This is one of the concrete matters which I spoke of previously in a more abstract way. At the beginning of the lecture in regard to a certain eventuality, I said that the spiritual world might have withheld itself; but it did not. What has actually happened is that since the Christmas Conference and above all because of the opportunities vouchsafed to me for occult work, the demons that hitherto prevented these things from being voiced have now been compelled to remain silent and end their obstruction. The things to which I refer are of course not entirely new for they were experienced a long time ago in the way I have indicated to you. But it must be remembered that in occultism things that are discovered one day cannot be communicated the next.

ii
### The Three Forms of Thinking.
*Paths for Cognition of Higher Worlds*
(GA 79, 26 November 1921)

If I may put it this way, a person who wishes to become a spiritual inves-
tigator in an anthroposophical sense must set out from the point where he
stands in ordinary life and ordinary science; from there he must take his
own development in hand. The forces which should be developed first of
all are the forces of thinking. This is a first step in such a development,
and we shall see that this does not imply a one-sided development of intellectual forces or thinking, but the unfolding of the whole human being.
But a beginning must be made with a particular exercise in thinking.
The kind of thinking to which we are accustomed in ordinary life and also
in ordinary science is given up to external observation and follows, as it
were, the thread of external observation. We direct our senses towards the
external world and link our thoughts with perceptions transmitted by the
senses. The observation of the external world provides a firm support,
enabling us to connect our experiences with the contents of our soul.
It has been the endeavour of science, and rightly so, to develop the support
given by external observation more and more. This observation has been
enhanced by the use of scientific experimental research where every single
condition leading to different manifestations can be clearly surveyed so
that the processes become quite transparent, as it were.

For the attainment of its task, the spiritual science of
Anthroposophy must deviate from this way of thinking which is entirely
directed towards the objective reality outside. Anthroposophy must above
all strengthen and intensify thought within the human being. In the public
lecture which I gave yesterday I remarked that a muscle grows stronger if
it does a certain work routinely, and this also applies to the forces of the
soul. When certain definite concepts which can easily be surveyed are set
at the centre of our consciousness by systematic practice again and again
so that we completely surrender to such concepts with our entire nature,

then our thinking power in particular grows stronger. This intensification of the forces of thinking must of course be reached in such a way that clear and thought-imbued forces of will are maintained in all that we do.

[...]

The first thing which should be borne in mind when treading the path to higher knowledge [cognition] is that our thinking, which is free from sense impressions, acquires an inner activity, mobility, that completely claims the attention of our soul in the same way that this attention is ordinarily claimed only by an external sense perception. One might say: What we ordinarily experience in connection with an external sense impression, we should learn to experience in connection with that intensified thought-activity which is completely pervaded by a clear and conscious will.

[...]

Then one arrives at a point where a new way of thinking is acquired. The old thinking that one utilizes in ordinary life and science remains fully intact. But a new way of thinking is added to the former old thinking when in a corresponding manner we practice those exercises that have principally been characterized as thought exercises – these exercises are described in my book, *Knowledge of the Higher Worlds and Its Attainment* or in my *Occult Science, an Outline* – and practice these exercises systematically over and over for the purpose of an inner soul development. One person will need longer periods of time for the attainment of results, and another person a shorter period when such exercises are carried out in one's consciousness. The new way of thinking which is added to the old way of thinking is something I would like to describe in the following manner.

Perhaps you will allow me to make a personal remark, but one that is not meant personally. It is one that you will readily admit belongs to the objective part of my descriptions. In the early nineties of the nineteenth century, I wrote my *Philosophy of Freedom* in order to show that freedom really lives in man's ethical moral life. There it has its roots. This book has evoked many misunderstandings because people simply cannot penetrate into the way of thinking which is employed in this book.

My *Philosophy of Freedom* already employs that form of thinking which must be gained by systematic practice in order to reach cognition of higher worlds. It is a first beginning in this direction, a first step which anyone can make in ordinary life; yet at the same time it is a first step leading to knowledge of higher worlds.

Now, ordinary thinking – you need only consider the ordinary form of thinking to see how what I say is justified – ordinary thinking is a thinking that consists of spatial perceptions. In our ordinary thinking everything is arranged spatially. Just think how you trace back time-related issues to spatial thinking. For time is expressed through movements of the clock. Fundamentally speaking, we also find the same process in our physics formulae. In short, we must conclude that ordinary thinking is a combining way of thinking, one that collects separate elements. We use this way of thinking in healthy ordinary conditions of life, and also for ordinary science.

However, the kind of thinking that must be added for the purpose of knowledge of higher worlds, and that one acquires through the aid of exercises as previously described, is a thinking that I might call morpho-logical thinking, one in which we think in pliable or flexible forms. This thinking is not limited to space; it is definitely one that lives in the medium of time in the same way thinking lives within the medium of space. This thinking does not link one concept to another; it places before the soul something like a "conceptual organism". When we have a conception, an idea or a thought, we cannot simply pass on from one thought to another in any way one likes. Taking the human organism as an example, one cannot pass from the head to any of the other bodily forms but first must pass over the neck, then the shoulders, chest, etc., to see how everything in an organism hangs together, so to speak. Every thing has a definite structure in an organism which must be considered in its entirety, and likewise the thinking which I call morphological thinking must be inwardly mobile in order to do so. As previously stated, morphological thinking exists in the medium of time, not space, but this thinking is inwardly so mobile that it calls forth one form out of the other. It constantly members itself in an organic sense; it constantly grows.

It is this morphological thinking that must be added to the other and that can be attained through such meditation exercises as I have indicated in principle in some of my books. These exercises strengthen and intensify thinking. With this morphological thinking, with this thinking that takes its course in forms ("Gestalten") and in images, one attains to the first level of cognition of higher worlds, namely what I have described in my writings as imaginative knowledge.

[...]

Therefore, a person who arrives at such organic-morphological thinking – a thinking that develops itself, so to speak, into a living process of growth – cannot retain the results of this thinking in ordinary memory. Freedom too can only be characterized when one ascends to such self-developing growing thinking. This is why my *Philosophy of Freedom* gave rise to so many misunderstandings, and was in effect "covered up". Yet it had to be given [to the public] by way of this method because freedom is indeed a spiritual experience and one cannot attain to it with ordinary combinatory thinking.

[...]

If we have reached the point of developing this picture-like, imaginative thinking, we must then proceed further with the strength thus gained. I have stated that just as a muscle grows stronger through physical work, our thinking-force can also grow in strength when we carry out the exercises which are described and further delineated in the books mentioned above. When we develop within ourselves an intensified thinking that extends to a picture-like formative quality which lives in the dimension of time, then we reach a level where other forces of our soul may be developed and strengthened.

Ordinary conceptions of life arise and go away or we can also try to rid ourselves of them, either by seeking to discard them from our soul, or the organism sees to it that we forget them, and so on. However, those conceptions that we cause to be present in our conscious mind for the purpose of higher cognition – as I have described it – are harder to be brought to the point of forgetfulness than ordinary conceptions. Quite an effort must be made to forget them. This is a second kind of exercise: an artificial forgetting, as it were; an artificial suppression of thought.

If we have practiced this artificial suppression of concepts for a sufficiently long period of time depending on our individual development and predispositions, we become able to suppress the entire tableau of which I have spoken, so that our consciousness becomes completely empty. The only thing which should remain for us is the thinking that is permeated by our will and composure; but this thinking now appears in a new form.

So far, I have described two ways of thinking to you: the ordinary space-bound way of thinking, and the way of thinking which has a growth-process all its own where one thought or concept grows forth out of the other, as it does out of an organism where one part is connected with another. If this morphological way of thinking is practiced for a certain span of time, we gradually develop a third way of thinking, which we need in order to ascend to a higher stage of supersensible knowledge. I will describe next what happens when one ascends to a higher world; to what is more than a mere overview of one's own organisation.

Through imaginative cognition we come to the point where we have a "survey" over our own organisation so that we tell ourselves: The soul-spiritual element, something that is super-sensible, works in earthly life on the physical-corporeal element. And we need this morphological thinking, for otherwise it is not possible to understand what takes place in time nor what works out of the super-sensible realm into the sensory one, for this morphological thinking is present while undergoing continual metamorphosis. We have to make our thinking mobile and our thoughts inwardly connected. Mere "combining" thinking cannot grasp the life which proceeds from the spirit; this can only be grasped, or comprehended, by an inwardly living thinking. We must attain to a still different thinking if we wish to rise up to the next stage of super-sensible knowledge. Let me use an example in order to explain this to you. Even this example is somewhat difficult to comprehend, but I think you will be able to understand what I mean.

I ask all of you to recall that Goethe tried to understand the individual cranial bones as metamorphosed bones of the vertebra. In the single bones of the skull Goethe beheld a metamorphosis of the vertebra. Though somewhat modified, modern science also adopts this view, but it is no longer entirely in keeping with Goethe's conception; nevertheless this view is valid today.

It does not suffice, however, to consider the purely morphological derivation of the cranial bones. We must go further if we wish to understand the relationship of the human head with the remaining human organism – we will restrict ourselves to the skeleton. We must not only envision a transformation, but something very different. Let us ask for instance: What kind of relationship exists between the bony system of the arms or legs and the bony system of the cranial bones, the bones of the head? Here it is the case that the metamorphoses through which one form gives rise to the other can only be grasped if we bear in mind that this is not only a spatial re-forming that takes place in the medium of time, but that quite another process takes place which is very difficult to understand, namely a kind of inversion; a turning inside-out.

For, if you wish to understand the mutual relationship of the leg-bones to those of the head, you have to compare the outer surface of the skull-bones with the inner surface of a hollow bone, let us say the upper hip. The inner side of the upper hip-bone would have to be turned inside out, and its elasticity would also have to change. Its inner surface would then be turned outward, and the outer surface of a skull-bone would correspond to the inner surface of a hollow bone of man's limbs, and the other way around. The external surface of the shin-bone [tibia] does not correspond to the outer surface of the cranium, but to its inner surface.

Imagine this process of metamorphosis like a glove which is turned inside out, but at the same time the elasticity of the glove undergoes a change. A new form arises. It is as if the glove is not only turned inside out, but after having done so it would assume a completely different shape through its forces of elasticity.

You see, I must mention something extraordinarily complicated already as a first indication to you concerning this third kind of thinking, which not only lives in constantly changing forms, but is also capable of turning the formation of the inner content to the outside and in so doing changes its form. This is only possible through the fact that our thinking now no longer lives in the medium of time, for in this turning inside-out our thoughts transcend space and time and penetrate into a reality that lies beyond space and time.

I know very well that we cannot immediately become familiar with this third kind of thinking which differs so greatly from the combining and the formative ways of thinking. It is not easy to penetrate into this third kind of thinking, which dives down, as it were, into "space-lessness and timelessness" [a dimension totally lacking in space and time]; and what reappears is changed as to its form; its inside is turned outwards and the outer is turned inwards. But Anthroposophy does not wish to offer the kind of amateurish nonsense about higher worlds that many people have resorted to. Anthroposophy, because it is as honest as any honest science, must point out that it is not only necessary to leave the realm of ordinary science but that it is even necessary to acquire a completely new way of thinking. Inwardly, we must hold the nature of the human being together quite differently if we try to advance to a qualitative thinking in the above manner, for it is nothing less than a changing of the entire quality of thinking which originates in this turn-around, this changing from the inside to the outside. Only when one has in this way brought one's thinking to the point of submerging, penetrating, "into the qualitative", can one ascend to that stage of knowledge of super-sensible worlds that follows the stage of imaginative thinking.

If the tableau about which I have spoken – referring to the tableau in which the work of the soul-spiritual forces on the physical organism becomes visible on the etheric level – has been suppressed so that an empty consciousness has been brought about, then one does indeed have an empty consciousness for a certain time. It is possible to bring about an empty consciousness for a while merely by suppressing one's perception. But when such a reality is suppressed, when we suppress forces, for example, that are constantly at the service of growth and nutrition during our earthly existence, we dive down into a completely new world. Then we really are in the higher worlds and the ordinary physical world lies behind us like a memory. We must have this as a memory for otherwise we would not be healthy individuals of sound mind; without memory we would be psychopathic human beings subjected to hallucinations and illusions.

If we proceed in the right way along the path of spiritual investigation, we maintain our sober-mindedness; our calm thoughtful consciousness permeated by the will even when we ascend to the highest worlds, and there need be no mention of falling prey to hallucinations or suggestions.

If we are subjected to hallucinations or suggestions, it means that the ordinary consciousness has been completely pushed aside by a pathological state of mind. In the state of consciousness which Anthroposophy strives to reach for the attainment of knowledge of higher worlds, the essential thing is to maintain our ordinary consciousness to the full extent, so that we keep our sound common sense and calm state of mind while ascending to higher worlds. And even what I have communicated to you about the turned upside-down thinking, the supra-morphological thinking, even that exists for the purpose of entering into these higher worlds with full consciousness. We then really experience the higher worlds and their spiritual contents.

### iii
### Freedom and Intellectuality
(GA 257, 30 January 1923)

Now, my dear friends, as I have often pointed out, we have to be clear when we are presenting Anthroposophy that we are now living in the age of consciousness-soul development. This in turn means that the rational or intellectual state of mind has become the most preferred and best soul-condition for human beings of the present time. Ever since the time of the philosopher Anaxagoras in ancient Greece, we have been sifting every judgment, even those based on external observation, through our intellectuality.

If you examine the rationalistic science of today, particularly mathematics which is the most rationalistic of all, and also consider the rationalistic working over of empirical data by the other sciences, you will form some idea of the actual thought-content of our time. This thought-content, to which even the youngest children are exposed in modern schools, made its appearance at a fairly definite point in human evolution. We can clearly pinpoint this at the beginning of the first third of the fifteenth century [AD], for it was only then that this intellectuality appeared on the scene in unmistakable form.

In earlier times people thought more in pictures even when they were dealing with scientific subject matter, and these pictures expressed the growth forces inherent in the things they thought about. They did not think in abstractions such as those that come so naturally to us today.

Now these abstract concepts educate us inwardly for the pure-thinking" described in my *Philosophy of Freedom*, and make it possible for us to become free beings. Before people were able to think in abstractions they were not free self-determined souls. Human beings can develop freely only because they are no longer determined by anything inward anymore, since moral impulses are grasped in pure thinking – you can read about that in my *Philosophy of Freedom*. Pure thoughts, however, are not reality they are pictures, images that cannot exercise any sort of compulsion on us. They leave us free to determine our own actions. So on the one hand mankind has evolved to the level of abstract thinking, and on the other hand to freedom. This has often been discussed here from several other angles.

Let us now consider how things stood with mankind before earthly evolution brought him to the point of grasping abstract thoughts, and so to freedom. The humanity that was incarnated on earth in earlier periods was incapable of abstract thinking; not even in ancient Greece was this yet possible, not to mention still earlier periods. People living in those early days thought entirely in pictures, and were therefore not as yet endowed with the inner sense of freedom that became theirs when they attained the capacity for pure, that is abstract, thinking. Abstract thoughts leave us cold, but the moral capacity given us by abstract thought makes us intensely warm for it represents the very peak of human dignity.

What was it like before abstract thought, with its accompaniment of freedom, was conferred on human beings? Well, you know that when human beings pass through the portal of death and cast off their physical body, for the first few days they still retain around themselves the etheric body and experience an all-inclusive, all-encompassing review of their life, not in a presentation of details but in equalized universal images of their course of life as far back as the moment of their first memory. This tableau of one's life confronts a person as picture-content for several days after he has died. Yes, my dear friends; that is the way it is today. But during the time when people living on earth still possessed a picture consciousness, their experience immediately after death was that of a rational and logical grasp of the world such as human beings have today here on earth, but which those who lived in earlier times did not have during the period between birth and death.

That is something that in the most eminent sense guides us into an understanding of the human entity. What a person experienced only after death in ancient as well as in somewhat later periods of history – namely a brief "review" in abstract concepts and an impulse to freedom which then remained for him or her during the life between death and a new birth – has gradually shifted in the course of human evolution to be an experience we have during life on earth. This constant pressing through of super-sensible experience into earthly experience is one of the great secrets of existence. The capacity for abstraction and freedom that presently extends into earthly life was something that came into an earlier humanity's possession only after death, in the form of this review following death as I have described. Nowadays, human beings living on earth possess rationality, intellectuality and freedom, exchanging these after death for a mere picture consciousness in their reviewing of their lives. There is a constant passing over of this kind going on, and with that actual super-sensible matters move into sense experience.

From this you can see how, quite objectively and by observation of the spiritual world, Anthroposophy obtains the truths of which it speaks. Nothing of subjective arbitrariness flows into the handling of these facts. But once we have these facts, do they not influence our feelings and our impulses of will? Can it ever be said of Anthroposophy that it is merely a theory? It appears theoretical when we simply say that the human being of the modern age is a being of abstraction and freedom! But how permeated by artistic feelings and religious devotion things appear when we realize that what gives us – as modern human beings in this earthly life – freedom in our earthly experience and the faculty of abstraction is something which has passed out of heavenly worlds into the earthly one; making its way to us in a direction exactly opposite to the direction we take when we pass through the gate of death to enter them. We go out through the gate of death into spiritual realms.

Our freedom and faculty for abstraction come to us as a divine gift that has been given to earthly worlds by the spiritual. It pervades us with a sense, a feeling, of what we are as human beings, making us aware not only of the fact that we are bearers of something spiritual in ourselves, but also the source from where this spiritual element derives. We look on death with the realization that what lies beyond it was experienced by people of an earlier time in a way that has now been carried over into the modern experiencing of people here on earth. Intellectuality and freedom has now moved into us, and the human being of the present age learns to become acquainted with it.

The fact that this heavenly element of intellectuality and freedom has thus been transferred into earthly life makes it necessary to look up to the divine in a different way from that of earlier ages. This different way of looking up to the Divinity has become possible for humanity through the Mystery of Golgotha. The fact that Christ came to live on earth enables humans to sanctify elements of heavenly origin that might otherwise tempt man to arrogance and similar attitudes. We are living in an age that calls on us to recognize that our loftiest modern capacities, the capacity for freedom and pure concepts, must be permeated by the Christ-impulse. Christendom is not perfected yet. It is great just because all the various evolutionary impulses of the human race must gradually be saturated by the Christ-impulse. We must learn to think purely with Christ, to be a free being with Christ, for otherwise we will not have the proper relationship to the super-sensible world that enables us to perceive correctly what it gives us.

As modern human beings, we realize that the super-sensible penetrates into earthly life in a direction opposite to the one we take when passing through the portal of death. With the descent of Christ, the spiritual sun enters into the earth realm from spiritual heights so that the human element that has made its way from the super-sensible to the sense world comes together with the cosmic element that has taken the same path, in order that man may find his way to the spirit of the cosmos. The spirit that for ancient mankind dwelled in the world beyond death can rightly be taken hold of by people in the present age only when they are irradiated by the Christ, who descended to earth from that same world out of which rationality, intellectuality and freedom also made their way into the experience of incarnated human beings.

iv

**Michael and Rosicrucianism.**
*Occult Foundations of Occult Science, an Outline*
(GA 233a, 13 January 1924)

A personality like Christian Rosenkreutz knew that initiates of ancient times have lived with their visions; that they affirmed what they had beheld by means of knowing that it was there reflected somewhere in the heavens – be it in the Moon-sphere, be it in the planetary sphere, be it at the end of the universe. It was reflected. Now, however, nothing was reflected; for the immediate wide-awake vision of man, nothing at all was reflected. But people could now find ideas about nature; the Copernican world-system could arise, and all manner of ideas could be formed. In the warmth-ether they spurt out into widths of worlds.

Thus it came about that Christian Rosenkreutz, by inspiration of a higher spirit, found a way to perceive the reflection after all, in spite of the fact that it was only a reflection by the warmth-ether. [In ancient times] this occurred by means of utilizing other dull and unconscious conditions of consciousness as aids or support, conditions in which a person is normally outside his or her body. Then it became perceptible that what is discovered with modern abstract ideas is after all inscribed in the spiritual world, though not in space. This is what we see then in the Rosicrucian movement: the Rosicrucians, as if in a transition stage, made themselves acquainted with all that could be discovered about nature in their epoch of time. They received it into themselves and assimilated it as only a human being could do. They enhanced into true wisdom what for the others was only science. Then they protected it in their souls attempting with the greatest possible purity to pass over into sleep with this wisdom following intimate meditations. And then it came to pass that the divine-spiritual worlds brought back to these Rosicrucians in a spiritually real language what had first been apprehended in abstract ideas.

In Rosicrucian schools, not only was the Copernican cosmology taught, but in special states of consciousness its ideas came back in the form

I explained here during recent days. It was the Rosicrucians in particular who realized that what one receives initially with modern cognition must first be borne up, as it were, towards the gods so that they can re-translate it into their language and then give it back again to human beings.

That this can be possible has indeed remained so up to the present time. For, it is indeed true my dear friends; if you are touched by the Rosicrucian principle referred to here, study the system of Haeckel [referring to Ernst Haeckel, German zoologist, 1834-1919], study Haeckelism today with all its materialism, and at the same time let yourselves be pervaded by what are methods of cognition as indicated in *Knowledge of the Higher Worlds and Its Attainment*. Take what you learn in Haeckel's *Anthropogeny (Anthropogenesis)* concerning the human ancestors. In that form it may perhaps disgust you. Learn about it nevertheless, appalling as it may be. Learn all about external natural science and then bear it up to the gods, and you will receive in return what is narrated in my book *Occult Science* concerning evolution.

Such is the connection between the feeble, weak knowledge that we can acquire here on earth with our physical body, and that which the gods can bestow on us, if with a proper attitude we duly prepare ourselves through the learning of this knowledge. But human beings must first bear upwards to the gods what they can learn here on earth, for times have indeed changed.

[...]

This is the curious thing about Rosicrucianism that in a time of transition, this spiritual movement had to stand still, had to desist from advancing into dream-like conditions and, as it were, to dream the higher truth of what ordinary science soberly finds here in nature.

That, however, is the peculiar thing since the beginning of the Michael-epoch, namely that since the end of the 1870's what had been achieved during the ancient Rosicrucian age can now be achieved in a conscious way as described above. Thus, it can be said nowadays that the other condition which was half-conscious is no longer required but a higher conscious condition is needed. And then, along with the insights one acquires in nature, one can penetrate into higher worlds, and what has been acquired as ordinary natural science emerges out of the higher world towards us inasmuch as what is inscribed in the astral region can be read once again. It emerges and comes to meet us in spiritual reality. And what one does there, namely that we carry up into the spiritual world the natural scientific knowledge that is acquired here, is then carried out into a spiritual world; and likewise the creations of naturalistic culture or the feelings of naturalistically working religion within the human soul – even religion has become naturalistic nowadays. As we carry all of this upwards, one does in fact encounter Michael if one's faculties have been developed for this.

We can therefore say that the old Rosicrucian movement is characterized by the fact that its most brilliant minds had an intense longing to encounter Michael. They could do so only as if in a dream. But since the end of the last third of the 19th century, human beings can encounter Michael in the spirit in a conscious way.

Now, Michael is indeed a strange being; a being who in a manner of speaking reveals nothing, unless we bring something towards him based on our diligent spiritual work here on earth. Michael is a silent spirit. He is a spirit that is silent and reserved. While other ruling Archangels are loquacious talkative spirits – naturally in a spiritual sense – Michael is definitely a reserved taciturn spirit, one who says little and who at most offers sparse indications. For what one learns from Michael are not words in themselves but – if I may so express it – the look, the power of his glance.

And the reason for this is that Michael concerns himself most of all with what human beings *create* out of the spiritual element. He dwells in the consequences of what is created by human beings. The other spirits live more in the causes; Michael lives more with the effects, the consequences. The other spirits kindle in man the impulses for what human beings are supposed to do. Michael will become the actual champion of freedom. He lets human beings do what they do, and then he takes what becomes of human deeds, and carries this on and out into the cosmos, so that what human beings cannot as yet themselves "accomplish" will continue working in the universe.

In regard to other entities from the Hierarchy of the Archangels, we have the feeling that from them come the impulses to do this or that to a greater or lesser degree. But Michael is that spirit from whom no impulses come to begin with, because his truly representative perspective of ruling is the one that is now at hand – when matters are to arise out of human freedom. But when human beings do things out of spiritual activity or inner freedom, consciously or unconsciously stimulated by reading in the astral light, then Michael carries what is a human earthly deed out into the cosmos so that it becomes a cosmic deed. Michael cares for the consequences; other spirits care more about the causes.

Yet, Michael is not only a silent taciturn spirit. As he approaches human beings, Michael comes towards us with a clear rejection of much that we do inasmuch as we still dwell here on earth. For example, all that forms itself in either human, animal or plant-life and tends to lay stress on inherited characteristics – inherited faculties in physical nature – is of such a kind that it appears to us as if Michael were pushing it away from himself in rejection. He wants to demonstrate with this gesture that such insights bear no fruit whatsoever for us in regard to the spiritual world. Only what we discover in the human, animal and plant kingdoms independently of purely inherited elements can be borne upwards by Michael. Then we receive, not a rejecting gesture of deprecation, but the acquiescent look of approval which tells us that this is a thought justifiably conceived in harmony with cosmic guidance. For, this is what one learns to strive for more and more: to ponder, as it were, in order to push through to the astral light, to behold the secrets of existence and then to come before Michael and receive his approving glance that tells us: That is right, that is in harmony with the guidance of the cosmos.

v
## Spiritual Warmth and Spiritual Light Essay:
### *Michael's Mission in the Cosmic Age of Human Freedom*
### and an extract from the text of the Spiritual
### Foundation-Stone-Laying during the Christmas Conference
(GA 26, 9 November 1924 and GA 260, 25 December 1923)

Human beings know themselves to be in a reality when they confront the Sun and receive warmth and light from it. In the same way, we must live in regard to the presence of Christ, the spiritual Sun, who has united His existence with that of the earth. From Him, we must receive in an alive way what in the spiritual world corresponds to warmth and light.

We will feel ourselves permeated by "spiritual warmth" when we experience the "Christ in ourselves". Feeling ourselves thus permeated we will say to our own inner being: "This warmth frees my soul-nature from attachments within the cosmos in which I must not remain. The divine-spiritual existence of primal times had to lead me through struggle to freedom in regions where divine-spiritual existence could not remain within me. Yet, it has given me the Christ, so that His forces might bestow on me as a free human being, what the divine-spiritual existence of primal times bestowed on me by way of nature, which was then also the spiritual path. This warmth guides me back to the Divine from which I once came."

In this feeling-experience of inner [devoted] soul-warmth, the human being will grow together with the experiencing in and with Christ, and the experience of genuine and true humanity. "Christ gives me my human nature" – this feeling wafts and weaves in us as our fundamental emotion of soul. Once this feeling is there another arises as well; we feel lifted by Christ beyond mere earthly existence and feel at one with the starry firmament around the earth, and with that the Divine-Spiritual is recognized in this firmament.

It is the same with spiritual light. We can feel ourselves fully in our true human nature inasmuch as we become aware that we are free individualities. However, a certain process of darkening is still connected with this. The Divine-Spiritual of primal times no longer radiates. In the light that the Christ brings to the human "I", the primal light is once again present. In such a living together with the Christ, this bliss-endowing thought can shine throughout the entire soul like a Sun. The primordial majestic divine light is back once again; it shines even though its radiance is not a nature-like shining. And in the present age, human beings unite themselves with the spiritual-cosmic light-forces of the past at a time when they were not yet free individualities. In light of these considerations, we can now find the directions that can guide our human nature properly, when we unite ourselves with the Michael-mission comprehensively in our souls.

Then in warmth of spirit we shall feel the impulse that will carry us across into our cosmic future in such a way that we will remain faithful to those primal gifts bestowed on us by divine-spiritual entities despite the fact that we developed in their realms to the point of being free individualities. And we shall sense in the spirit's light the power that leads us – cognizing with a higher and ever expanding consciousness – into the universe where, as free human beings, we rediscover ourselves along with the Gods of our origin.

*

The proper soil into which we must lower today's Foundation Stone, the proper soil consists of our hearts in their harmonious collaboration – in their good love-filled desire together to bear the will of Anthroposophy through the world. This will shines towards us like a reminder of the light of thought that can radiate toward us at any time from the dodecahedral Stone of Love which we want to lower into our hearts today.

Dear friends, let us take this deeply into our souls. With it let us warm our hearts and minds; with it let us enlighten our souls. Let us cherish this warmth of soul, this soul-light which out of good will we have now planted into our hearts.

We plant it at a moment, my dear friends, when human memory that truly understands the universe looks back to the point in human evolution at the Turning Point of Time, when out of the darkness of night and out of the darkness of human moral feeling, shooting like light from heaven, was born the divine being who had become the Christ; the Spirit-being who had entered into humankind.

We can best bring strength to warmth of soul and that light of soul which we need if we enliven them with the warmth and light that shone forth at the Turning Point of Time as the Christ-light in the darkness of the universe. In our hearts, in our thoughts, and in our will let us bring to life that original consecrated night of Christmas which took place two thousand years ago, so that it may help us when we carry forth into the world what shines toward us through the light of thought of that dodecahedral Foundation Stone of Love which is shaped in accordance with the universe and has been laid into the human realm.

So may feelings of our hearts be turned back towards the primal Christmas night in ancient Palestine:

> At the Turning Point of Time
> The Spirit-Light of the World
> Entered the stream of earthly being.
> Darkness of night
> Had held its sway,
> Day-radiant light
> Streamed into souls of men:
> Light that gives warmth
> To simple shepherds' hearts,
> Light that enlightens
> The wise heads of kings.
>
> Light Divine!
> Christ-Sun
> Warm thou our hearts,
> Enlighten thou our heads,
> That good may become
> What we from our hearts would found
> What we from our heads would direct
> In conscious
> Willing.

Thus feeling our way back to the primal Christmas night can give us the strength for the warming of our hearts and the enlightening of our heads which we need in order to carry out in the right way, working anthroposophically, what can emerge out of threefold human cognition that harmonizes into a unity.

### vi
### Cosmic Address by Michael in his Sun-School
(GA 240, 20 July 1924)

It can be said that once, at the end of the fifteenth century, Michael gathered his hosts of divine and human beings in the realm of the Sun and spoke to them in an address that extended over long periods of time approximately as follows:

Since the age when the human race first populated the earth in human form, the Mysteries have existed upon the earth: Sun-mysteries, Mercury-mysteries, Venus-mysteries, Mars-mysteries, Jupiter-mysteries, Saturn-mysteries. The gods sent their secrets into these mysteries, and those human individuals deemed fit for initiation were initiated into them. Human beings here on earth could therefore know what occurred on Saturn, Jupiter, Mars and so on, and also know how happenings in those spheres work into humanity's evolution here on earth. There have always been initiates who communed with the Gods in the Mysteries. With an old instinctive clairvoyance, these initiates received what approached them in the Mysteries by way of impulses. Except for a few meagre traditions – thus spoke Michael to his disciples – this has almost completely vanished from the earth. The impulses can no longer stream into the earthly region. Only in the lowest-lying subordinate area of procreation, Gabriel still has the power to let the Moon-influences flow into the evolution of humanity. The ancient traditions have almost vanished from earth, and therewith the possibility to nurture and cultivate the impulses that stream into subconscious life and into the various corporealities of human beings. We now look back, however, to all that was brought down to human beings in the Mysteries a long time ago like a gift from heaven; we survey this wondrous tableau; we glance down into the course of time. We behold the Mystery-sites and we see how celestial wisdom streamed down into them, and how human beings were initiated by this wisdom. In particular, we behold how from our sanctified realm in the Sun, the cosmic intelligence thus came down and imbued humankind; how the great teachers of mankind received ideas, thoughts, and concepts that were spiritual but were inspired from our hallowed realm in the Sun. That has disappeared from earth. We realize this when we reflect on the ancient times on earth; we see it gradually disappearing from earth-evolution during the age of Alexander and its aftermath. Down below among human beings, we see how the intelligence that has become earthly spreads gradually among human beings. Now this outlook has remained with us. We still behold the secrets into which the initiates were instructed long ago. Let us bring these secrets to awareness in us. Let us bring them to awareness in those spiritual entities that never appear in a physical body "around" us but have their existence only in an etheric form. Let us likewise bring these secrets to those souls who have frequently lived on earth in physical bodies; those who are actually here now, and who belong to the Michael-community. Let us bring these secrets to the awareness of these human souls. May we start on the grand initiate-teaching that once in the ancient way poured down through the Mysteries; let us introduce these initiate teachings to the souls of those who in an intelligent way were linked with Michael. Let us "image forth" the great initiation-teaching that once streamed down in the ancient fashion through the Mysteries to the earth. We will present this to the souls of those who in their life of intelligence were linked with Michael.

And there, in Michael's region, instruction was given – if I may use such a terrestrial expression which sounds almost trivial in such a context – instruction was given on the ancient initiate-wisdom. A mighty all-encompassing heavenly school existed. In it Michael offered what he now no longer could administer himself.

**vii**
## Conclusion of *The Last Address*
## Introduction to the Michael-Meditation
[GA 238, 28 September 1924)

Only then when this work, the mighty tremendous penetration with the Michael-power, the Michael-will, into the whole of life takes place – which is none other than what precedes the Christ-will so that this Christ-force can be implanted into earthly life in the right way; when this Michael-power can truly be victorious over the demonic dragon-like forces (that each of you know well); when all of you who in the light of anthroposophical wisdom have received the Michael-thought with faithful hearts, devoted love, and safe-guard it; when you endeavour to go forward with this year's Michael-mood of holiness and dedication, and make it the starting-point of what is not only revealed in your soul but can also live in your deeds in all its strength and power; only then will you be devoted servants of this Michael-thought; then you will be noble co-workers of what must come to pass through Anthroposophy in accord with Michael making himself felt in earth-evolution.

In the near future, when in four-times-twelve human beings the Michael-thought becomes fully alive; in four-times-twelve human beings who are recognized not through their own means but by the leadership of the Goetheanum in Dornach; when in such four-times-twelve human beings leaders arise having the mood of soul that belongs to the Michael festival, then we can look upon the light that through the Michael-stream and Michael-deeds will spread out in the future among human beings.

That this is so, my dear friends, for this I have attempted to pull myself together and rise up to speak to you today, if only in these few short words. My strength would not suffice for more today. But out of the words today it is this that might speak to your souls: That you can receive this Michael-thought in accord with what a Michael-devoted heart can feel, when – clothed in the light-ray garment of the Sun – Michael appears and initially gestures and points us to that which must now take place. For it must be so that this Michael-garment – this garment of light – will become the waves of the words that are Christ-words, and the Word of Worlds that can transform the Logos of Worlds into the Logos of Humanity.

Therefore let my words to you today be these:

> Springing from Powers of the Sun
> Radiant Spirit-powers, blessing all Worlds!
> For Michael's garment of rays
> You are predestined by Thought Divine.
>
> He, the Christ-messenger, reveals in you –
> Bearing mankind aloft – the sacred Will of Worlds.
> You, the radiant Beings of Ether-worlds
> Bear the Christ-word to man.
>
> Thus shall the Herald of Christ appear
> To the thirstily waiting souls,
> To whom your Word of Light shines forth
> In cosmic age of Spirit-Human.
>
> You, the disciples of Spirit-knowledge,
> Take Michael's Wisdom beckoning,
> Take the Word of Love of the Will of Worlds
> Into your souls' aspiring, actively!

# Notes

## Quotations from Rudolf Steiner

1.  In GA 152
2.  In GA 240
3.  In GA 233a
4.  In GA 214

## Preface

1.  In this book the Michael-verse is depicted in a twofold manner, first as the Michael-*Imagination* when we are considering the eurythmy presentation, and the other time as the Michael-*meditation* when this refers to the inner path of schooling in the Michael-mysteries.
2.  See for this also in S. O. PROKOFIEFF, *The Foundation Stone Meditation; A Key to the Christian Mysteries*, Chap. 6, "The Union of the Rosicrucian and the Michaelic Stream in the Foundation Stone Meditation", Temple Lodge 2006.

## Chapter I
## Three Meditations

1.  See the text of the "Butterfly-meditation" by Rudolf Steiner in GA 265. Esoteric Lesson of 23 October 1923.
2.  Rudolf Steiner gave this meditation to Henriette Maria Wegman, the mother of Ita Wegman for her 73rd birthday. See on this in P. SELG, *Die beseelte Menschen-Sonne: Eine Herzmeditation Rudolf Steiner* [The Ensouled Sun of Man: A Heart Meditation by Rudolf Steiner], Arlesheim, 2011.

3.  This refers to the concluding lecture of the weekend conference on Sunday, 8 May 2011.

4.  See for more detail in S. O. PROKOFIEFF, *Rudolf Steiner and the Founding of the New Mysteries*, Chap. 6, "The Foundation Stone Meditation", Temple Lodge 1994.

5.  Throughout the year 2011 in many locations, the 150th anniversary of the birth of Rudolf Steiner was commemorated in different ways as was his life and work.

## Chapter II
### Rudolf Steiner and his relationship to Michael

1.  See on this in his autobiographical lecture of 4 February 1923 in Berlin, published in *Briefe von Rudolf Steiner* [Letters from Rudolf Steiner], Vol. 1, Dornach 1955, 2nd Edition.

2.  Reference is to a cycle of ten lectures of which the first three were dedicated to these Michaelic motifs in the life of Rudolf Steiner.

3.  For example, before Rudolf Steiner had publically presented the spiritual scientific truths of the three systems of the human physical body in his book, *Riddles of the Soul* (GA 21) for the first time in 1917, he had already worked privately on this book for thirty years, even though as an inner (personal) experience it had stood before his spiritual gaze since 1887.

4.  Lecture of 4 February 1913, published in *Briefe von Rudolf Steiner* [Letters from Rudolf Steiner], Vol. 1, Dornach 1955, 2nd Edition. Likewise the courses about physiology and anatomy that he delivered after taking appropriate elective university coursework belong to this.

5.  Already in his early childhood, and then especially in Vienna, Rudolf Steiner had ample opportunity to become acquainted with the Catholic religion and its theology.

6.  First edition 1901, then 1914 in an enlarged new form published under the title, *The Riddles of Philosophy: Presented in an Outline of its History* (GA 18).

7.  In early lectures Rudolf Steiner named the path into the spiritual world

that he described in this book, "The Christian Rosicrucian Path".

8.     This was the case with Rudolf Steiner in his Weimar period when he went through the development of his own intellectual or mind-soul (28$^{th}$ to 35$^{th}$ year of life).

9.     See the complete text of this description in this book's Appendix.

10.    In his book, *Occult Science, an Outline* (or *Esoteric Science, an Outline*), Rudolf Steiner even writes about two paths into the spiritual world; one by means of the spiritual schooling depicted in *Occult Science, an Outline*, and the other through *The Philosophy of Freedom*. (See GA 13, Chap. "Knowledge of the Higher Worlds".)

11.    Reference to those human beings who, like Rudolf Steiner, are able to behold the spiritual world adjacent to the earth.

12.    That we actually have to do with the Ahrimanic dragon which is connected with today's development of natural science, can also be gathered from the following words in the same lecture: "Michael did not battle the dragon in the age that preceded this one, for then the dragon that is now meant was not yet a dragon. It will become a dragon when those concepts and ideas that are merely natural scientific laws are supposed to be developed into the world view of the coming age. And what tries to rear up its head here is in turn conceived correctly in the picture as the dragon that must be overcome by Michael, whose era begins in our years" (ibid.).

13.    From the preface of the French translation of the book *Christianity as Mystical Fact and the Mysteries of Antiquity* (GA 8), published in German translation in *Beiträge zur Rudolf Steiner Gesamtausgabe*, [Contributions to Rudolf Steiner's Complete Works], No. 42, summer 1973.

14.    Rudolf Steiner describes this illusory region as the "eighth sphere". (See GA 254, 18 October 1915).

15.    What this "jump" signifies in concrete human life as a kind of crowning point of modern Christian initiation, Rudolf Steiner described elsewhere in more detail. See on this in S. O. PROKOFIEFF, *Rudolf Steiner's Path of Initiation and the Mystery of the Ego*, Temple Lodge 2013.

16. Rudolf Steiner introduces the name "Michael-Christ" in his essay, *The Michael-Christ Experience of Man* (GA 26).

17. GA 224, 23 May 1923. It is to the great credit of Peter Selg, who was the first who related these words directly to experiencing the Mystery of Golgotha in Rudolf Steiner's life. (See P. Selg, *Michael als Genius der Zivilisationsentwicklung. Rudolf Steiners Abschied von Berlin. Potsdamer Strasse 39a, 23 Mai 1923* [Michael as the Genius of the Evolution of Civilization. Rudolf Steiner's Farewell from Berlin. Potsdamer Strasse 39a, 23 May 1923], Arlesheim 2013.) From what was said, it follows that in our age only the *purely spiritual* path to the Mystery of Golgotha is justified and in accord with Michael.

18. This remark is necessary here because these words by Rudolf Steiner are again and again put in question by some Anthroposophists either directly or in a surreptitious manner, something by which his moral integrity is massively attacked.

## Chapter III
## The Nature of the Michael-Mystery

1. See regarding this in S. O. Prokofieff, *The East in the Light of the West*, Part III, "The Birth of Christian Esotericism in the Twentieth Century and the Occult Powers that Oppose it", Temple Lodge 2009.

2. See regarding this in the Esoteric Lesson of 1 June 1907 (GA 266/1).

3. Esoteric Lessons of 9, 18 and 23 October, and 5 December 1907 (GA 266/1).

4. How fundamental this interest, this concern, was to the Michael-mysteries since 1913 is made evident by the fact that, within the esoteric school conducted by Rudolf Steiner in its symbolic section, he now no longer speaks (as he did earlier) of a "Misraim-service" but of the "Michael-service" (GA 265, p. 155 and p.170 f.).

5. "What I have only been able to indicate in a few words [concerning the Second Mystery of Golgotha] will gradually penetrate into human souls, and the mediator, the herald, will be Michael who now is the messenger of the Christ" (GA 152, 2 May 1913).

6.  Rudolf Steiner speaks about this basic characteristic of true Rosicrucianism in the following words: "I ask you ... not to accept on authority and faith anything I have ever said or shall say ... I am not concerned. What is stated out of the sources of Rosicrucianism, you can by all means prove" (GA 121, 17 June 1910).

7.  "And thus we behold the spirit Michael ... doing battle for the purity of the spiritual horizon" (GA 174, 3 December 1914). For the etheric return of the Christ can only take place when "the spiritual world work is done, so to speak; in the pure shaping of the approaching, etherically coming Christ who is intended to appear to the human being as an etheric figure. However, for that it is necessary that he, Michael, who moves in front of the Sun-spirit [Christ] faces a battle in the spiritual world" (ibid.).

8.  Or in another lecture, Rudolf Steiner states: "It is Michael who has to prepare the appearance of the Christ as an etheric entity" (GA 174, 14 February 1915).

9.  The actual appearing of the Christ in etheric form has only begun in the middle of the nineteen-thirties of the twentieth century, and this means that during the year 1914 this time still referred to the future. According to Rudolf Steiner, the actual appearing of the Christ in etheric form will still last for three thousand years. (See GA 130, 17 September 1911).

10. See regarding the Michael Culture in GA 194, 30 November 1919.

11. This *Christian* path to the three spirit-members which becomes possible beginning in our time through the connection with the etheric Christ must – because these matters are complicated and manifold – be distinguished from the Luciferic path leading there, which is depicted in the lecture of 9 January 1912 (GA 130).

12. See also GA 93a, 24 October 1905, and GA 94, 29 May 1906. The here mentioned work on the three spiritual members of the human being has its limits, however, within the earth aeon. For the *complete development* of the Spirit-Self, Life-Spirit and Spirit-Human will only become possible in future aeons on Jupiter, Venus and Vulcan. The same point likewise relates to the reference of these three spiritual

members of the human being above in this chapter.

13.  "But he [Michael] appears with the pointed sword through which he indicates the higher human nature" (GA 229, 15 October 1923).

14.  Concerning this, Michael's openness to the world, Rudolf Steiner states: "As a *being*, he moves about *like a world*, only affirming himself inasmuch as he affirms the world, as if guiding forces from out of all cosmic sites down to the earth" (GA 26, 16 November 1924; italics by Rudolf Steiner). These represent part of the description of the Michael-Imagination that Rudolf Steiner places over against the Ahriman-imagination in the same essay. It follows from this that Michael only "affirms the world" when all Ahrimanic elements are excluded.

15.  For more detail on this, see in the lecture cycle, *The Spiritual Backgrounds of the Outer World. The Fall of the Spirits of Darkness* (GA 177).

16.  That the three pre-stages of the Mystery of Golgotha were at the same time the three stages of the Christ's descent from the Sun to the earth is mentioned by Rudolf Steiner in the lecture of 30 March 1914 (GA 152).

17.  See GA 152, and S. O. PROKOFIEFF, *The Appearance of Christ in the Etheric. Spiritual-Scientific Aspects of the Second Coming*, Chap. 1, "The Cosmic Dimension of the Etheric Return of the Christ", Temple Lodge 2012.

18.  See in more detail in S. O. PROKOFIEFF, *Anthroposophy and The Philosophy of Freedom, Anthroposophy and its Method of Cognition. The Christological and Cosmic-Human Dimension of The Philosophy of Freedom*, Temple Lodge 2009.

19.  To this "endurance" ["Geschehen" in German, translated as "enduring"] of mankind in the cosmos likewise belongs the afore-mentioned "pre-stages" of the Mystery of Golgotha. They were carried out for the salvation of humanity by Christ through the Nathan-soul in various localities and during different evolutionary stages of our solar system. Michael too participated in them so that humankind could continue to exist on earth.

20. Rudolf Steiner states in this regard: "He pushed the Luciferic spirits opposing him down to earth." This means that through the casting down of Michael's opposing spirits to earth, the human being was initially pervaded with reason, and with that what corresponds to the human head" (GA 194, 22 November 1919).

21. See in more detail concerning the Nathan Soul in S. O. PROKOFIEFF, *The Cycle of the Year as a Path of Initiation Leading to an Experience of the Christ-Being: An Esoteric Study of the Festivals*, Chap II, "The Advent Mystery as Mystery of the Nathan Soul", Temple Lodge 2014; and on the same subject: "The Humanitarian Task of the Nathan Soul," published in the anthology, *Gemeinschaftsbildung im Lichte Michaels* [*Community Building in the Light of Michael*]. Dornach 2010.

22. Humankind has retained a wondrous imagination of this third Christ event in the picture: "St. George overcomes the Dragon" or "The Archangel Michael overcomes the Dragon" (GA 152, 27 May 1914).

23. See in more detail in S. O. PROKOFIEFF, *The Appearance of Christ in the Etheric. Spiritual-Scientific Aspects of the Second Coming*, Chap. 1, "The Cosmic Dimension of the Etheric Return of the Christ", Temple Lodge 2012.

24. GA 211, 24 April 1922. See on this also in S. O. PROKOFIEFF, *The Twelve Holy Nights and the Spiritual Hierarchies*, Part 1, Chap. 2, "The Starry Script as a Key to Anthroposophical Christology", Temple Lodge 2004.

25. What is said here does not contradict the fact that Michael was also the herald of Yahweh. For in the pre-Christian Sun-Mysteries, Michael was the herald of the Christ, but in the Moon-Mysteries on the other hand, he was the herald of Yahweh. In the first form of his appearance he inspired the birth of man's independent thinking in Greek philosophy; in the second form the Hebrew religion and above all the Old-Testament prophets. Then as the guide of the Ancient Hebrew folk, he had the task of preparing the physical appearance of the Christ through generations on earth.

26.  Rudolf Steiner defines the Heavenly Intelligence as "the mutual rules of demeanour of the higher hierarchies. What they do, how they interact with each other, and how they are with each other – that is Cosmic Intelligence" (GA 237, 8 August 1924).

27.  In the karma lectures, Rudolf Steiner says nothing about a cosmic sacrifice offered up by Michael. The fact that intelligence falls away from him, however, is described there as a universal necessity which stands in a direct relationship to the Mystery of Golgotha since, due to that, Michael himself comes into a completely new connection with Christ. This is why one can assume that it was actually a sacrifice here, due to which Michael allows the most precious subject that he administered from the primal beginning in the cosmos to now sink down into human beings. I think that Rudolf Steiner, in further karma lectures that should have accompanied the founding of the Second Class of the School of Spiritual Science, would also have indicated this aspect of the Michael-Mystery where in doing so Michael's cosmic path of the imitation of Christ would have revealed itself more clearly.

28.  The reason this happened was probably because the demons had not yet been brought to silence at that time, and prior to the Christmas Conference had not allowed Rudolf Steiner directly to express these secrets which are connected with the Michael-Mystery in the cosmos. (See Rudolf Steiner's comments at the end of page 215 above.)

29.  It is also noteworthy that Rudolf Steiner introduces this entire theme along with a review of his book, *The Philosophy of Freedom*. Now, its two main parts precisely reveal the nature of the concepts: intellectuality and freedom. In its first part, *The Science of Freedom*, we deal among others with the transformation of abstract thoughts into pure thinking; on the basis of this in the second part of the book, *The Reality of Freedom*, the nature of free deeds is depicted.

30.  For "Christ [has] moved down to the earth ... from out of those worlds [of the Sun], out of which rationality, intellectuality, and freedom have moved into human life between birth and death" (ibid.).

31. It is just this motif of the connection of the microcosm (of the Spirit in Man) with the macrocosm (of the Spirit in the World) that was already placed as the basic thought into the "building concept" of the First Goetheanum with its two cupolas.

32. Both faculties are in an archetypal manner described in the book, *The Philosophy of Freedom* and brought into a form in which they can then be permeated through Anthroposophy by the Christ-impulse.

33. In the book *Cosmic Memory* (GA 11, Chap. "The Separation of the Genders"), Rudolf Steiner describes that process like this: "The force with which humankind forms a thinking brain is the same force with which the human being fructified itself in ancient times. Thinking is 'dearly acquired' through the unisexual condition."

34. Owing to the separation of the sexes, the human brain originated in humanity and was from the beginning the bastion of Ahriman as the "Lord of Death" in the human body. Even viewed medically, the largest concentration of death-forces in us is contained in the brain.

35. What is stated here does not contradict the fact that the entry of death-forces into humanity's evolution has likewise still deeper reasons. To go into them would lead us beyond the context of this description, but here in the framework of the quoted words by Rudolf Steiner it is only important to show that, as a presupposition of freedom, the death forces had to pervade brain-thinking, and that it was Michael who, as builder of the human form, had already created the possibility for this.

36. In this regard, Rudolf Steiner speaks of "living thinking" that in slightly different terminology is also called "pure" or "sense-free" thinking. (See more on this later in the chapter.)

37. As we have already seen, this spiritual world is the Michael-kingdom on the Sun (from where Christ also descended to the earth). This is why Rudolf Steiner states that the Sun is the cosmic source of freedom on one hand, and on the other that of intellectuality. Regarding freedom, he expresses himself in an almost hymn-like way saying that, "Addressing the Sun, we can feel like this: Oh, thou Cosmic Son of Freedom, I feel thee related to all that in my own

being bestows freedom and the faculty of decision for the future!" (GA 240, 25 January 1924)   Regarding intellectuality, he says concisely: "The Sun is the fount of all that is intellectual" (GA 240, 21 August 1924).   Elsewhere he states, "All human intelligence originates from Michael in the Sun" (GA 237, 8 August 1924).

38.   This relates to the two parts of *The Philosophy of Freedom* that deal with these qualities which likewise cannot be separated from each other.

39.   He characterizes "combining thinking" like this: "The thinking which we are nowadays used to, not just in external life but also in science, surrenders to outer observation [of sense perceptions]; it runs on the 'thread' of outer observation, as it were" (GA 79, 26 November 1921).

40.   Some characteristics of Michaelic thinking can already be traced on the preceding stage of thinking, and above all in *The Philosophy of Freedom*.

41.   In connection with the terminology of *The Philosophy of Freedom*, Rudolf Steiner also mentions this shift from the second to the third kind of thinking like this: "What confronts an individual first only in pure thinking condenses, as it were, to a spiritual reality" (GA 79, 29 November 1921).

42.   In this regard, one must distinguish between sense-free and body-free thinking.   Sense-free thinking only causes a person to be independent of the body's sense impressions, something that is already the case when one deeply ponders something and where, for a short time, one's sense impressions are completely forgotten.   Body-free thinking by contrast guides the soul in full consciousness out of the physical body.   Thereby, one consciously enters on the modern path of inner schooling into the spiritual world.

43.   This statement by no means signifies that the fundamental direction of the later *Philosophy of Freedom* did not indwell Rudolf Steiner's soul much earlier.   Already in 1881 in a letter to a friend during his youth, he wrote about his project of penning a "philosophy on freedom", namely in connection with the philosophical works of Schiller (GA 38, 1st Letter of 27 July 1881).   This affirms that already

at age twenty he was far advanced on his path of pure thinking.

44. "That personality [the Master] ... actually made use of Fichte's works in order to connect with it certain considerations from which particular insights resulted. In these works, the seeds for 'spiritual science' could be found that the man who the youth becomes ... wrote later on" (Lecture of 4 February 1913 in *Briefe von Rudolf Steiner* [Letters from Rudolf Steiner], Vol. 1, Dornach 1955, 2nd Edition).

45. See GA 233a, 13 January 1924. What the gods entrusted to Rudolf Steiner, he once again returned back to them on the same pathway, meaning from the level of the third kind of thinking back to the second and further to the first, back to human beings. Thereby, spiritual scientific contents could become accessible to contemporary humanity.

46. Rudolf Steiner mentions the spirituality that is contained in modern natural science in various passages of his work, its one-sided materialistic direction notwithstanding, for example in the following words: "According to its character, this newer age is really extraordinarily spiritual. A greater number of spiritual concepts and spiritual perceptions than those that had been brought to the surface through recent natural science have never before existed in humanity's evolution ... One can utilize them in the way they are used by academic science today. Now, there [in natural science] they are spiritual, yet when they are only applied to the external material world their spirituality is denied. One can, however, apply these natural scientific concepts in such a way that they can also serve as meditation-substance by meditating about them. Then they lead most surely into the spiritual world" (GA 174, 24 February 1918). Later, Rudolf Steiner formulates this thought in a still more concisely meaningful manner: "But while the consideration of this epoch [of the so-called newer age] had to be limited to the external physical world, there unfolded in the inner essence of the human soul a *purified, self-subsisting spirituality* of the human being as an experience" (GA 26, *The Condition of the Human Soul before the Dawn of the Michael Age*; italics by Rudolf Steiner.)

47. See Chapter 2.

48. "One can, however, likewise apply these natural scientific concepts in such a way [that instead of one 'only ... directing them to the external material world'] they can also serve as substance for meditation, so that then one meditates on them. They then lead most surely into the spiritual world" (GA 174, 24 February 1918).

49. GA 26, *The Condition of the Human Soul before the Dawn of the Michael Age*; italics by Rudolf Steiner.

50. As we already saw, pure thinking already represents the transition to the third kind of thinking.

51. GA 26, *Michael's Mission in the Cosmic Age of Human Freedom*.

52. GA 26, *The Experience of Michael in the course of his Cosmic Mission*.

53. The people referred to here who still think their freedom could be curtailed because they owe this independence to the Christ, are persons who have as yet not entered upon the described path, or put differently, have remained caught up in its very beginnings.

54. See more details in S. O. PROKOFIEFF, *Anthroposophy and The Philosophy of Freedom, The Christological and Cosmic-Human Dimension of 'The Philosophy of Freedom'*, Chap. 9, "Metaphysical Foundations of the Unconditionality of *The Philosophy of Freedom*", Temple Lodge 2009.

55. With these six lines, Rudolf Steiner has concluded the fourth part of the Foundation Stone Verse on 1 January 1924.

56. In the Letter to the Galatians by Paul, it says verbatim: "I live but, now no longer "I", but Christ lives in me" (2: 20).

57. In his lectures concerning the "eighth sphere" or the sphere of evil, Rudolf Steiner describes the joint struggle by Lucifer and Ahriman against human freedom in an impressive way. Among other points he says: "Now, Lucifer and Ahriman however have the desire to drag man's free will into their eighth sphere, but not to allow anything in their sphere that stems from free human will" (GA 254, 18 October 1915).

58. "Such individuals behold how a human being in freedom passes through the image of Michael in Ahriman's sphere, and is to be guided away from Ahriman to the Christ" (GA 26, *The Experience of*

*Michael in the course of his Cosmic Mission*). A person can only take with him the image of Michael, for in that case his/her inner freedom remains fully intact.

59.  See in more detail in S. O. PROKOFIEFF, *Das Rätsel des menschlichen Ich. Eine anthroposophische Betrachtung* [The Riddle of the Human Ego. An Anthroposophical Consideration], Dornach 2013, 2nd Edition. That human freedom is likewise connected with the nature of the "I" in an existential way, results moreover from the following statement by Rudolf Steiner: "What is 'free' can proceed only from out of the 'I' [the ego]" (GA 26, *Michael's Mission in the Cosmic Age of Human Freedom*.

60.  In the book *A Way of Self-Knowledge*, these four stages are summed up as follows:

   I.   *The Physical Body in the Physical-Sensory Surrounding World.* Through it, the human being recognizes him or herself as an independent individual ("I") ...

   II.  *The Delicate Etheric Body in the Elemental Surrounding World.* Through it, the human being recognizes him or herself as a member of the earth-body ...

   III. *The Astral Body in a Spiritual Surrounding World.* Through it, the human being is a member of a spiritual world. In this "body" the "other I" of man is contained that brings itself to expression in repeated earth-lives ...

   IV.  *The 'true I' in a Supra-Spiritual World.* Through it, the human being finds him or herself as a spiritual being ...
       (GA 17; italics by Rudolf Steiner).

61.  This is why Goethe, who fully understood this second stage of thinking, authored his *Metamorphosis of the Plant* not in prose but in verse-form.

62.  Concerning the full clarity of the nature of occult time that he had already attained during his youth, Rudolf Steiner wrote, looking back on it later: "At this time [around age eighteen] full clarity was attained concerning the perception of time ... It was the insight that there exists another stream of time that along with the forward-moving

evolution moves backwards – the occult-astral stream of time. This insight is the condition for spiritual beholding" (GA 262, Manuscript of Barr-I).

63. See on this also in S. O. PROKOFIEFF, *The Mystery of the Resurrection in the Light of Anthroposophy*, Chap. II, "Easter, Ascension, and Whitsun in the Light of Anthroposophy", Temple Lodge 2010.

64. See GA 13, Chap. "World Evolution and Man".

65. This withdrawal in four stages of the hierarchies out of the cosmos is depicted in Rudolf Steiner's article *The Activity of Michael and the Future of Mankind* (GA 26, 25 October 1924).

66. See GA 121, 11 June 1910. This is why, in his *Fairytale of the Green Snake and the Beautiful Lily*, Goethe designated it as the mysterious fourth power.

67. This image of the bridge is likewise contained as a result of the snake's offering in Goethe's Fairytale.

68. For Rudolf Steiner, the terminology, "Rosicrucian-path", refers to the anthroposophical path of inner schooling that is depicted above all in his books, *Knowledge of the Higher Worlds and Its Attainment* (GA 10), and *Occult Science, an Outline* (GA 13).

69. See about this new relationship to Christ that is feasible today through occupying oneself with Anthroposophy in GA 175, 6 February 1917.

70. It was around the year 1413 AD that the present epoch of the consciousness-soul had begun.

71. Rudolf Steiner speaks of Anthroposophy as a "gift from Michael" in GA 152, 2 May 1913.

72. In recent attacks against Anthroposophy and the personality of Rudolf Steiner, one can clearly recognize traces of such an Ahrimanic possession.

73. See on the incarnation of Ahriman in GA 193, 27 October 1919 and 1 January 1919.

74. Rudolf Steiner speaks of the fact that the entire second half of earth evolution will be under the predominant influence of Ahriman and his hordes (see GA 193, 27 October 1919 and 4 November 1919).

75. This is why Rudolf Steiner mentions in some passages of his work that Sorat himself has an Ahrimanic character (see GA 184, 11 October 1918). However, considered from a cosmic aspect there exists on the other hand a decisive difference. According to his origin, Ahriman belongs to the evolution of humanity. He remained behind on the Old Sun and even had a positive task there. When he moves, however, beyond the limitations of that task, he turns into an opponent for human beings. An example is when he brings it about that the human intelligence becomes evil. Sorat, by contrast, never had a positive task in humanity's evolution. As to his origin, he does not belong to it. He only represents evil and from the beginning is not only the opponent of man but even the cosmic opponent of the Christ. He is only interested in the destruction of the earth and humankind because Christ united with both. (See on this in GA 104, 29 June 1908.)

76. See further on these themes in S. O. PROKOFIEFF, *And the Earth becomes a Sun. The Mystery of the Resurrection*, Chap. 6, "The Cosmic Destiny of Evil", Wynstones Press 2014.

77. John the Evangelist likewise points to this ominous role of corrupted reason or misguided human intelligence respectively with his comment concerning the necessity to think with its capabilities about the number of the "beast", which at the same time is a human being's number, for it indicates the human being "who has allowed him or herself to be seduced" (ibid.). It is formulated in the Apocalypse as follows: "Here is wisdom. He who has reason let him who has understanding reckon the number of the beast, for it is a human number" (13:18).

78. See on this "Cosmic-will" in the text of the Michael-Imagination in Chap. 4 of this book.

79. See previous annotation.

80. In the lecture of 29 August 1923 (GA 227), Rudolf Steiner links the activity of the hierarchies with the cosmos in such a way that the Third Hierarchy is chiefly effective out of the Moon-sphere, which moreover encompasses the sphere of Mercury and Venus. The

Second Hierarchy is above all active out of the Sun-sphere which also includes the realms of the planets "above the Sun"; and the First Hierarchy unfolds its main activity from the starry world all the way down to the Saturn-sphere. (See also GA 110, 15 April 1909-II.)

81. The previous event of this kind occurred in the Atlantean Age, when the entities of the First Hierarchy transposed the cosmic intelligence out of the domain of the limbs of the physical body into the realm of the heart (see ibid.). A still earlier corresponding happening took place during the Lemurian time when the the human being received its "I" from the higher hierarchies, the Elohim (Spirits of Form). It was then that cosmic intelligence was guided from beyond the human cosmos by the entities of the First Hierarchy into the metabolic and limb system of humankind so that the proper preparation for the then following bestowal of his/her "I" could take place.

82. We must clearly distinguish between the above-described permeation of the human being with cosmic intelligence through the First Hierarchy and the intelligence coming from the kingdom of Michael that was subject to his administering. For the First Hierarchy had the task of transforming the human being three times all the way into the three systems of his/her physical body. (Only the First Hierarchy has the power to transform the material-physical out of the spiritual dimension.) The Michaelic intelligence on the other hand – that reached human beings on earth around the 8th until the 9th century – did not have the task to change human existence but above all human consciousness, so that they could attain to the experience of freedom.

83. GA 26, *Michael's Mission in the Cosmic Age of Human Freedom*.

84. Rudolf Steiner thus says in this regard: "And this is to begin in our age; it is supposed to be a guidance of Christendom into deeper truths; an explanation for the Christ in as much as He is to find His way into mankind in a living way through ... the Sun-spirit – Michael" (GA 240, 21 August 1924).

85. Concerning the relationship of the Christ-deed with the fall into sin, meaning the cessation of the latter's consequences, Rudolf Steiner speaks in GA 143, 17 December 1912.

86. See in this regard lectures by Rudolf Steiner concerning the intellectual fall into sin in the book, *Living Cognition of Nature, Intellectual and Spiritual Fall into Sin* (GA 220).

87. Michael could do this primarily because his Archai-nature meant that he experienced his "I" at the Spirit-Human [level] and was thereby especially linked with the Spirit-Human principle.

88. See in S. O. PROKOFIEFF: *The Mystery of John the Baptist and John the Evangelist at the Turning Point of Time. An Esoteric Study*, Temple Lodge 2005.

89. As the individual who was the first to discover and express the conformities with human thinking, which at that time still came from the Sun, Aristotle was particularly connected with Michael.

90. Rudolf Steiner formulates it like this: "I should like to say that the loosening, the freeing, of earthly intelligence from cosmic intelligence was contained in Aristotelianism" (GA 240, 19 July 1924). This meant that as the result of the Mystery of Golgotha, there was already prepared on earth during the fourth century BC, through this deed on Aristotle's part, what later took place in the Sun-kingdom of Michael when cosmic intelligence – which had been administered by Michael – took the Christ-path and descended to earth. Then, beginning from the 8th to the 9th century, the cosmic intelligence was gradually to become human intelligence.

91. At this point, Rudolf Steiner could even agree with an opinion by Kant in this regard: "In fact the founding of the technique of thinking was so significantly developed by Aristotle that Kant stated, and rightfully so, that logic actually had not progressed by one sentence since Aristotle's time. And basically, his logic is still valid for today" (GA 35, *Philosophy and Anthroposophy*, 17 August 1908).

92. The participation of all three kinds of entities of the Third Hierarchy in the Michael-School is spoken of by Rudolf Steiner in the lecture of 27 August 1924 (GA 240). In reference to the cosmic cultus on the other hand, he also mentions the participation of "the entities of the hierarchies" (GA 238, 16 September 1924). And in a somewhat earlier lecture he states in the same context that the "mighty, majestic,

cosmic imaginations of the supersensible cultus were woven by human souls together with the spirits of *the upper hierarchies* who were participating in the cosmic cultus" (GA 237, 6 July 1924).

93. Concerning the active participation of human souls in the supersensible cultus, Rudolf Steiner mentions the fact that they were all together there in the spiritual world "in order to carry out a super-earthly ritual [cultus] in which, by means of actual and mighty imaginations, there was depicted what in a spiritual sense was to be established again in the new Christendom of the twentieth century on the earth" (GA 240, 19 July 1924). This means that it was human souls themselves who, together with hierarchical beings, carried out this cultus.

94. To affirm at this point here how this process is connected with the secret of the resurrection-body of the Christ would go beyond the scope of this consideration.

95. *Goethe's Complete Works*, Vol. 9, Zürich 1949.

96. Rudolf Steiner moreover states the following about the supersensible cultus itself: "The souls were united there – just as they are now united here in human bodies on earth – in order for them to fit together (out of what I would like to call cosmic substantiality and cosmic forces) what in mighty pictures had cosmic significance and what was the first sounding forth of what is to take its course here now as teaching, as *anthroposophical deed* on earth" (GA 240, 18 July 1924).

97. See in more detail in S. O. PROKOFIEFF, *Rudolf Steiner's Sculptural Group. A Revelation of the Spiritual Purpose of Humanity and the Earth.* Chap. 1, "On the Pre-History of the Sculptural Group", Temple Lodge 2013.

98. At that time Rudolf Steiner still used the designation "Theosophists".

99. See more details on this in S. O. PROKOFIEFF, *The Esoteric Significance of Spiritual Work in Anthroposophical Groups*, Chap. 4, "The Threefold Source of Karma", Temple Lodge 2007.

100. See in S. O. PROKOFIEFF, *Rudolf Steiner and the Founding of the New Mysteries*, Part III, "Anthroposophy – the World-Whitsun-Message",

Temple Lodge 1994, and *Wie stehen wir heute vor Rudolf Steiner?* [How Do We Face Rudolf Steiner Today?], Arlesheim 2012.

101. What was said does not contradict the fact that Rudolf Steiner could research all contents of Anthroposophy himself in the spiritual world. For even the contents of the Michael-school had to be rediscovered by him in this manner. Moreover, the translation of these purely spiritual contents into earthly words was Rudolf Steiner's unique accomplishment.

102. In the last preface that Rudolf Steiner wrote only eleven weeks prior to his death, he writes literally: "The book indeed contains the outlines of Anthroposophy as a totality ... All that I myself have been able to say appears as a further explanation of the original sketch when fitted into this book in the correct place" (GA 13).

103. Quoted from T. Meyer, *Ludwig Polzer-Hoditz. A European,* Annotation VI, "Conversations with Rudolf Steiner", Temple Lodge 2014.

104. For the first lecture on Nietzsche, Rudolf Steiner was invited to speak at Count Brockdorff's home on a theme that had previously been requested.

105. The gradual "incarnation" of Anthroposophy on earth corresponds to the fourth stage of its cosmic-telluric development as described above.

106. Concerning this, Rudolf Steiner reports, "Now, what does the main activity of the Ahrimanic spirits consist in as regards their battling against the coming Michael-age? The chief means they use are that, during occasions when the consciousness of human beings is dampened down, they cause our minds to become possessed by them, as it were; they interfere in human consciousness" (GA 240, 20 July, 1924). And this possession can at times even lead to a temporary incorporation of Ahrimanic spirits in human sheaths. "Incarnation is not possible for them but temporary incorporation, temporary permeation of individual human beings is possible. Then the brilliant, dazzling, superior spirit of an Ahrimanic intelligence is stronger than what exists in some individual human beings; it is much much stronger" (GA 237, 4 August 1924).

107. See in this regard the book by Louis M. J. Werbeck, *Die wissenschaftlichen Gegner Rudolf Steiners und der Anthroposophie durch sie selbst widerlegt* [The Opponents of Rudolf Steiner and Anthroposophy, refuted by themselves], re-print of the first edition of 1924, Wallisellen 2003, and the book by Karl Heyer, *Wie man gegen Rudolf Steiner kämpft: Materialien und Gesichtspunkte zum sachgemäßen Umgang mit Gegnern Rudolf Steiners und der Anthroposophie* [How Rudolf Steiner is Opposed. Materials and Viewpoints for a Factual Handling of Rudolf Steiner's and Anthroposophy's Opponents], Perseus Verlag, Basel 2008, 3rd edition.

108. A further detailed and considered example for this from modern times can be found in the two parts of the article by S. O. Prokofieff, *Ein Buch und seiner Hintergründe* [A Book and Its Backgrounds], published in "Nachrichten für Mitglieder" ["News for Members"], No. 45 and 46, 2007.

109. That such a transformation of evil into good belongs to the mighty actions of the true spiritual Masters, is described by Rudolf Steiner as follows: "The Masters are not a protective wall against evil but rather a protective wall for the leaders in the absorption of evil. We are not supposed to eliminate evil; rather we are to *confront and engage evil* and then utilize it in the sphere of the good" (GA 264, page 188 in the German edition).

110. See in more detail in S. O. Prokofieff, *May Human Beings Hear It! The Mystery of the Christmas Conference*, Chap. 5, "The Esoteric Archetype of the Original Council", Temple Lodge 2014.

111. When Theophrast's teacher had to leave Athens, not of his own free will, he passed this task on to Theophrast which he fulfilled by continuing the Lyceum. It is also said that during the following years Theophrast authored almost as many works as had his teacher. But almost none of these works reached posterity. After Aristotle left Athens, Theophrast fully finished construction of the Lyceum and decorated it with busts of his teacher. The actual name of Theophrast was "Tirtam". He received the name "Theophrast" – meaning "one who speaks divinely" – because he had a most unique gift for languages

from Aristotle himself. (See on this in: DIOGENES LAERTOS, *Über Leben und Meinungen berühmter Philosophen* [*Concerning the Life and Opinions of Famous Philosophers*], Book V, Chap. 2, "Theophrast").

112. This appeal was written in 1942, hence at that time "twenty years" after the First Goetheanum's fire. Quote from MARIE STEINER, *Briefe und Dokumente, vornehmlich aus ihrem letzten Lebensjahr* [*Letters and Documents, Mainly from the Last Year of Her Life*], Dornach 1981; italics by Marie Steiner.

113. ITA WEGMAN, *An die Freunde* [To the Friends], Article: "In Erinnerung an die Weihnachtstagung" ["In Memory of the Christmas Conference"], 26 April 1925, Arlesheim 1986, 3rd Edition.

114. Although Rudolf Steiner speaks in this connection repeatedly in a number of passages of the "spiritual powers" in plural form (this occurs furthermore similarly in the Class Lessons), in doing so he is nevertheless referring to Michael and the spiritual beings serving him. This is proven by Rudolf Steiner in the following words: "Viewed in the supersensible realm, matters stand like this: All the spiritual powers that one can designate with the name Michael administer the ideas in the spiritual cosmos" (GA 26, *The Condition of the Human Soul Before the Dawn of the Michael Age*).

115. "One may say that unceasingly since the founding of the Anthroposophical Society at the Goetheanum, those spiritual powers from whom we have received our revelations look down upon us with a still greater benevolence than was the case earlier, so that in this direction already for sometime a heavy weight could be lifted from the Anthroposophical Society" (GA 260a, 12 August 1924).

116. "Now it can actually be stated ..., that it is not only since the Christmas Conference that revelations out of the spiritual world are no longer held back, but that on the contrary the spiritual world looks down on what takes place through the anthroposophical movement in the Anthroposophical Society with much greater benevolence than was earlier the case, and that the gifts since this Christmas Conference have essentially become more abundant" (GA 260a, 24 August 1924).

117. ITA WEGMAN, *An die Freunde* [To the Friends], Article of 17 June 1925, Arlesheim 1986, 3rd Edition.

118. Rudolf Steiner describes it like this: "Our karmic account will be balanced in the future – meaning that it will be placed into the cosmic or world order in future times when we will have found the path to Christ – in such a way that the settlement of it will call forth the greatest possible human benefit for the remainder of earth-evolution – that will be the concern of Him who beginning in our time becomes the 'Lord of Karma' – that will be the concern of the Christ" (GA 130, 2 December 1911).

119. About the nature and significance of unselfishness in the present time and in anthroposophical contexts, see PETER SELG, *Die Kultur der Selbstlosigkeit. Rudolf Steiner, Das Fuenfte Evangelium und das Zeitalter der Extreme* [The Culture of Selflessness. Rudolf Steiner, The Fifth Gospel and the Age of the Extremes], Dornach 2006.

120. See concerning the Sun and Moon-karma in GA 240, 25 January 1924. The difference existing in them must be understood to mean that the Sun-karma is what pertains to the future. On the objective foundation of this a new "karma community" can come into being; a community that Rudolf Steiner moreover calls "the foundation that is built on the 'I'-nature of humankind in the future" (GA 123, 11 September 1910). Moon-karma on the other hand is what produces the personal hindrances from the past, on the inner journey. These hindrances have a "separating" affect between human beings and must be overcome in the course of the further ongoing evolution. In the same lecture, Rudolf Steiner furthermore describes the new karma community established on the Sun-karma in the following words: "Due to the fact that the threads pertaining to the individuals are woven into the karma of the entire Society, a kind of web is spun. And through what the Christ has brought down out of spiritual heights, this net is supposed to be a replica of the order in the heavens through its characteristics. This means that in accordance with the order in the spiritual world, the karma of an individual is to be linked with the totality of karma, not in any arbitrary way but in such a way that the

entire organism may become a replica of the order in heaven" (ibid.). Rudolf Steiner therefore says later on in the karma lectures that one cannot enter into the "Michael-community" – this is what he calls the Anthroposophical Society after the Christmas Conference – unless that decision by the individual to become a member is "completely sincere and deeply takes hold of the entire human soul and affects the person's destiny *in the most essential way*" (GA 237, 3 August 1924).

121. The fact that such a transposition from what is beheld in the astral light into the earthly thought element – and with that becomes accessible to all human beings – belonged among the most important tasks for Rudolf Steiner, this is a matter that in a conversation with Maria Roeschl was later on recounted in Ernst Lehrs's autobiography as follows: "Maria Roeschl once asked Rudolf Steiner whether there existed initiates during his age who were capable of beholding spiritual truths as high and wide as he was able to do. His reply, so she told me later, was that indeed there existed such individuals, but none who could clothe what they had beheld into the form of thoughts that would make it possible for other persons to trace [such thoughts] in their own mind. For that required taking what was spiritually beheld all the way into one's brain, and this was a sacrifice that no other person could offer up." E. LEHRS, *Gelebte Erwartung* [Lived Expectation], Chap. "Hellsehen und Geistesforschung" ["Clairvoyance and Spirit Research"], Stuttgart 1979.

122. The attentive reader will notice from this passage that likewise in regard to the contents of the supersensible Michael-School, Rudolf Steiner speaks of "world secrets" which were likewise considered there by Michael. (See the words by Rudolf Steiner on pages 19-20).

123. See for this the text of the Foundation Stone Laying (GA 260, 25 December 1923) as well as S. O. PROKOFIEFF: *May Human Beings Hear It! The Mystery of the Christmas Conference.* Chapter "The Mystery Act of the Foundation Stone Laying of 25 December 1923", Temple Lodge 2014.

124. ERNST LEHRS, *Gelebte Erwartung* [Lived Expectation], Chap. XXI, Stuttgart 1979; italics by E. Lehrs.

125. Only a few days prior to his death, Rudolf Steiner asked for the production of the first outlines for the sculptural work on the interior shapes of the Second Goetheanum.
126. From Ita Wegman's notebook, quoted in accordance with her, *Erinnerung an Rudolf Steiner* [*Recollections of Rudolf Steiner*], Chap. 3, published by Peter Selg, Arlesheim 2009; italics by Ita Wegman.
127. GA 26, *The Experiences of Michael in the course of his Cosmic Mission*.
128. Concerning this designation, see *Epilogue* in this book.

## Chapter IV
## The Michael-Imagination as a Revelation of the Michael-Mystery

1.   See likewise on this in S. O. PROKOFIEFF: *The Esoteric Significance of Spiritual Work in Anthroposophical Groups and the future of the Anthroposophical Society*, Chap. 8, "The New Group Souls", Temple Lodge 2007.

2.   It is not without significance that in the same lecture Rudolf Steiner moreover speaks of the "unbreakable agreement" between Platonists and Aristotelians in the spiritual world in regard to the end of the twentieth century.

3.   Likewise in the esoteric instructions of the Class Lessons, Rudolf Steiner speaks again and again of these spiritual "Powers" who guide the entirety.

4.   GA 26, *The Condition of the Human Soul Before the Dawn of the Michael Age*.

5.   Concerning the relationship of the Angels to Michael and to the "cosmic intelligence" administered by him, see also GA 237, 8 August 1924.

6.   This reality stands as a primal image behind the imagination of the twelve Bodhisattvas in the Buddhi-sphere (see on this in GA 116, 25 October 1919). And behind each of them stands an Archangel (see GA 110, 16 April 1909-II). Within the Third Hierarchy, the Archangels are above all connected with the Christ (the Archai with the Father, and the Angels with the Holy Spirit).

7. See regarding this in GA 211, 24 April 1922. Even the sequence "word of Christ", "Shining-word" and "Love-word" reveals among others the secret of the threefold Sun, out of which Christ works as Sun-word.

8. See the variation of the Foundation Stone Meditation published in Rudolf Steiner's time in 260a, 13 January 1924.

9. See GA 227, 29 August 1923. They are moreover the original "owners" of the substance of "Cosmic Intelligence" that have already three times been guided by the First Hierarchy into human beings on earth. (See on this in Chap. 3).

10. See on this the lecture cycle, *Genesis: Secrets of Creation* (GA 122).

11. See GA 13.

12. GA 260a, 13 January 1924.

13. Rudolf Steiner speaks of Anthroposophy as "initiation science", for example in GA 187, 28 December 1918.

14. For this reason, Rudolf Steiner speaks in his early lectures of the Anthroposophical-Rosicrucian initiation as the one that is linked with the will of the human being – not directly but rather through the mediation of the Spirit (See GA 131, 5 October 1911). He describes the will as follows: "This initiation counts chiefly on the strengthening, the empowering, of the inner will ... Thus, Rosicrucian schooling is directed towards the development of the will" (GA 97, 30 November 1906). And in the *Michael-Letters*, Rudolf Steiner points in the same way to Michael who, out of the spiritual world, stimulates the contemporary path of inner discipline, or schooling: "It is Michael's task to guide human beings back again once more on paths of will to where we as human beings have come down from, when with our earthly consciousness we descended on paths of thinking from the living experience of the supersensible to the experience of the sensory world" (GA 26, Leading Thought 105).

15. The fact that these two lines relate to human will and karma at the same time does not represent a contradiction. For karma always works through the will, be it in the human being or in the universe. This is why the entire karma of our solar system begins on Ancient Saturn with the "Act of Creation" by the Spirits of the Will (Thrones).

16. See GA 131, 11 and 12 October 1911.

17. This third stage corresponded at the Turning Point of Time to the Event of Whitsun on the fiftieth day following the Resurrection.

18. According to Rudolf Steiner, the age of the etheric second coming will last for three thousand years (see GA 130 and GA 118).

19. Rudolf Steiner speaks of 1930 until 1935 as the time when the etheric appearance of the Christ begins for all of humankind (see GA 118).

20. To attain the Christ-comprehension in the way Rudolf Steiner represented it all his life in Anthroposophy, is simply impossible to attain without its being infused with Christ-consciousness.

21. In this book Rudolf Steiner writes furthermore of those Angeloi who did not accept the Christ-impulse into themselves after the conclusion of their guidance in the Egyptian-Chaldean epoch, and have therefore presently become the inspirers of contemporary materialism.

22. GA 26, *The Activity of Michael and the Future of Mankind*; italics by Rudolf Steiner.

23. GA 26, *At the Dawn of the Michael Age*; italics by Rudolf Steiner.

24. Rudolf Steiner likewise calls this "heart-thinking" the "logic of the heart", and states that everything he has ever researched in the spiritual world was attained through making use of this quality of thinking (GA 119, 29 and 30 March 1910).

25. During the earth aeon, human beings will not yet fully attain to Spirit-Self. Nor will they attain to the other two still higher Spirit-members. Rather they will receive them as if prophetically; as a gift from on high, not as a part of their own "I". The latter will occur only during the future conditions of Jupiter, Venus and Vulcan – normally called New Jupiter, New Venus and Vulcan in anthroposophical literature.

26. GA 26, *The Condition of the Human Soul Before the Dawn of the Michael Age*; italics by Rudolf Steiner.

27. See in more detail in S. O. PROKOFIEFF, *The Esoteric Nature of the Anthroposophical Society*, Wynstones Press 2014.

28. In 1909, Rudolf Steiner still used the term, "Theosophists".

29. See on this in GA 93a, 24 October 1905 and GA 94, 28 October 1906.

30. See more on the first human Manu in GA 93, 11 November 1904.

31. This characteristic of Michael corresponds exactly to what Rudolf Steiner states in his lecture of 28 December 1918 concerning the Spirits of Personality (Archai), who are beginning "today" to ready themselves for becoming the new creators in earth's evolution. They no longer give revelations to human beings, as the Spirits of Form did earlier. The Spirits of Personality wait until the Spirits of Form bring towards them the fruits of their own free spiritual work in the form of new imaginations that are self-created, to which they reply with their inspirations and intuitions which subsequently are bestowed on human beings.

32. Here, it must be recalled once more that our approach to Michael in the spiritual world is possible for human beings in three ways: through initiation, after death, or during sleep.

33. Concerning the imagination of Michael's hands, see in the Epilogue.

34. GA 26, *The Experiences of Michael in the course of his Cosmic Mission.*

35. See in more detail in Chap. 3 and GA 233a, 13 January 1924.

36. GA 26, *At the Dawn of the Michael Age.*

37. We are not talking about some arbitrary spiritual streams, but only those streams that are connected with Michael and that have passed through his supersensible school and the cosmic cultus. Concerning these streams, Rudolf Steiner speaks above all in the lecture of 21 August 1924 (GA 240); to them belong also the Rosicrucian stream, the stream of true Manicaeism, as well as the Platonic and Aristotelian streams. This is what Rudolf Steiner refers to in the following words: "Only because such a spirituality like the one that flows through the anthroposophical movement unites itself with other spiritual streams, will Michael find those impulses that will unite him once again with the intelligence that has become earthly, yet actually belongs to him" (GA 237, 28 July 1924). It is almost superfluous to mention here that these words by the spirit-teacher are completely misunderstood if one links them with something other than what originates in the great Michael-stream in the spiritual world.

38. It is not difficult to recognize in this duality of love and light the two parts of *The Philosophy of Freedom* (GA 4) in which the path to thinking's light of cognition and to action out of love of the object are quite accurately depicted. In the second edition of the book (1918) in the addition to Chap. 10, Rudolf Steiner even mentions the "power of love in the spiritual sense".

39. It becomes clear from the shorthand notes that in *The Last Address* Rudolf Steiner always pronounced the name "Michael" as "Mee-ka-el" ("Mi-ka-el" in German).

40. Compare the two versions of the Foundation Stone Meditation in GA 260, 25 December 1923, and in GA 260a, 13 January 1924.

41. What is being referred to here is principally the connection to the contents and impulses of the supersensible Michael-School and the cosmic cultus, something that is possible through Anthroposophy.

42. The principle of Spirit-Human is connected chiefly with the will and physical body of the human being.

43. See the introductory words for the Michael-Imagination in *The Last Address* on page 146 above.

## Chapter V
## The Michael-Imagination in Eurythmy and its Esoteric Backgrounds

1. See in more detail in S. O. PROKOFIEFF, *Eurythmie als christliche Kunst. Vom Ursprungsimpuls und Wesen des Eurythmischen* [*Eurythmy as Christian Art. Concerning the Original Impulse and Nature of the Eurythmic Element*], Article: "Eurythmie. Ein kosmischer Impuls durch Rudolf Steiner" ["Eurythmy. A cosmic Impulse through Rudolf Steiner"], published in the Collected Works: Günther von Negelein (Publ.), Dornach 2007.

2. She replied verbatim: "I believe one could dance anything that one feels". M. WOLOSCHIN, *Die grüne Schlange. Lebenserinnerungen* [The Green Snake. Recollections], Chap. "Der Lehrling" ["The Apprentice"], Stuttgart 2009, 8th Edition.

3. The Foundation Stone Meditation was presented for the first time

on 20 April 1924 in the Carpentry Hall and repeated on 22 April. In regard to eurythmy, Rudolf Steiner stated in his introductory words on this occasion that with this "what has begun at Christmas [during the Christmas Conference] has been advanced by one step".

4.  The conversation took place at Christmas time 1919 in Stuttgart. Quoted from the collective volume; *Zur religiösen Erziehung. Wortlaute Rudolf Steiners als Arbeitsmaterial für Waldorfpädagogen* [*Religious Education. Verbatim Quotes by Rudolf Steiner as Working Material for Waldorf School Teachers*], Stuttgart 1997; in this book: HERBERT HAHN: *Vom Entstehen des freien christlichen Religionsunterrichts in der Waldorfschule und vom Einrichten der Sonntagshandlungen* [*Concerning the Origination of the Free Christian Religious Instructions and the Establishment of Sunday Ceremonies*].

5.  Rudolf Steiner reports in this regard: "While it may still seem astounding, today, it is nevertheless true that occasionally when people sit together and can't find their way out of a problem one way or another; and even when a large number of people meet and wait for something to take place, that they will then behold the etheric Christ! He will actually be there, will help in giving advice and join in having His say in whatever problem the crowd faces. We shall definitely encounter such occasions" (GA 130, 1 October 1911).

6.  See more detail about the Foundation Stone Meditation and eurythmy in S. O. PROKOFIEFF, *May Human Beings Hear It! The Mystery of the Christmas Conference*, Chap. 4, "The Foundation Stone Meditation in Eurythmy. An Esoteric Contemplation", Temple Lodge 2014, and S. O. PROKOFIEFF, *The Foundation Stone Meditation. A Key to the Christian Mysteries*, Chap. 9, "The Foundation Stone Meditation in Eurythmy and the Mystery of the Two Jesus Children", Temple Lodge 2006.

7.  In other deliberations on the eurythmic presentation of the Michael-Imagination, the attention of the reader is above all directed to the eurythmy forms given by Rudolf Steiner, their artistic forms, the inner relationships and connections of certain elements. The attempt is made to bring about an interconnection with the

Meditation's text that expresses these forms. It goes without saying that from the aspect of the professional eurythmist many other discoveries are made, but this must be left to eurythmists. I very much hope that the content of this chapter will elicit and promote further impulses on the part of experienced eurythmists for this unique work of art by Rudolf Steiner.

8.   All space-related indications are to be considered as being viewed by the audience.

9.   The "H" sound is especially linked with the creation of the human being. It says for example in Genesis 2, verse 7: "... the LORD GOD ... breathed into his nostrils the breath of life, and thus man became a living soul".

10.  The primal cosmic image for this is represented by the Seraphim who since the beginning of Ancient Saturn permeate its entire sphere with their enthusiasm. (See for this GA 233a, 4 January 1924).

11.  Rudolf Steiner speaks about this entry of the Michael-power into the hearts of human beings in many different passages, for example in the following words: "In earlier times, human beings close to Michael beheld this Archangel unfolding his activity in the spirit-realm; now they realize that they should allow Michael to live in their hearts; they now dedicate their thought-borne spiritual life to him; now they allow Michael to instruct them in their free and individual thought-life about what the proper directions are for the human soul" (GA 26, *At the Dawn of the Michael Age*). In the prelude, the straight lines performed by the five eurythmists demonstrate the "*thought-borne spiritual life*" of the human beings close to Michael who dedicate this life voluntarily to him. In the ongoing text of the meditation, there is made clear what instructions they subsequently receive from Michael.

12.  It is a matter of "turning around" in the Gospel of John, namely in that scene where Mary Magdalene is the first person to recognize the resurrected Christ and likewise in the very first Class lesson of the School of Spiritual Science.

13.  GA 26, *Second Study (continued): Hindrances and Helps to the Michael Forces in the Dawn of the Age of the Spiritual Soul*, 6 December 1924.

14. From a slightly different standpoint, Rudolf Steiner described this mood at the beginning of his book, *Knowledge of the Higher Worlds and Its Attainment* (GA 10).

15. Concerning Michael's effect on human beings insofar as they seek for an inner connection with him, Rudolf Steiner states: "Michael's impulses are strong, they are powerful, and they work from out of the spiritual directly through the entire human being. They work into the spiritual, from there through the soul-element, and from there into the corporeal [physical] body of the human being. And in karmic relationships these supersensible forces are always active. Entities of the higher hierarchies work together with human beings and on human beings. Karma is thereby formed. And by virtue of the fact that the Michael-forces affect the entire human being, they are moreover forces that work especially powerfully into the karma of mankind" (GA 237, 3 August 1924). Now these karma forces in human beings dwell particularly in the unconscious depths of the will, in the same way that only consciously adopted powers of will can work into the transformation of the physical body. See also words to this effect by Rudolf Steiner concerning Michael's relationship to the element of will on pages 146-147 above.

16. "Deeds" moreover refer to inner deeds as well, for example a meditation that is performed correctly in which thinking is permeated with consciousness and human will; or the study of spiritual science that – if lifted up to the first stage of the modern path of initiation – leads to the beginning of a spiritualization of Michaelic intelligence.

17. See for this, note 110 in Chapter III.

18. Concerning the Kings and Shepherds in connection with the 4th part of the Foundation Stone Meditation and their reflection in the karmic streams, see H. P. VAN MANEN, *Twin Roads to the New Millennium. The Christmas Conference and the Karma of the Anthroposophical Society*, Rudolf Steiner Press 2014.

19. Concerning this front-facing direction and its connection with the "I" axis in eurythmy, see in more detail in S. O. PROKOFIEFF: *May Human Beings Hear It! The Mystery of the Christmas Conference*,

Chap. 4, "The Foundation Stone Meditation in Eurythmy. An Esoteric Contemplation", Temple Lodge 2014.

20.   In the postlude, with the last sounds of the "hallelujah" ("...luja"), the group of eurythmists turns away from a front facing direction to the left front.  This brings to expression the resolute transposing of the Michael-thought power into deed.  With three concluding steps to the rear while simultaneously guiding the A-gesture powerfully downwards into the will-region, the group of eurythmists once more congregates into a front facing direction and furthermore leaves the stage in this orientation.

21.   Viewed by the eurythmists, the movement leads to the right.

22.   Viewed from the eurythmist, the movement leads to the left.

23.   He himself will only descend into this earthly surrounding, following the conclusion of the cultus in the year 1879, in order from there to begin his contemporary guidance of mankind.

24.   In the third scene of the *First Mystery Drama: The Portal of Initiation*, Benedictus speaking of himself states:

> "When on the pilgrim's path of soul
> I had attained the stage
> That granted me the honour
> Of serving with my counsel in the spirit-spheres" (GA 14).

25.   More on this in S. O. PROKOFIEFF, *May Human Beings Hear It! The Mystery of the Christmas Conference*, Chap. 5, "The Esoteric Archetype of the Original Council", Temple Lodge 2014.

26.   In 1413 the fifth post-Atlantean epoch, or consciousness-soul development, began on earth.  From that time forward, the human being's point of view was initially to be directed predominantly towards the outer physical-sensory world, something that nowadays represents the fundamental basis of earthly civilization.  By contrast in the Michael-School, which assumed its activity in the Sun-sphere approximately at that same time, it was above all a matter of participants properly orientating themselves in regard to newly arising spiritual questions in their consciousness-souls.  The older mystery-school contents, because they were being transformed, could

henceforth be absorbed for the first time into the consciousness-soul. Rudolf Steiner states concerning this: "Above in the spiritual world, a sublime 'school' existed in the supersensible realm that in a new way summarized the ancient wisdom of the initiates. This school called up into the consciousness-soul – for human beings between death and rebirth who were predestined for this – what in earlier times had existed in the rational or intellectual-soul, and sentient-soul and so on, what had been the wisdom-property of humankind" (GA 240, 20 July 1924).

27. GA 10, Chap. 7, "Changes in the Dream Life of the Spiritual Disciple".
28. As already mentioned earlier on in this book, the cosmic "I" of Michael works out of the sphere of Spirit-Human.
29. Concerning the Michaelites, see in more detail in the Epilogue.
30. See note 110 in Chapter III.
31. See more of the "upper and lower gods" in GA 129, 25 August 1911.
32. See a detailed description of the two paths in the book by MALTE DIEKMANN, *Der Weg der Initiation. Anthroposophie und die neuen Mysterien* [The Path of Initiation. Anthroposophy and the New Mysteries], Sammatz 2010.
33. See note 20 in Chapter V.
34. See more about the Moon-karma of the past and the future Sun-karma in GA 240, 25 January 1924; concerning the two karmic groups within the Anthroposophical Society in GA 240, 18 July 1924.

## Epilogue
### Michael and the Michaelites

1. Such human hands that were spiritually stretched out from the earth to Michael were, so to speak, the forms and colours of the First Goetheanum in which the spatial element was transformed into the time element for the artistic experience of human beings.
2. See GA 26, *At the Dawn of the Michael Age*.
3. See GA 26, *The World-Thoughts in the Working of Michael and in the Working of Ahriman*; italics by Rudolf Steiner.

4.   GA 26, *The Experiences of Michael in the course of his Cosmic Mission*; italics by Rudolf Steiner.

5.   Within the Third Hierarchy, the Archai are specially connected with the virtue of courage; for they absolved their "human stage" on ancient Saturn, where their external sheath – their "body" at that time – had consisted of warmth, and their innermost being pervaded by the substance of the courage of the Thrones, who at that stage had become the "beginning point" for a new creation. (See GA 132, 31 October 1911).

# Bibliography

The following list includes writings and lectures by Rudolf Steiner quoted in this book and is shown in chronological order in accordance with the bibliographical GA numbers in the Collected Works. The English titles of translated works are given in italics.

Abbreviations:
Rudolf Steiner Press: RSP
SteinerBooks / Anthroposophic Press: SB
Mercury Press: MP
Completion Press: CP

GA/CW

2    *The Science of Knowing*, MP 1988
     *Goethe's Theory of Knowledge*, SB 2008
     The Theory of Knowledge Implicit in Goethe's World Conception
4    *The Philosophy of Freedom*, RSP 2011
     *The Philosophy of Spiritual Activity*, SB 2007
     *Intuitive Thinking as a Spiritual Path*, SB 1995
8    *Christianity as Mystical Fact and the Mysteries of Antiquity*,
     SB 2006
9    *Theosophy*, SB 1994 / RSP 2005
10   *How to Know Higher Worlds*, SB 1994
     *Knowledge of the Higher worlds: How is it Achieved?* RSP 2009
11   *Cosmic Memory*, SB 2006
13   *Occult Science: an Outline*, RSP 2011
     *An Outline of Occult Science*, SB 1972
     *An Outline of Esoteric Science*, SB 1997
     *Esoteric Science, an Outline*

103 *The Gospel of St. John,* SB 1984

104 *The Apocalypse of St. John: Lectures on the Book of Revelation,*
   SB 2004

107 *Disease, Karma and Healing. Spiritual-Scientific Enquiries into the*
   *Nature of the Human Being,* RSP 2013
   *The Being of Man and his Future Evolution*

109 *The Principle of Spiritual Economy,* RSP 1986 / SB 1986
   *Rosicrucian Esotericism*

110 *The Spiritual Hierarchies and the Physical World,* SB 2008

112 *The Gospel of St. John and Its Relation to the Other Gospels,*
   SB 1982

114 *The Gospel of St. Luke,* SB 2001

116 *The Christ Impulse and the Development of Ego-Consciousness,*
   RSP 2014

118 *The Reappearance of Christ in the Etheric,* SB 2004
   *True Nature of the Second Coming*

119 *Macrocosm and Microcosm*

121 *The Mission of the Folk Souls,* RSP 2005
   *The Mission of the Individual Folk Souls*

122 *Genesis: Secrets of Creation,* RSP 2002
   *Biblical Secrets of Creation*

123 *The Gospel of St. Matthew,* SB 2003

129 *Wonders of the World*

130 *Esoteric Christianity and the Mission of Christian Rosenkreutz,*
   RSP 2005
   *Rosicrucian Christianity,* MP
   *The Mission of Christian Rosenkreutz*

131 *From Jesus to Christ,* RSP 2005

132 *Inner Experiences of Evolution,* SB 2006
   *The Inner Realities of Evolution*
   *Evolution in the Aspect of Realities*

142 *The Bhagavad Gita and the West,* SB 2006
   *The Bhagavad Gita and the Epistles of St. Paul*

214 *Das Geheimnis der Trinität.*
Fragments in English: *The Mystery of the Trinity,* SB 1991

218 *Spirit as Sculptor of the Human Organism,* RSP 2014
*Spiritual Relations in the Human Organism,* MP 1984

219 *Man and the World of Stars,* SB 1982

220 *Living Cognition of Nature*
*Awake! For the Sake of the Future,* SB 2015
*Fall and Redemption,* MP
*Truth, Beauty and Goodness*

223 *The Cycle of the Year as Breathing Process of the Earth,* SB 1984
*Michaelmas and the Soul Forces of Man,* SB 1982

224 *Die menschliche Seele in ihrem Zusammenhang mit*
*göttlich-geistigen Individualitäten.* The lecture of 23 May 1923
is included in *The Festivals and Their Meaning IV Michaelmas*

227 *The Evolution of Consciousness,* RSP 2006

229 *The Four Seasons and the Archangels,* RSP 2002

233a The lectures of 4 and 13 January 1924 are included in
*Rosicrucianism and Modern Initiation,* RSP 2000

236 *Karmic Relationships. Esoteric Studies, Volume II,* RSP 1997

237 *Karmic Relationships. Esoteric Studies, Volume III,* RSP 2002

238 *Karmic Relationships. Esoteric Studies, Volume IV,* RSP 1997

240 *Karmic Relationships. Esoteric Studies, Volume VI,* RSP 2002
*Karmic Relationships. Esoteric Studies, Volume VIII,* RSP

243 *True and False Paths in Spiritual Investigation,* RSP 1985

245 *Guidance in Esoteric Training: From the Esoteric School,* RSP 2001

254 *Occult Movements in the 19ᵗʰ Century,* RSP 1973

257 *Awakening to Community,* SB 1975

260 *The Christmas Conference for the Foundation of the General*
*Anthroposophical Society, 1923/1924,* SB 1990

260a Fragments in English: *The Foundation Stone / The Life, Nature &*
*Cultivation of Anthroposophy,* RSP 2011 and *The Constitution*
*of the School of Spiritual Science,* RSP 2013.

262 *Correspondence and Documents 1901-1925: Rudolf Steiner/Marie*
*von Sievers: Exchange of Letters and Documents,* RSP / SB

# Other books by Sergei O. Prokofieff

**Published by Wynstones Press:**
*And the Earth becomes a Sun – The Mystery of the Resurrection*
*The Esoteric Nature of the Anthroposophical Society*
*'Time-Journeys' – A Counter-image to Anthroposophical*
*Spiritual Research*

**Also available in English:**
*Eternal Individuality*
*Rudolf Steiner and the Founding of the New Mysteries*
*Prophecy of The Russian Epic*
*The Case of Valentin Tomberg*
*Rudolf Steiner's Research into Karma*
*The East in the Light of the West*
*The Cycle of the Seasons and the Seven Liberal Arts*
*The Cycle of the Year as a Path of Initiation*
*Rudolf Steiner's Path of Initiation and the Mystery of the Ego*
*The Encounter with Evil and Its Overcoming through*
*Spiritual Science*
*The Esoteric Significance of Spiritual Work in*
*Anthroposophical Groups*
*The Foundation Stone Meditation*
*The Heavenly Sophia and the Being Anthroposophia*
*The Mystery of John the Baptist and John the Evangelist at*
*the Turning Point of Time*
*The Occult Significance of Forgiveness*
*The Spiritual Origins of Eastern Europe*
*The Twelve Holy Nights and the Spiritual Hierarchies*
*Valentin Tomberg and Anthroposophy*

*What is Anthroposophy?*
*Relating to Rudolf Steiner*
*Anthroposophy and The Philosophy of Freedom*
*The Mystery of the Resurrection in the Light of Anthroposophy*
*The Whitsun Impulse and Christ's Activity in Social Life*
*The Guardian of the Threshold and The Philosophy of Freedom*
*The Appearance of Christ in the Etheric*
*Why Become a Member of the Anthroposophical Society?*
*Why Become a Member of the School of Spiritual Science?*
*Crisis in the Anthroposophical Society*
*Rudolf Steiner's Sculptural Group*
*May Human Beings Hear It! The Mystery of the Christmas Conference*

**Other work not translated into English:**
*Maximilian Woloschin. Mensch – Dichter – Anthroposoph.*
*Novalis und Goethe in der Geistesgeschichte des Abendlandes.*
*Friedrich Schiller und die Zukunft der Freiheit. Zugleich einige*
    *Aspekte seiner okkulten Biographie.*
*Das Rätsel des menschlichen Ich. Eine anthroposophische*
    *Betrachtung.*
*Die Grundsteinmeditation als Schulungsweg. Das Wirken der*
    *Weihnachtstagung in 80 Jahren.*
*Das Rätsel des Demetrius. Versuch einer Betrachtung aus histo-*
    *rischer, psychologischer und geisteswissenschaftlicher Sicht.*
*Die geistigen Aufgaben Mittel- und Osteuropas.*

# And the Earth becomes a Sun
## *The Mystery of the Resurrection*

This book forms a direct continuation of the book *The Mystery of the Resurrection in the Light of Anthroposophy*, which appeared in 2008 (and in English translation in 2010). Because of the complexity and manifold nature of the various aspects of the book's theme, many questions had to remain open during its composition – and additional ones have arisen. In the light of this I was prompted by a number of friends to take up the threads of this publication in a renewed way.

We can constantly find questions raised in Rudolf Steiner's work to which he himself suggests answers or states the direction for further research. One experiences this also – and especially – in the realm of anthroposophical Christology. If one tries to come closer to a solution, one will soon discover that what may perhaps have appeared to be a contradiction or an initially insoluble problem is suddenly resolved and opens up entirely new, surprising perspectives. Some of these perspectives will be found in the present publication.

Whilst it is not necessary to have read the earlier book before reading this one, the foundations of what is presented here lie in the previous publication. A familiarity with the other book will therefore be of significant help for understanding the overall context.

The aim of this book is to reveal the spiritual dimension of Rudolf Steiner's Christological research, to make visible its significance and importance for our time and to place it in the perspective of the entirety of human evolution.

576 pages. 240 x 165 mm. Hardback.
ISBN 9780 946206 773

# The Esoteric Nature of the Anthroposophical Society

In 2012, two books by Sergei O. Prokofieff, *Why Become a Member of the Anthroposphical Society*, and *Why Become a Member of the School of Spiritual Science*, were published by Temple Lodge Publishing.

*The Esoteric Nature of the Anthroposophical Society* is the third and final book in this series, now published by Wynstones Press.

"With regard to the question of the esoteric nature of the Anthroposophical Society, the answer most often follows that this esotericism is primarily connected with the Independent School for Spiritual Science. It is less often taken into consideration, however, that at the Christmas Conference Rudolf Steiner ascribed to the Anthroposophical Society itself a decidedly esoteric character, which since then was to permeate all of its activities. Only when this is achieved can the Society fulfil its central task in our time: 'to unite the greatest conceivable openness with genuine, true esotericism' (Rudolf Steiner).

*The Esoteric Nature of the Anthropsophical Society* attempts to answer the question as to what the unique nature of this esotericism consists in, and how it can be brought concretely to realisation."

168 pages. 210 x 150 mm. Paperback.
ISBN 9780 946206 766

## 'Time-Journeys' – A Counter-image to Anthroposophical Spiritual Research

In our time there exist in the world various occult, religious and mystical streams. Some of these have long since incorporated themselves into the Anthroposophical Society; others have done so only recently. This gives rise to a vital, perhaps even decisive question for the future of the anthroposophical movement: How do such streams relate to Rudolf Steiner's spiritual science, and to what extent is their blending with Anthroposophy justified?

One such stream, which has more than a few supporters within the anthroposophical movement, is here analysed in the light of this question. The facts cited here may form the basis for an independent judgment on the part of the reader.

In this concise study Sergei Prokofieff addresses the nature of spiritual scientific research as well as a number of central Christological themes.

156 pages. 210 x 150 mm. Paperback.
ISBN 9780 946206 742

**Wynstones Press**
publishes and distributes a range of
Books, Advent Calendars, Cards and Prints.
For further information please see:

www.wynstonespress.com
info@wynstonespress.com